THE NEW DEMAGOGUES

'The optimistic world of globalization and neo-liberal economics has rapidly disappeared in the last decade with financial instability, refugee crises, political extremism, Brexit and the potential breakup of the European Union. Donald Trump's foreign policy appears to be designed to undermine the UN, NATO, EU, and WHO. In response we have a plethora of explanations and definitions, especially of populism, but no comprehensive social science perspective. The crises are global and cannot be understood in a national context. Joshua Roose offers an original and innovative analysis exploring issues often overlooked by commentators: religion and masculinity. The erosion of key social institutions, especially citizenship and patterns of normative behavior such as civility, has created a social and political vacuum now filled by strong man politics and populist ideologies. Combining comparative empirical research, historical depth and theoretical inquiry, *New Demagogues* is sociology at its best.'

— **Bryan S. Turner**, *The Graduate Center, City University of New York, USA*

Focused on the emergence of US President Donald Trump, the United Kingdom's departure from the European Union, and the recruitment of Islamic State foreign fighters from Western Muslim communities, this book explores the ways in which the decay and corruption of key social institutions has created a vacuum of intellectual and moral guidance for working people and deprived them of hope and an upward social mobility long considered central to the social contract of Western liberal democracy. Examining the exploitation of this vacuum of leadership and opportunity by new demagogues, the author considers two important yet overlooked dimensions of this new populism: the mobilization of both religion and masculinity. By understanding religion as a dynamic social force that can be mobilized for purposes of social solidarity and by appreciating the sociological arguments that hyper-masculinity is caused by social injury, Roose considers how these key social factors have been particularly important in contributing to the emergence of the new demagogues and their followers. Roose identifies the challenges that this poses for Western liberal democracy and argues that states must look beyond identity politics and exclusively rights-based claims and, instead, consider classical conceptions of citizenship.

Joshua M. Roose is a Senior Research Fellow in Politics and Religion at the Alfred Deakin Institute for Citizenship and Globalisation, Deakin University, Australia. He is the author of *Political Islam and Masculinity: Australian Muslim Men*.

ROUTLEDGE STUDIES IN POLITICAL SOCIOLOGY

For a full list of titles in this series, please visit:
https://www.routledge.com/sociology/series/RSPS

Performance Action
The Politics of Art Activism
Paula Serafini

Agonistic Articulations in the 'Creative' City
On New Actors and Activism in Berlin's Cultural Politics
Friederike Landau

Talking Collective Action
A Sequential Analysis of Strategic Planning in Anti-Nuclear Groups
Ole Pütz

Brains, Media and Politics
Generating Neoliberal Subjects
Rodolfo Leyva

The New Demagogues
Religion, Masculinity and the Populist Epoch
Joshua M. Roose

The Political Attitudes of Divided European Citizens
Public Opinion and Social Inequalities in Comparative and Relational Perspective
Christian Lahusen

THE NEW DEMAGOGUES

Religion, Masculinity and the Populist Epoch

Joshua M. Roose

LONDON AND NEW YORK

First published 2021
by Routledge
2 Park Square, Milton Park, Abingdon, Oxon OX14 4RN

and by Routledge
52 Vanderbilt Avenue, New York, NY 10017

Routledge is an imprint of the Taylor & Francis Group, an informa business

© 2021 Joshua M. Roose

The right of Joshua M. Roose to be identified as author of this work has been asserted by him in accordance with sections 77 and 78 of the Copyright, Designs and Patents Act 1988.

All rights reserved. No part of this book may be reprinted or reproduced or utilised in any form or by any electronic, mechanical, or other means, now known or hereafter invented, including photocopying and recording, or in any information storage or retrieval system, without permission in writing from the publishers.

Trademark notice: Product or corporate names may be trademarks or registered trademarks, and are used only for identification and explanation without intent to infringe.

British Library Cataloguing in Publication Data
A catalogue record for this book is available from the British Library

Library of Congress Cataloging-in-Publication Data
A catalog record has been requested for this book

ISBN: 978-1-138-36469-1 (hbk)
ISBN: 978-1-138-36470-7 (pbk)
ISBN: 978-0-429-43119-7 (ebk)

Typeset in Bembo
by Taylor & Francis Books

To the Strong Women in My Life

Kristine, Arielle, Mietta and Mary

CONTENTS

List of tables viii
Preface xi
Acknowledgements xiii
Abbreviations xv

1 Introduction 1
2 Populism in the West: Democratic fault lines and the rise of the new demagogues 21
3 Religion and populism 51
4 Male supremacism 80
5 Brexit and the white working-class 110
6 Trump and blue-collar workers 140
7 Western Islamic State foreign fighters and jihadi masculinity 167
8 Religion, masculinity, and the new populism 192

Index 209

TABLES

4.1 Women deserve equal rights to men (percentage of respondents who disagree or strongly disagree), by gender, country, age (Great Britain, United States, and Australia)   103

4.2 Rights for women have gone too far (percentage of respondents who agree or strongly agree), by country, gender, age (Great Britain, United States, and Australia)   103

5.1 Frequency of gender references in Nigel Farage's pre-EU Referendum public statements   119

5.2 Frequency of emotional tone (anger, anxiety, sadness) in Nigel Farage's pre-EU Referendum public statements   120

5.3 My employment and income are stable and secure (percentage of respondents who agree or strongly agree) by gender and age, Great Britain   127

5.4 Hard work will ensure I can build a better future (percentage of respondents who agree or strongly agree), by gender and age, Great Britain   129

5.5 I feel that I can make a better life for my family in this country (percentage of respondents who agree or strongly agree), by gender and age, Great Britain   131

5.6 Minorities undermine or threaten national unity (percentage of respondents who agree or strongly agree), by gender and age, Great Britain   133

6.1 Frequency of gender references in Trump 2016 campaign material   150

6.2 Frequency of emotional tone (anger, anxiety, sadness) in Trump 2016 campaign material   150
6.3 My employment and income are stable and secure (percentage of respondents who agree or strongly agree) by gender and age, United States   153
6.4 Hard work will ensure I can build a better future (percentage of respondents who agree or strongly agree), by gender and age, United States   155
6.5 I feel that I can make a better life for my family in this country (percentage of respondents who agree or strongly agree), by gender and age, United States   158
6.6 Minorities undermine or threaten national unity (percentage of respondents who agree or strongly agree), by gender and age, United States   159
7.1 Frequency of gender references in Islamic State recruitment material   179
7.2 Frequency of emotional tone (anger, anxiety, sadness) in Islamic State recruitment material   181

PREFACE

In December 2016, as Director of the Institute for Religion, Politics, and Society at the Australian Catholic University, I was afforded the opportunity to visit Rome and the Holy See. I had several meetings at the Vatican, including with the Secretary for Relations with States and the Prefect of the Secretariat of the Economy. Noticeable on the latter's bookshelves were a number of biographies of Margaret Thatcher, which were particularly striking to me at the time due to Thatcher's association with neoliberal economics and her claims that there is no 'society'. The Cardinal shared his concerns on a number of issues and identified identity politics and Islam as the key challenges facing the Church. This was at the height of the marriage equality movement, which was sweeping across the globe with remarkable success, and the peak of the Islamic State movement's physical presence in the Middle East and international terrorist activities. This meeting, in particular, demonstrated to me that, at its very highest levels, the Catholic Church stood in direct political opposition to another faith and to those asserting their human rights in the public sphere.

Several days later I was fortunate to meet arguably *the* key figure in the study of political Islam, Professor Olivier Roy in *Firenze*, near the European University Institute. Over lunch and a couple of bottles of wine, we discussed the core thesis of his (then) new edited book (with Nadia Marzouki and Duncan McDonnell): *Saving the People: How Populists Hijack Religion*. It struck me that the book's thesis was directly at odds with my recent experience at the Vatican. Also, more broadly, it was at odds with what I had observed within my role at the Catholic University and what was my experience having been raised in the Protestant evangelical tradition, in which textualism was absolutely central. Indeed, it appeared to be a conception of religion that assumed leaders were almost always, if not entirely, representative of a faith. My experiences demonstrated to me that each religion has deep undercurrents whereby those not in the ascendancy, be it within the religion itself or in the nation, believe it is god's will that they should be.

These initial thoughts stewed until the 2017 International Conference on Populism at the University of Potsdam led by Professor Bryan S. Turner and Professor Jürgen Mackert, where I was invited to present and spoke to broad themes on the intersection of religion and masculinity. It was a privilege to listen to some of the world's great scholars on populism, yet many of the papers were theoretical and focused primarily on definitions. Furthermore, both religion and masculinity were largely overlooked. This led to the first steps toward writing this book and testing its core claims at the British Sociological Association Conference held at the University of Manchester, where I was fortunate to meet the Commissioning Editor of this Routledge series, Neil Jordan.

This book serves as a modest attempt to cast a light on what I believe are critical, yet largely overlooked, dimensions of the new demagogues and their use of populism as a tactic to mobilise support. It is necessarily broad, covering three contrastive case studies in the United Kingdom, United States, and Australia. The book brings to light core patterns across international contexts that help us better understand the dawn of the populist era, though it also, by necessity, leaves considerable areas that require further study and elaboration. As the COVID-19 pandemic rages and protests sweep the globe, the book seeks to demonstrate that, in order to break out of this epoch of demagogic strongmen, social division, the erosion of democracy and citizenship, and, increasingly, the breakdown of international institutions, we need to both learn from our past and think creatively about our future.

ACKNOWLEDGEMENTS

This book is dedicated to the strong women in my life. My wife Kristine, daughters Arielle Solange and Mietta Elizabeth Anne, and mum, Mary Roose. No book is an easy undertaking. It required fieldwork in the United Kingdom and United States, late nights, early starts, and long days. I could not have done this without your understanding, support, and, indeed, inspiration. Thank you! To my wider body of family, including my dad, David, and aunty, Margaret, who have taken interest in my work, I also thank you and look forward to reacquainting myself with you all.

At an intellectual level, I owe a debt of gratitude to those scholars whose work and conversations have contributed to my formation of ideas, including Professor Bryan S. Turner, Professor Jack Barbalet, Professor Jocelyn Cesari, Dr. Rosario Forlenza, Professor Olivier Roy, Professor Pam Nilan, Dr. Mario Peucker, Dr. Milad Milani, Dr. Maria John, Dr. Michael Casey, Associate Professor Michael Flood, and Professor Jürgen Mackert at Potsdam, whose centre and staff held the 2017 Conference on Populism that sparked many of the ideas shaping this work. I thank Mark Davis at Ipsos Public Affairs for his work and generosity in assisting to develop the Global Masculinity survey. I thank the staff at the Alfred Deakin Institute at Deakin University, in particular Professor Fethi Mansouri, the Director and UNSECO Chair for Cultural Diversity and Social Justice, and Professor Shahram Akbarzadeh, the Deputy Director, for their support.

This book started out as a paper at the British Sociological Association Conference in Manchester in 2017. I thank the organisers for the invitation to present as well as Commissioning Editor Neil Jordan and Senior Editorial Assistant Alice Salt for their support and patience throughout the process. I thank the copyeditor for this project, Ann M. Hale, for her excellent work. I also thank the International Centre for Law and Religion Studies at Brigham Young University for their generosity in funding my trip to the United Kingdom in 2019, and I am grateful to the Oxford-BYU Religion and the Rule of Law program, which made a side trip to conduct fieldwork in Birmingham possible.

Finally, I thank those interviewed for their openness and generosity with their time. Many of those I spoke with, particularly in working-class, blue-collar communities, stated that it was the first time they had been interviewed in any capacity. Whilst I might differ significantly in my personal views, it has been my aim as a researcher scholar to ensure that our conversations and interviews were reflected accurately and that your voices on the matters central to this book are heard.

Joshua M. Roose. June 2020

ABBREVIATIONS

ABC	Australian Broadcasting Corporation
ABS	Australian Bureau of Statistics
ACLU	American Civil Liberties Union
ACOSS	Australian Council of Social Service
AFIC	Australian Federation of Islamic Councils
AFP	Agence France-Presse
AIHW	Australian Institute of Health and Welfare
APS	American Philosophical Society
BBC	British Broadcasting Corporation
CAN-DO	Community Area New Development Organisation
CNN	Cable News Network
CVE	Countering Violent Extremism
DHS	Department of Homeland Security
DoD	Department of Defense
EDL	English Defence League
EU	European Union
IIRA	Illegal Immigration Relief Act
KOZ	Keystone Opportunity Zone
LIWC	Linguistic Inquiry and Word Count
LGBTIQ	Lesbian, Gay, Bisexual, Trans and Gender Diverse, Intersex, Queer, and Questioning
LSE	London School of Economics
MGTOW	Men Going Their Own Way
NHS	National Health Service
OECD	Organisation for Economic Co-operation and Development
SPLC	Southern Poverty Law Centre
UK	United Kingdom

UKIP	United Kingdom Independence Party
UN	United Nations
US	United States of America
VE	Violent Extremist
WHO	World Health Organisation

1
INTRODUCTION

Introduction

In 2020 the world seems barely recognisable compared with just half a decade before. Political populism, a tactic employed by a new generation of demagogic strong men, has gone some way toward undermining the rule of law and established global order. Exhibiting a nostalgia for imagined past greatness and harbouring a deep animosity towards faceless 'elites', a new generation of demagogues have exploited the emotions of those who feel 'left behind', democratic processes, mass and social media, and years of benign neglect by career politicians to gain the helm of their national governments or develop formidable opposition movements that threaten to do so. As the COVID-19 pandemic sweeps the globe, it is evident that many of these demagogues will seek to use sweeping new emergency powers to entrench themselves further.

This book aims to understand how and why Western liberal democracies have become dominated by a new class of demagogic strongmen. It is focused in particular on the emergence of President Donald J. Trump in the United States, the United Kingdom's 'Brexit' from the European Union, and the recruitment of foreign fighters from Western Muslim communities to join the Islamic State Caliphate. Far from 'one off' events, these are ongoing developments that signal deep discontent by a significant proportion of the population at the current state of local and world affairs. President Trump has survived a December 2019 impeachment trial in the United States House of Representatives and is, despite his flawed handling of the COVID-19 Pandemic and a Presidency defined by controversy, in a strong position to be re-elected in 2020. Irrespective of whether this occurs, his election in 2016 resulted in deep-seated change to the composition of American courts and emboldened both far-right and evangelical-Christian actors to move further into the mainstream of American political life. The detrimental impact of the Trump presidency has been felt by key global institutions, including NATO and the World Health Organisation. After over three years of delays, the December 2019 election of Boris Johnson by a compelling margin on a platform of 'getting it done' looks similarly set to change the political, economic, and social landscape of Britain – and Europe – for decades, if not centuries, to come. After many years of efforts by Nigel Farage, the demagogic figurehead of the 'Brexit' movement, Britain commenced withdrawal from the European Union at 11:00 p.m. on the 31st of January 2020. Some other nations, including Italy and Poland, are reconsidering their EU membership. The March 2019 land defeat of the Islamic State and the death of its demagogic leader, Abu Bakr al-Baghdadi, in October 2019 appear to signal the defeat of the radical self-proclaimed Islamic Caliphate, yet the expansion of the movement into other war zones and simultaneous resurgence of Al Qaeda indicate that the threat of global Islamist extremism and terrorism is far from over. As the COVID-19 crisis and its aftermath, including deep economic impacts, will likely reveal, we may not yet have seen the worst of the highly politically charged, dynamic decade. Rather, as the book title suggests, we may be at the beginning of an era: a *populist epoch*.

This book investigates how the decay and corruption of key social institutions, including (but not limited to) trade unions, churches, and formal political parties, in the context of the enactment of neoliberal economic policies has created a vacuum of intellectual and moral guidance for working people and deprived them of hope and the upward social mobility long considered central to the social contract of Western liberal democracy. This vacuum of leadership and opportunity has been skilfully exploited by new demagogues who have proven particularly adept at exploiting social media as a force multiplier for their campaigns.

I explore two important yet overlooked dimensions of this new populism: the mobilisation of both religion and masculinity by the new class of demagogues. By understanding religion as a dynamic social force that can be mobilised for purposes of social solidarity and by appreciating the sociological arguments that hyper-masculinity is caused by social injury, I consider how these key social factors have been particularly important in contributing to the emergence of the new demagogues and their followers, how this poses challenges for Western liberal democracy, and how states must look beyond identity politics and exclusively rights-based claims and, instead, consider re-engaging classical conceptions of citizenship.

Overview: The new populism

The global demagogic and populist surge is not limited to Western, English-speaking, liberal democratic nations. From Hungary, Poland, and Turkey to India, the Philippines, and Brazil (not to mention the many parties across Europe, Africa, Asia, and South America that are electorally successful but not yet in power,), a new breed of strongmen has emerged, replacing liberal predecessors with vitriolic politics centred on various forms of ethno- and religious-nationalism. These leaders promote nostalgia for imagined past national glories and claim to stand against a raft of internal enemies (elites) and external enemies (international organisations, other nations, migrants, minority religions) that have allegedly held their nation back from greatness.

Despite considerable recent progress, scholarship is yet to adequately grasp the dimensions of this new and profoundly modern form of demagoguery and populism. Indeed, the study of both has only recently re-emerged from an extended hibernation. For historians, political scientists, sociologists, and interdisciplinary scholars, the new demagoguery and, in particular, new populism represent significant conceptual challenges as they seek to grapple with how they are constituted, key social and intellectual influences, the extent to which there are parallels with the emergence of Fascism and National Socialism in the twentieth century, and the extent to which demagoguery and populism pose an existential threat to Western liberal democracy.

The majority of emerging scholarship on populism is theoretical. Defining the challenge is a critical element of shaping further questions. Yet this quest for a definition extends back at least half a century. In 1967 the London School of Economics (LSE) hosted a conference, *To Define Populism*, which featured some of the twentieth century's great social and political theorists, including Alain Touraine, Donald McCrae, Ernest Gellner, and Isiah Berlin. The latter noted the difficulty of a singular definition of the concept at one of the conference sessions:

> I think we are all probably agreed that a single formula to cover all populisms everywhere will not be very helpful. The more embracing the formula, the less descriptive. The more richly descriptive the formula, the more it will exclude. The greater the intension, the smaller the extension. The greater the connotation, the smaller the denotation.
> *(London School of Economics 1967: 139)*

Long serving LSE Professor of Sociology Donald McCrae noted that the roots of populism are found in the relationship between men and social harm:

> Populism cannot be a consciously minority movement. Whether falsely or truly, it stands for the majority of man, the majority of men who have somehow been damaged. By whom have they been damaged? They have been damaged by an elite, either economic, political, or racial, some kind of secret or open enemy – capitalism, Jews, and the rest of it. Whoever the enemy is, foreign or native, ethnic or social, does not much matter.
> *(London School of Economics 1967: 141)*

These individual characteristics may sound remarkably cogent today. Yet as Allcock argues, the major feature absent from lists of characteristics of this type is any understandable connection between the diverse elements included in them. They are 'arbitrary, eclectic, and theoretically isolated' (1971: 379). This is a problem that has, in large part, remained to the present day.

It is telling that 50 years later at the 2017 Potsdam International Conference on Citizenship and Populism, which brought together leading scholars on the topic, there was a unanimous acknowledgment of the difficulty in defining populism, noting its 'lack of conceptual and analytical clarity' (Rucht 2017). Rogers Brubaker considered the concept to be 'defined so broadly as to be ubiquitous' and that scholarship is almost resigned to the proposition that you can 'recognise it when you see it' (2017). Muddying the waters for scholars is the fact that populism is an integral component of the election cycle in liberal democracies; the party with the highest electoral appeal (popularity) wins office. Furthermore, the new populism may be cloaked in traditional notions of 'right' and 'left' activism as well as contemporary labels such as 'alt-right,' not to mention the increasing, yet under studied, dimension of religious populism.

Despite the conceptual challenge, contemporary scholarship has converged on key elements defining the new populism, including mobilisation against faceless and 'corrupt' elites (McCarthy 2017), public attacks against migrants (Wodak 2017; Berezin 2017; Yuval-Davis 2017), 'superfluous populations' (Snow 2017), attacks on women's rights (Moghissi 2017; Hadj-Abdou 2017), and an imagined national community comprised of the 'majority' (Snow 2017; Brubaker 2017; Bulli 2017). Moffitt asserts that populism is a political style that is performed, embodied, and enacted across diverse political and cultural contexts (2016). Brubaker goes so far as to consider new populism to consist of a 'discursive and stylistic repertoire' including 'antagonistic depoliticisation', 'majoritariansim', 'anti-institutionalism', and 'anti-intellectualism' (2017).

There is a general consensus that key causal factors of contemporary global populism include the 2009 sovereign debt crisis and associated policies emphasising austerity (Berezin 2017), securitisation (Brubaker 2017; Turner 2017), and mass migration (Yuval-Davis 2017; McCarthy 2017). Calhoun (2017) has noted that populism is not just a politics of interests, it is expressly directed against 'interests' that divide the people. These interests directly undermine the notion of meritocracy and upward mobility through hard work. Milbank (2017) has adopted a theological perspective and sought to represent liberalism and secularism as culpable for a deeper spiritual dissatisfaction amongst the population that, in turn, drives populism. Milbank collaborator and Blue Labour advocate Adrian Pabst similarly claims that 'liberalism contains the secular roots of populism', using the example of identity politics that 'has tended to celebrate the diversity of difference at the expense of civic ties that bind people together above the divides of class, colour, and creed' (2018). John Keane claims that populism is a 'democratic phenomenon' and a public protest by the demos, who feel 'annoyed, powerless, and no longer "held" in the arms of society' (2016).

Populism as tactic

Populism has been described as a 'thin ideology' (Mudde 2004; Stanley 2008), elevating 'the people' and emphasising their betrayal by elites (Elchardus & Spruyt

2016: 113). This is an inherently problematic framing that leads to the concept of populism having little meaning at all.

The concept of ideology, like populism, has long been considered difficult to define (Converse 1964; Mullins 1972). The French term *idéologie* was first framed by Destutt de Tracy, a philosopher, with the etymology of the concept stemming from the Greek *ideo* (of ideas) and *logy* (discourse or doctrine). The concept was arguably first popularised by Marx in his work *The German Ideology*. However, Gerring noted the 'semantic promiscuity of the word' and that 'few concepts in the social science lexicon have occasioned so much discussion, so much disagreement, and so much self-conscious discussion of the disagreement …' (1997: 958–959). Teun van Dijk commented that 'Ideology has been dealt with in literally thousands of books and articles (but as many authors also conclude) its definition is as elusive and confused as ever' (1998: vii).

Knight, by contrast, argued that the core definition of ideology in political science as a *'coherent and relatively stable set of beliefs or values'* has remained constant over time', even if the connotations associated with the concept have undergone transformation (2006: 625). For Knight, the utility of the term is situated in its ability to articulate a broad, abstract concept – a set of beliefs – efficiently (2006: 623). After an exhaustive consideration of 27 elements of ideology across literature, Hamilton defined ideology as 'a system of collectively held normative and reputedly factual beliefs and attitudes advocating a particular pattern of social relationships and arrangements, and/or aimed at justifying particular pattern of conduct which its proponents seek to promote, realise, pursue, or maintain' (1987: 28).

To view the new populism as a 'thin ideology' neglects the fact that both the left and right of the populist political spectrum meet these very same aspects of the definition of populism. These are core characteristics or 'attributes' of populism, however beyond rhetorical flourishes about the people and the elites, there is very often no consistent philosophical basis of belief or intellectual consistency. To believe in or at least speak to the supremacy of one social group over another does not in and of itself constitute an ideological orientation. Indeed, those programs put in place by populists very often undermine 'the people' and enrich the very elites they state they stand against. Populism is, in effect, *an empty shell devoid of belief.* One could go so far as to label populism as a form of political nihilism centred on destruction. This does not prevent religious actors and those claiming cynically moral legitimacy from working closely with those deploying populist tactics to further their political agenda. Populism is deployed in equal measure by the political left, right, and independents seeking to make a name for themselves and to mobilise populations through the use of emotion. Populism is a means for those at the fringes of a political system to seek to attain power. It is why very often wealthy men not accepted within their own elite circles – including Trump and Farage – are at the fore of populist movements. Populism is first and foremost a political tactic that targets the centre of gravity of the established system: the consent of the governed. It stokes distrust and undermines social cohesion through dividing society into 'us' and 'them'.

Populism thrives in the absence of the bonds of citizenship – the package of rights and responsibilities that coheres society. Citizenship serves as the glue that holds a society together. Whilst often imperfect, when enacted, citizens feel a part of something and 'held in the arms of society'. Extreme narratives based on social division hold no traction and can develop no critical mass of followers. Populism as a political tactic fails where citizenship is strong. In contrast to populism, masculinity does have the potential, at its extreme edge, to form the base of a coherent political ideology centred on expansive social change. It is for this reason that populists are particularly keen to use and adept at mobilising masculinity to strengthen their deployment of populist tactics aimed at dividing society.

To this extent, it is important to understand that demagoguery and populism go hand in hand. The concept of the demagogue, despite its origins in the classic Greek word '*Demos*', from which we derive 'democracy', has long been framed in a pejorative sense, referring to the 'leader of the mob' or those who 'rouse the rabble' (Allison 2009). By exploiting emotion, ignorance, and prejudice to gain and maintain political power, demagogues have always had a disproportionate and detrimental impact on the world around them. They subvert democratic processes and the rule of law, deepen social divisions grounded in an ideal conception of the nation and people, and very often seek the violent expulsion (or extermination) of non-peoples. Demagogues, historically and in the present, are almost entirely men who seek to attain power and hold it whatever the cost. The 'discursive and stylistic repertoire' of populism is but a means to an end. As conservative philosopher Roger Scruton has argued, the new breed can win elections, disrupt the status quo, and use the popular vote to upend the expectation of political elites, but they also have one thing in common:

> their preparedness to allow a voice to passions that are neither acknowledged nor mentioned in the normal course of politics … They are not democrats, but demagogues – not politicians who guide and govern, but agitators who stir the unthinking feelings of the crowd.
>
> *(Scruton 2017)*

The vast majority of published work on contemporary populism is theoretical, rather than empirical. To this extent it is preoccupied with avoiding (or countering) critique rather than informing public debate and providing potential policy solutions The empirical work that has been published has focused primarily on large-scale analysis of discourse (Jagers & Walgrave 2007; Hawkins 2009; Caiani & Della Porta 2011; Hawkins et al. 2012; Wodak 2015). Whilst valuable in outlining top-down factors, contemporary scholarship is distant from the often challenging lived 'everyday' existence and the social influences shaping those drawn to populist narratives. Importantly, given the influence of masculinity and religion in the lives of working men, contemporary scholarship fails predominantly to engage with how both have been mobilised (and weaponised) by the new demagogues to build their base. Understanding this requires an interdisciplinary approach that draws on sociology, political science, and, importantly, history, for current developments are the result of the cumulative effect of decades of social policies and hundreds of years of framing ideas about the ideal ordering and governance of society.

Relatively little empirical work has been undertaken into right-wing populist supporters or organisations. While Mabel Berezin notes that such work has been stigmatised in academia – 'if you do that sort of work you might be seen as a closet right-winger' – she comments that 'more ethnographic work is needed looking at specific locales' (2017). Ethnographic work, including digital ethnography, has the potential to reveal deeper insights into the dimensions of social injury, anger, anxiety, and humiliation shaping support for populism. It is arguable that it is precisely because of the lack of qualitative and ethnographic work bridging the gap between the reader and subject, who is typically at the opposite end of the spectrum from the academic reader, that the emotionally raw and visceral nature of contemporary populism is overlooked and misunderstood. The metaphorically and literally violent propositions put forward by the new demagogues must be understood in the context of deep-seated emotional and morally driven responses. The notion that violence is caused by a deficit of morality and justice is misplaced. Indeed, 'on the contrary, violence is often caused by a surfeit of morality and justice, at least as conceived in the mind of the perpetrator' (Pinker 2011: 84).

Main themes and objectives

This book aims to break new ground by examining the underexplored contribution and complex interrelationship of populism, masculinity, and religion. In doing so, it seeks to contribute to a more holistic and nuanced understanding of the new demagogues and populism and, importantly, explore its potential future trajectories in Western contexts. It does so by examining three contrasting studies and specific sites of the new populism in action: the election of US President Donald Trump (Hazleton, Pennsylvania); the United Kingdom 'Brexit' from the European Union driven by the United Kingdom Independence Party (UKIP) (Kingstanding, Birmingham); and the recruitment of young Western Muslim men by the Islamic State movement with particular reference to Australia (Melbourne and Sydney), which produced a disproportionate number of fighters per capita. Despite local differences, the narratives employed to appeal to and recruit primarily male supporters and the social characteristics of these supporters are remarkably similar. This demonstrates a significant global issue amongst men who feel marginalised and resentful. This book explores five interrelated theses:

1. The decline of citizenship, the welfare state, and key social institutions has created an intellectual and moral vacuum for populists to exploit;
2. Demagogic actors are using religious motifs and narratives to strengthen their appeal, however organised religion is also seeking to exploit populism to gain greater political influence;

3. Populist hyper-masculinity, irrespective of the national context in which it is displayed, is indicative of deep-seated social and emotional injury;
4. The combination of religious invective, social injury, and wounded masculine pride signals the emergence of a new form of violent extremism that can have global implications; and
5. Paradoxically, it is in both the religious and hyper-masculine dimensions of the new populism that potential conceptual and policy solutions to the challenge are situated.

The first thesis requires an exploration of the decline of classic sociological conceptions of citizenship as outlined by Marshall (1950) and Turner (1990) defining the rights and duties of citizenship. An exploration of this theses will draw upon Turner's subsequent exploration of the erosion of citizenship (Turner 2001), critiques of neoliberalism as a driver of state policy (Harvey 2007) and contributor to the expulsion of citizens from the economy (Sassen 2014), an exploration of the transition of identity politics from a basis in honour and dignity to 'victimhood' (Campbell & Manning 2014), and dissection of the concept of meritocracy (Littler 2017).

The broad crux of this thesis is that as the welfare state has retracted in the face of neoliberal ideology and economic programs, so too has the influence, credibility, and reach of institutions that have traditionally played a central role in the lives of working people and the organizations that supported them. This includes trade unions (intellectual leadership) and the Church (moral leadership). Trade unions have traditionally played an important role in advocating for working people (particularly men) and in offering intellectual leadership on key social issues. For working men, trade unions, and their related institutions, including mechanics institutes, working men's clubs, and sporting teams, unions provided both an intellectual framing of the working-class predicament and a sense of working-class solidarity. With a combination of increased casualisation alongside anti-trade union laws and sentiment, trade unions have been able to maintain membership in the public sector, but they declined in both influence and reach amongst the working-classes. They represent a small fraction of the workforce in the countries examined (Roose 2017), and key leadership positions are filled, not by workers, but by ambitious white-collar professionals seeking to use such positions as entry points to higher political office.

In a similar vein, formally working-class-focused political parties, including Labour (UK), the Democrats (US), and Labor (Australia), have become dominated by professional politicians, many of whom have never worked outside of politics, and have been amongst the first parties to embrace neoliberal policies. The inequitable distribution of wealth has grown markedly, with corporations and individuals moving beyond the reach of the state, as highlighted recently in the leaked 'Paradise Papers'. If taxation is a key dimension of citizenship, then it becomes clear that the corporation in the new economy has little interest in a substantive contribution to wider society. As a consequence, the primary vote for all major parties, often seen to be aligned with corporate interests, has been declining significantly over time.

Whilst not immune to short bursts of populist rhetoric, the Christian churches, particularly those aligned broadly with national political leadership, have acted as a strong shaper of community and moral guidance, which plays a key role in traditional working-class masculinity. Morality remains central to the lived experiences of working men and, along with a sense of dignity, is a key dimension of their self-worth (Lamont 2000). It has also played a key and long-forgotten role in the formation of the welfare state, Keynesian economics, and citizenship. Churches across the denominations have historically been pivotal in forging community belonging, a sense of identity, and solidarity in the face of economic and social challenges. Importantly, however, church attendance (as well as marriage) has been declining for several decades amongst the working-class, and religion is considerably less important in the lives of the younger generation (Pew Research 2015). Working-class families are consequently more fragile than ever before, and working-class men are increasingly unlikely to marry at all (Wilcox & Wang 2017). Importantly, the moral authority of churches has been denigrated by a multitude of issues, including child sexual abuse, allegations of corruption, a refusal to include women and LGBTIQ communities, and out of touch elite leadership. Similarly, corruption amongst Muslim governing bodies, very often run by first-generation, older migrants in Western contexts, has similarly undermined trust and moral authority, resulting in anger and alienation from the wider community, This has led to a decline in their influence, particularly amongst locally born Muslims who have increasingly sought guidance online and who have been the primary focus of recruitment efforts by the Islamic State movement.

As the 'new economy', defined by amorality, precarious labour, and individualised conceptions of the workforce, has seen traditional male roles marginalised and honour and dignity stripped away, these traditional support mechanisms, be they economic, solidaristic, familial, or communal, have simultaneously retracted. Their absence has created a vacuum of ideas that has been filled by identity politics and a politics of victimisation that has been so readily exploited by the new demagogues.

The second thesis concerns the role of religion in contemporary developments. Religion has become central to the narratives of contemporary populists worldwide. The notion of a 'Christian' civilization facing existential threat from immigrants and Islam is a central element of the new populism. As religious institutions, which have acted to consolidate working-class identity, decline, the void has been filled by a multitude of other faiths and practices, including the rise of non-religion. Populists and religious leaders alike decry this situation. It is argued here, however, that rather than reject populist references to the religious, some religious leaders, in particular evangelicals, are actively aligning with the argument for a more cohesive 'Christian' identity as a matter of survival. Catholicists, a well-resourced textualist grouping within the Catholic Church, seek to undermine not only their leader, but the division of Church and State across the West. Salafist groups similarly lead the push for a more cohesive global Muslim community of believers (*Ummah*) that stands in contrast to non-Muslims. Those churches (or indeed Imams) that do enjoy state support or sanction, on the other hand, often reject these calls as being motivated by xenophobic sentiments, which further marginalises them from their working-class base.

The role of religion is a key overlooked dimension of the new populism. This could be considered reflective of mainstream disdain for religion in the academy. Brubaker (2017), for example, described Christianity as an 'empty nodal signifier' and questioned its relevance in contemporary European populism. However, Cas Mudde (2016) referred to knowledge on the relationship between religion and populism as 'an important black spot'. There is currently just one significant book exploring the relationship between religion and the new populism: *Saving the People: How Populists Hijack Religion* (2016) edited by Marzouki, McConnell, and Roy. It is a comparative work focused on the European context. Its core (cumulative) argument is that Christianity in Europe has been appropriated (and, indeed, held hostage) by populists to develop their anti-Islam and anti-Muslim narrative, and the faith and theological dimensions of Christianity remain abstracted from populist identity politics. However, as Forlenza (2019) has noted, this argument deprives those drawn to populist narratives who actively identify as Christian of the possibility that they may experience the emotions of fear, anger, and resentment related to the notion of an existential threat to their faith and identity (no matter how imaginary the threat might be). Furthermore, *Saving the People* fails to engage with either denominational differences (and competition) or the broader political manoeuvring of Christian churches across Europe and the United States as they engage with or challenge populist leaders and movements to enhance their social and political standing. I argue that, on the one hand, religion has been politicised by external actors, however, on the other, organised religion is far from passive in the current political climate. Any attempt to understand populism must take into account the strategies and tactics employed by the leadership of different church factions, denominations, and faiths in the competition for adherents and political influence.

The relationship between religion and populism has a long history that is almost entirely disregarded by arguments identifying 'religion' as appropriated. Attempts by religious actors to shape national and international economic programs are also largely overlooked. Furthermore, many members of the Church establishment and Muslim leaders alike frame themselves as victim of a faceless, liberal, secular elite bent on their destruction. This raises important questions: Where do different religious actors stand in relation to the new demagogues and their populist narratives? Do they seek to mobilise them for political gain or reject them outright? Are different denominations pursuing different political strategies? If so, how does their standing in relation to the state, power, and authority shape this? These questions must be addressed in seeking to better understand the new populism.

The third thesis requires an exploration of how displays of populist hyper-masculinity, irrespective of the local context, are indicative of deep-seated social injury and wounded masculine pride. It is argued that the alienation, anxiety, and resultant anger of working- and, increasingly, middle-class men is a key contributor to the new populism. The new demagogues derive their primary support from disenfranchised working men marginalised by neoliberal economic policies in which casualisation, automation, and mass retrenchments have decimated the traditional working-class base.

Contemporary scholarship, with some notable exceptions, largely overlooks the relationship between masculinity and populism. No monograph adequately examines the manner in which populist movements and leaders have successfully mobilised and weaponised masculinity (and, in particular, religion-inflected masculinity) to build their support base. Comparatively, more empirical work has been done amongst working men and women (Gest 2018; Standing 2011; McDowell 2003; Lamont 2000), with studies dating back to Orwell's *The Road to Wigan Pier* (1937) and beyond. However, these and other works on this spectrum overlook almost entirely the interaction between religion and masculinity as well as how religion offers a space for the reassertion of masculinity, status, and meaning for men at the margins. Further, they fail to engage with how religion shapes and actively engages with populist narratives, movements, and leaders to benefit the faction, denomination, or particular faith.

McDowell asserts that the successful transition to employment is 'a key element of the establishment of an acceptable version of manhood' (2003: 58), and she poses a series of questions that are central to understanding the challenges faced in contemporary society: 'What happens to men's sense of themselves as masculine when the sort of work associated with masculinity disappears, as it has in many urban localities? Will young men be prepared to undertake feminised servicing work for low wages in common with increasing numbers of young women, or do they feel it is an affront to their sense of dignity?' (McDowell 2003: 58) Hegemonic working-class masculinities grounded in roles represented as 'heroic, with punishing physical labour that involved different degrees of manual skills and bodily toughness' (Ward 2013: 4) have been undermined and, in the context of neoliberalism and the 'new economy', subordinated to masculinities equipped with the requisite cultural capital and bodily dispositions to achieve in a world where manual labour is less valued. There has been a very public naming and shaming of these young men and women. Labels such as 'chav' (UK) and 'deplorable' (US), as Jones (2011) has noted, constitute an attack on the poor and speak to a wider societal contempt. 'Chavs' as a pejorative term is less than two decades old (Oxford Dictionary 2015), whilst the term 'deplorable' was used in the 2016 presidential campaign by Democratic candidate Hilary Clinton. For men on the receiving end of these terms, they contrast strongly with the notion of the 'heroic' masculine, working-class male ethos.

It is primarily these alienated working men that form the base of contemporary populist movements whose narratives promote empowerment, honour, belonging, and, most ominously, revenge. The experience of working- and lower-middle-class masculinities is grounded in real world struggle defined by alienation from labour, anxiety due to the precarious nature of their work, anger due to their downward social trajectories, and anomie based in a deficit of moral guidance and social bonds (Standing 2011). One need only look at the crowds at many populist events or online propaganda videos for groups such as the Islamic State to see that such men form the base of support for the new demagogues, a representation supported by numerous statistical sources (Pew Research 2016; Ipsos MORI (2016); Statista 2016). These men demonstrate what Connell (2012) refers to as 'subordinated masculinities' driven by humiliation, social injury, a lack of respect and recognition, and perceived stripping of honour and dignity. Hage (2011) refers to this process as 'misinterpellation' – the process of shattering that occurs when the promise of society that hard work will result in upward social mobility is found to be false. The process of misinterpellation is central to increased receptibility to populist narratives when a sense of victimhood functions to provide an alternate source of meaning defined in opposition to a blameworthy 'other' and access to upward social and spiritual mobility through action. However, these are also deeply personal experiences, and I will argue that the role of emotion in responses to this profound sense of vulnerability and helplessness must be considered.

Barbalet (1993: 133) notes that it is 'through emotions that actors are engaged by others and through their emotions that they alter their relations with them'. He notes further that subjection to arbitrary power, punishment where there should be reward, and frustrated attempts to satisfy needs are likely to evoke strong emotions including depression, fear, and anger. The current political context evolved over a period of sustained economic and political pressure and degradation of social status. With the stripping of honour and dignity from work, we are witnessing the death of working-class stoicism – emphasising endurance, self-control, and inner strength – and its replacement with what Campbell and Manning (2014) frame as a culture of victimhood. At its extremes (and most obscene), this has led some men across the class spectrum to gravitate to men's rights groups and coalesce around a common sense of persecution on the basis of their gender. Paradoxically, this collapse of working-class masculine stoicism parallels increased displays of physical hyper-masculinity.

We have witnessed the emergence of a virulent new form of anti-women ideology, which has come to the fore in the past half-decade in particular. It includes reinvigorated efforts to exclude women as religious leaders and confine them to the domestic sphere; groups, such as Men Going Their Own Way (MGTOW), framing women as money hungry whores; calls for the legalisation of physical violence and sexual assault against women; and violent Incels, who carry out acts of terrorist violence against women on the basis of gender. Framing is imperative, and the chapter considers the dimensions of 'ideological masculinity' as a base for understanding these developments and, in particular, male supremacism as a new form of violent extremism.

Interestingly, social injuries and wounded masculine pride are shared by both males drawn to the new populism and the new demagogues, who almost without exception have been individuals at the fringes of the establishment who, despite their wealth, have been shunned by their peers. This relationship between the demagogue and supporter may be experienced by the supporter as deeply visceral and personal, inspiring a loyalty that withstands public critique and scrutiny as well as a view that the demagogue is 'one of us'.

The fourth thesis explores the relationship between religious invective, social injury, and wounded masculine pride, the nature of which is profoundly modern and volatile. In the context of the alienation, anxiety, and expulsion outlined above, a number of new, highly politicised anti-women movements as well as movements within both Christianity and Islam are seeking to rehabilitate traditional notions of masculinity with the male as head of the family and breadwinner. These new movements within the 'manosphere' actively seek the subjugation of women and a willingness to use violence against women on ideological grounds, making this a new form of violent extremism. These new currents, which are a key yet underexplored dimension of the new populism, have global implications.

Du Mez (2017) has explored the relationship between US president Donald Trump and 'militant evangelical Christianity' by conducting a brief survey of evangelical literature on manhood to assert that white evangelical support for Trump is 'the culmination of a decade long embrace of militant masculinity' seeking to enshrine a warrior culture for men and passivity for women. In a similar vein, amongst the cut and thrust of pre-Brexit debate was a clarion call for a reassertion of the eighteenth-century movement of 'Muscular Christianity' as an anecdote to the decline of British international prestige and a reassertion of the centrality of men to British culture and church life. UKIP leader and key figure in the Brexit movement Nigel Farage has similarly called for a 'muscular defence' of Christian heritage and 'our Christian Constitution' (2015), releasing a 'Christian manifesto' titled 'Supporting the Family'. This is a response to the perception by both Farage and a number of clerics that the Archbishop of Canterbury and Church leadership have lost touch with their core constituents. For Islamic state militants, an Islamic 'warrior masculinity' is a central trope of efforts to recruit young Westerners. Foreign fighters, typically young men drawn from the margins of society who have experienced downward social and economic trajectories (Roose 2016), are promised honour, status as warriors of the Caliphate, and wives – things lacking in their home countries. Islamic State obituaries represent dead fighters as 'knights', 'commandos', and heroes of the caliphate (Roose 2016). In all cases, irrespective of local context, populist narratives emphasise the emasculation and victimisation of men, their marginalisation and disempowerment, and a solution in the form of an honourable 'militant' or 'warrior' masculinity in the service of God.

This religious-warrior masculinity is highly volatile, placing real world struggles in millenarian and very often apocalyptic terms and providing a justification for extreme political action, including the use of violence. In this sense, violent political discourse by the new demagogues must be viewed as more than mere rhetorical flourish; it is, in fact, a call to arms. It must be taken seriously as a threat to local, national, and international security. Importantly, this is a profoundly modern incarnation of past forms of religious extremism. Social media has acted as a force multiplier for identity-based movements to both project their voices and to recruit. These groups have interconnected strands locally, nationally, and internationally and are seeking to change the global landscape in a context where the use of force is not only acceptable, it is very often preferable.

The fifth and final thesis in this book is that it is paradoxically in both the religious and hyper-masculine dimensions of the new populism that potential conceptual and policy solutions to the challenge are situated. If hyper-masculinity may be understood as being caused by deep-seated social injury and wounded masculine pride (Humphrey & Islam 2002; Roose 2016), then religion has traditionally acted as a salve to such wounds, what Stark and Bainbridge (1985) describe as 'spiritual compensators' in the absence of earthly rewards. As outlined in the first thesis, the retraction of the welfare state and decline of both trade unions and the church have created a vacuum for populist narratives seeking not to heal, but to further open and exploit these wounds.

As identified above, I argue that in the context of social fragmentation and the decline of key social institutions, states must urgently rediscover and re-engage with citizenship as both a nurturing and rehabilitative concept for addressing the social injury of those drawn to populist narratives. This requires moving beyond binaries shaping political discourse around citizenship, prevalent amongst the political left (pro welfare state) and right (restrictive citizenship), and beyond the identity-rights-based approach that has come to dominate contemporary politics and that has, arguably, imploded (Raschke 2019). It requires a reinvigorated and redefined conception of citizenship that offers a sense of belonging, dignity, and, indeed, honour. As Heater (1990) has argued, citizenship can act to tame the divisive passions of other identities. This is particularly the case where emotions, including vulnerability, despair, anger, and resentment, create a potentially explosive fuel for action.

The state cannot fill the intellectual or spiritual vacuum created by the decline of trade unions and organised religion, however, it can and must become accessible to citizens (and particularly working-class men) in order to, as Keane (2016) argued, make them feel 'held in the arms of society'. Restoring honour and dignity to working-class men through developing highly calibrated and focussed government policies that, where necessary, incorporate the private sector to develop meaningful training and jobs that offer upward social trajectories, on the one hand, and instil a sense of duty and service to the community and nation, on the other, is a paradigm shift away from contemporary political discourses focussed on individual shortcomings and individual rights-based claims. It offers a sense of connection to wider society and directly challenges populist narratives emphasising disconnection, isolation, and anger. This also requires, in the context of contemporary identity politics, a quite radical reframing of masculinity from something to be deemphasised and hidden to something to be valued. It requires development of the presently unfashionable perspective that duty and responsibility to one's community and nation still have a role to play in a globalised world.

Book structure

Beyond this introductory chapter, the book is structured as follows. Chapter 2, 'Populism in the West: Democratic fault lines and the rise of the new demagogues', outlines and develops the first thesis of the book that the decline of citizenship, the welfare state, and key social institutions in the West has created an intellectual and moral vacuum for populists to exploit. This entails an examination of the theoretical basis for the thesis (outlined above) combined with an analysis of political discourses and statistical sources that examine union membership and church participation across Western nations, in particular the United Kingdom, United States, and Australia.

Chapter 3, 'Religion and populism', outlines and develops the second thesis of the book that religion is a dynamic social and political force. Whilst populist movements are using religious motifs and narratives to strengthen their appeal, organised religion is also jostling for social and political influence with or against government and populist movements. This requires an examination of dominant theoretical perspectives on the paradox of secularism and the fragmentation of religious authority alongside an exploration of the historic relationship between religion and populism.

Chapter 4, 'Male supremacism', explores both the third thesis, which asserts that populist hyper-masculinity, irrespective of the national context in which it is displayed, is indicative of deep-seated social and emotional injury, and fourth thesis, which asserts that the combination of religious invective, social injury, and wounded masculine pride is particularly volatile yet also profoundly modern. The chapter explores the expulsion of working-class men from the so-called 'new economy' and its impact on both communities and individual notions of honour and dignity. It moves beyond the working-class to consider the deep-seated prejudice against women that is increasingly evident in the white-collar, professional classes. The chapter also examines questions of intersectionality with an emphasis on race, gender, and class, exploring the concept of 'ideological masculinity' to understand how masculinity has been weaponised as a political motivation in and of itself.

The first of the three case studies, Chapter 5, 'Brexit and the white working class', features the United Kingdom's 2016 vote to withdraw from the European Union, known colloquially as the 'Brexit'. Birmingham, the United Kingdom's 'second city', is not only highly multicultural, it is marketed by city officials as a cosmopolitan and tolerant cultural hub. The city shocked the nation by narrowly voting to leave the European Union with a margin of 50.4 per cent to 49.6 per cent. However, in some areas, including Kingstanding in the city's northern Erdington Ward, over 70 per cent of residents voted to leave. With a particular emphasis upon the role of the United Kingdom Independence Party (UKIP), led by member of the European Parliament Nigel Farage, and the role of both established and minority religion in mobilising for the vote, this chapter explores how Farage, in particular, skilfully exploited working-class British masculinities and the religious terrain to guide the pro-Brexit coalition to a highly unexpected victory. The chapter draws on research conducted in Birmingham in July 2019, just months before the 2019 British election, the country's formal departure from the European Union, and the disproportionately detrimental impact of COVID-19 on the West Midlands.

Chapter 6, 'Trump and blue-collar workers', applies the core theses of the book in the context of the United States and, in particular, Hazleton, a blue-collar northern Pennsylvania town. Hazleton, a key city located in Luzerne County, is widely considered to have played a key role in the victory of Donald J. Trump in the 2016 presidential election. With its strong religious history, historic trade union footprint, and more recent social divisions based on immigration, Hazleton, Pennsylvania, preceded the rest of the United States by electing a populist mayor, Lou Barletta, known by some as 'Trump before Trump'. The chapter draws on research conducted in Hazleton in December 2019, just months before COVID-19 hit the town and transformed it into one of the worst hotspot cities in the United States.

The final case study, Chapter 7, 'Western Islamic State foreign fighters and jihadi masculinity', applies the core theses of the book to a contrastive case study of the Islamic State movement's recruitment of Western Islamic State foreign fighters to fight in Iraq and Syria and conduct terrorist operations across the West between 2014 and 2017. This is an important point of comparison to the previous two chapters. The chapter shows that, despite being born in the West, these young Muslim men have very often experienced similar downward social trajectories, including dishonour and a lack of empowerment compared to their non-Muslim peers, and they have been mobilised through recruitment propaganda that emphasises an Islamic warrior masculinity. In the absence of a charismatic demagogue within, these men looked to external figures, such as Abu Bakr al-Baghdadi or Western recruiters who had already made the move to join the self-proclaimed Caliphate. The chapter draws on linguistic inquiry and word count analysis of Islamic State recruitment materials, including the *Dabliq* and *Rumiyah* magazines as well as videos that have been central to recruitment efforts. While opportunities to interview members of Muslim communities with direct involvement in activities were limited, public statements by fighters and blogs made it possible to draw strong conclusions.

Chapter 8, 'Religion, masculinity, and the new populism' draws on the application of the book's theses in the three case studies (Chapters 5–7) to derive new insights into dimensions of the new populism and demagoguery. Importantly, it explores potential future trajectories in Western contexts. The chapter also develops the fifth and final thesis of the book, which argues that, paradoxically, potential conceptual and policy solutions to the challenges posed by new populism and demagoguery are situated in both the religious and hyper-masculine dimensions of the new populism. Solutions proposed include a recalibrated citizenship grounded in rights, responsibilities, and service; a reinvigorated and more inclusive secularism that contributes to the formation of values-based policymaking (in contrast to nihilist, neoliberal economic and social policies); a move beyond notions of male victimhood; and a return to the dignity of work and spaces for industrial citizenship to flourish. Such solutions obviously require political goodwill. These alternate policies are targeted simultaneously at contexts where policymakers may be dealing with the recent emergence of populist movements as well as contexts where there has been a recent change of government.

It must be noted from the outset that the language used by actors focused on in this book is confronting and is likely considered abhorrent by readers. Whether it be male supremacist views advocating violence against women, historic examples of anti-Semitism, prejudice based on religion, hate-fuelled rhetoric by politicians, or the more casual (though no less damaging) racism of those interviewed, it is clear that polarising and dehumanising violent language is a key element of demagogic populism and must be understood not only for its real world consequences, but its potential for genocidal violence.

This book covers broad terrain. It by no means proclaims to have all the answers to our current challenges. However, by exploring under examined and underutilised frames of analysis in order to understand the new populism and the emergence of new demagogic strongmen, who are intent on subverting the rule of law and democracy and exploiting social divisions for personal gain, it hopes to make a small contribution to better understanding the way forward.

References

Allcock, J.B. (1971). Populism: A Brief Biography. *Sociology*, 5 (3), 371–387.
Allison, L. (2009). Demagogue. In I. McLean & A. McMillan (Eds.), *The Concise Oxford Dictionary of Politics: 3rd Edition*. Oxford: Oxford University Press.
Barbalet, J.M. (1993). Citizenship, Class Inequality and Resentment. In B.S. Turner (Ed.), *Citizenship and Social Theory* (pp. 36–57). London: Sage.
Berezin, M. (2017). *Security Crises: Extreme Nationalism and Threats to Democracy in Europe*. University of Potsdam, Germany: International Conference of the Centre for Citizenship: Populism and Citizenship, 6–8 July.
Brubaker, R. (2017). *Conclusion: Populism and Citizenship*. University of Potsdam, Germany: International Conference of the Centre for Citizenship: Populism and Citizenship, 6–8 July.
Bulli, G. (2017). *Cultural Homogenous Community: The Populist Promise during the Migration Era*. University of Potsdam, Germany: International Conference of the Centre for Citizenship: Populism and Citizenship, 6–8 July.
Caiani, M. & Della Porta, D. (2011). The Elitist Populism of the Extreme Right: A Frame Analysis of Extreme Right-Wing Discourses in Italy and Germany. *Acta Politica*, 46 (2), 180–202.
Calhoun, C. (2017). *Populism, Polarization and Democracy: Thesis Eleven*. Public lecture at La Trobe University, Melbourne, Australia, 16 May. Retrieved from https://thesiseleven.com/2017/07/03/video-craig-calhoun-populism-polarization-and-democracy.
Campbell, B. & Manning, J. (2014). Microaggression and Moral Cultures. *Comparative Sociology*, 13 (6), 692–726.
Connell, R. (2012). Masculinities. *RaewynConnell.net*. Retrieved from http://www.raewynconnell.net/p/masculinities20.html.
Converse, P.E. (1964). The Nature of Belief Systems in Mass Publics. In D.E. Apter (Ed.), *Ideology and Discontent* (pp. 206–261). New York: Free Press of Glencoe.
Du Mez, K. (2017). Donald Trump and Militant Evangelical Masculinity. *Religion and Politics*, 17 January. Retrieved from https://religionandpolitics.org/2017/01/17/donald-trump-and-militant-evangelical-masculinity.
Elchardus, M. & Spruyt, B. (2016). Populism, Persistent Republicanism, and Declinism: An Empirical Analysis of Populism as a Thin Ideology. *Government and Opposition*, 51 (1), 111–133.
Farage, N. (2015). UKIP's Immigration Policy is Built on Fairness. *The Telegraph*. 3 March.

Forlenza, R. (2019). 'Abendland in Christian hands': Religion and Populism in Contemporary European Politics. In G. Fitzl, J. Mackert, & B.S. Turner (Eds.), *Populism and the Crisis of Democracy Volume 3: Migration, Gender, and Religion* (pp. 133–149). London: Routledge.

Gerring, J. (1997). Ideology: A Definitional Analysis. *Political Research Quarterly*, 50 (4), 957–994.

Gest, J. (2018). *The New Minority: White Working-Class Politics in an Age of Immigration and Inequality*. New York: Oxford University Press.

Hadj-Abdou, L. (2017) *The Populist Right and Gender-Nationalism*. University of Potsdam, Germany: International Conference of the Centre for Citizenship: Populism and Citizenship, 6–8 July.

Hage, G. (2011). Multiculturalism and the Ungovernable Muslim. In R. Gaita (Ed.), *Essays on Muslims and Multiculturalism* (pp. 165–186). Melbourne: Text Publishing.

Hamilton, M.B. (1987). The Elements of the Concept of Ideology. *Political Studies*, 35 (1), 18–38.

Harvey, D. (2007). *A Brief History of Neoliberalism*. Oxford: Oxford University Press.

Hawkins, K.A. (2009). Is Chávez Populist?: Measuring Populist Discourse in Comparative Perspective. *Comparative Political Studies*, 42 (8), 1040–1067.

Hawkins, K.A., Riding, S., & Mudde, C. (2012). Measuring Populist Attitudes on Three Dimensions. *International Journal of Public Opinion Research*, 30 (2), 316–326.

Heater, D. (1990). *Citizenship: The Civic Ideal in World History, Politics, and Education*. London: Longman Group.

Humphrey, M. & Islam, M. (2002). Injuries and Identities: Authorising Arab Diasporic Difference in Crisis. In G. Hage (Ed.), *Arab-Australians Today: Citizenship and Belonging* (pp. 49–87). Melbourne: Melbourne University Press.

Ipos MORI. (2016). How Britain Voted in the 2016 EU Referendum. *Ipsos*. Retrieved from https://www.ipsos.com/ipsos-mori/en-uk/how-britain-voted-2016-eu-referendum.

Jagers, J. & Walgrave, S. (2007). Populism as Political Communication Style: An Empirical Study of Political Parties' Discourse in Belgium. *European Journal of Political Research*, 46 (3), 319–345.

Jones, O. (2011). *Chavs: The Demonisation of the Working Class*. London: Verso Books.

Keane, J. (2016). Populism and Democracy: Dr Jekyll and Mr Hyde? *OXPOL Blog*, 3 November. Retrieved from https://blog.politics.ox.ac.uk/populism-and-democracy-dr-jekyll-and-mr-hyde.

Knight, K. (2006). Transformations of the Concept of Ideology in the Twentieth Century. *American Political Science Review*, 100 (4), 619–626.

Lamont, M. (2000). *The Dignity of Working Men: Morality and the Boundaries of Race, Class, and Immigration*. Cambridge, MA: Harvard University Press.

Littler, J. (2017). *Against Meritocracy: Culture, Power and Myths of Mobility*. London: Routledge.

London School of Economics. (1967). *Conference on Populism: Verbatim Report*. London School of Economics and Political Science, London: To Define Populism, 19–21 May. Retrieved from http://eprints.lse.ac.uk/102463.

Marshall, T.H. (1950). The Problem Stated with the Assistance of Alfred Marshall. In T.H. Marshall (Ed.), *Citizenship and Social Class* (pp. 1–9). Cambridge: Cambridge University Press.

Marzouki, N., McDonnell, D., & Roy, O. (Eds.). (2016). *Saving the People: How Populists Hijack Religion*. London: Hurst and Co.

McCarthy, J. (2017). *Specifying the Theoretical Factors Essential to Understanding Successful Contemporary Populist Mobilisation*. University of Potsdam, Germany: International Conference of the Centre for Citizenship: Populism and Citizenship, 6–8 July.

McDowell, L. (2003). *Redundant Masculinities?: Employment, Change, and White Working Class Youth*. Oxford: Blackwell Publishing.

Milbank, J. (2017). The Problem of Populism and the Promise of a Christian Ethics. *ABC Religion and Ethics*, 16 February. Retrieved from https://www.abc.net.au/religion/the-problem-of-populism-and-the-promise-of-a-christian-politics/10096050.

Moffitt, B. (2016). *The Global Rise of Populism: Performance, Political Style, and Representation*. Stanford, CA: Stanford University Press.

Moghissi, H. (2017). *Islamic Populism, Cultural Engineering, and Women's Quest for Rights*. University of Potsdam, Germany: International Conference of the Centre for Citizenship: Populism and Citizenship, 6–8 July.

Mudde, C. (2004). The Populist Zeitgeist. *Government & Opposition*, 39 (4), 541–563.

Mudde, C. (2016). Front Matter. In N. Marzouki, D. McDonnell, & O. Roy. (Eds.), *Saving the People: How Populists Hijack Religion*. London: Hurst and Co.

Mullins, W.A. (1972). On the Concept of Ideology in Political Science. *American Political Science Review*, 66 (2), 498–510.

Orwell, G. (1937 [2014]). *The Road to Wigan Pier*. London: Penguin Modern Classics.

Oxford Dictionary. (2015). Chav. In A. Stevenson (Ed.), *Oxford Dictionary of English* (3rd ed.). Oxford: Oxford University Press.

Pabst, A. (2018). 'Vox populi vox dei'?: Examining the Religious Roots of Populism. *ABC Religion and Ethics*, 23 August. Retrieved on 24 June 2019 from https://www.abc.net.au/religion/vox-populi-vox-dei-examining-the-religious-roots-of-populism/10214296.

Pew Research. (2015). *2014 Religious Landscape Study*. Pew Research Center.

Pew Research. (2016). An Examination of the 2016 Electorate, Based on Validated Voters. *Pew Research Center*, 9 August.

Pinker, S. (2011). *The Better Angels of Our Nature: The Decline of Violence in History and its Causes*. London: Penguin.

Raschke, C. (2019). *Neoliberalism and Political Theology: From Kant to Identity Politics*. Edinburgh: Edinburgh University Press.

Roose, J.M. (2016). *Political Islam and Masculinity: Muslim Men in the West*. New York: Palgrave.

Roose, J.M. (2017). Citizenship, Masculinities, and Political Populism: Preliminary Considerations in the Context of Contemporary Social Challenges. In J. Mackert & B.S. Turner (Eds.), *The Transformation of Citizenship Vol. 3: Struggle, Resistance, and Violence* (pp. 56–76). Oxon: Routledge.

Rucht, D. (2017). *Right-wing Populism in Context: A Cross-Time Perspective*. University of Potsdam, Germany: International Conference of the Centre for Citizenship: Populism and Citizenship, 6–8 July.

Sassen, S. (2014). *Expulsions*. Cambridge, MA: Harvard University Press.

Scruton, R. (2017). Populism, VII: Representation & the People. *New Criterion*, March. Retrieved on 20 June 2019 from https://newcriterion.com/issues/2017/3/populism-vii-representation-the-people.

Snow, D. (2017). *The Coterminous Rise of Populism and Superfluous Populations*. University of Potsdam, Germany: International Conference of the Centre for Citizenship: Populism and Citizenship, 6–8 July.

Standing, G. (2011). *The Precariat: The New Dangerous Class*. London: Bloomsbury.

Stanley, B. (2008). The Thin Ideology of Populism. *Journal of Political Ideologies*, 13 (1), 95–110.

Stark, R. & Bainbridge, W.S. (1985). *The Future of Religion: Secularization, Revival, and Cult Formation*. Berkeley, CA: University of California Press.

Statista. (2016). Share of Votes in the Brexit Referendum of 2016 in the United Kingdom, by Gender. *Statista*. Retrieved from https://www.statista.com/statistics/567922/brexit-votes-by-gender.

Turner, B.S. (1990). Outline of a Theory of Citizenship. *Sociology*, 24 (2), 189–217.
Turner, B.S. (2001). The Erosion of Citizenship. *British Journal of Sociology*, 52 (2), 189–209. doi:10.1080/00071310120044944.
Turner, B.S. (2017). *Religion and Populism: From Tea Party to Trump*. University of Potsdam, Germany: International Conference of the Centre for Citizenship: Populism and Citizenship, 6–8 July.
van Dijk, T.A. (1998). *Ideology: A Multidisciplinary Approach*. London: Sage.
Ward, M.R.M. (2013). *Working Paper 150: The Emos: The Re-traditionalisation of White, Working Class Masculinities Through the 'Alternative Scene'*. Cardiff: Cardiff University.
Wilcox, W.B. & Wang, W. (2017). The Marriage Divide: How and Why Working-class Families are More Fragile Today. *Opportunity America-AEI-Brookings Working Class Group*.
Wodak, R. (2015). *The Politics of Fear: What Right-Wing Populist Discourses Mean*. London: Sage.
Wodak, R. (2017). *The Micro-Politics of Right-wing Populism*. University of Potsdam, Germany: International Conference of the Centre for Citizenship: Populism and Citizenship, 6–8 July.
Yuval-Davis, N. (2017). *Everyday Bordering and Populist Constructions of 'The Migrant'*. University of Potsdam, Germany: International Conference of the Centre for Citizenship: Populism and Citizenship, 6–8 July.

2

POPULISM IN THE WEST

Democratic fault lines and the rise of the new demagogues

Introduction

This chapter explores the first thesis of the book, which argues that the rise of the new demagogues is linked directly to the deterioration of citizenship and the welfare state; the stripping of ethical values from policymaking, which stems from neoliberal economic policies; and the dramatic decline (in both membership and status) of key social institutions, including trade unions (offering intellectual leadership and solidarity to working people) and churches (offering moral and ethical leadership and community). This decline has resulted in a significant vacuum of intellectual and moral leadership for working people, which has been filled by populist narratives based on promoting nostalgia about a return to perceived past greatness and blaming other social groups for the loss of honour and place. The major political parties have come to consist of a class of professional politicians who are unable (or unwilling) to connect with working people at an everyday level. Consequently, populist narratives have become not only prevalent, but also at times dominant through the exploitation of democratic fault lines, with social and mass media acting as force multipliers for previously fringe voices.

The rise of the new demagogues

We live in a time of immense social, political, economic, and technological flux. On the one hand, tremendous strides have been made on a global scale towards the reduction of extreme poverty, illiteracy, and disease. The gender gap is slowly but surely closing. There has been a global reduction in violence. Technological innovation offers unprecedented global connectivity and solutions to critical challenges, including global warming. However, on the other hand, the gap between the extremely wealthy and ordinary working men and women has increased exponentially since the 'post-war egalitarian regime' (Alvaredo et al. 2018: 5). This is likely to be even more so the case post-COVID-19. The same technological change that has assisted in battling disease and improving efficiency has contributed to the expulsion of working men and women from blue- and, increasingly, white-collar sectors of the economy. Increased interconnectedness and the movement of people across the globe have created local tensions that have been readily exploited by previously marginalised, extremist political groups and contributed to the rapid development of the COVID-19 crisis, which expanded from a local epidemic in Wuhan, China, to a global pandemic in a matter of weeks in early 2020. Domestically, the 'war on terrorism' has seen entire communities targeted for securitisation. Violence towards women continues, particularly in the domestic sphere, and drug abuse, such as the methamphetamine and opioid epidemics, has shattered entire Western communities.

It is in this profoundly modern context that the new demagogues have found a receptive audience for their messages emphasising past greatness, national belonging, and exclusion of others and attacking the so-called 'establishment', which is seen as being responsible for prioritising international developments and interests over their own people and to the detriment of their own communities. Importantly, these challenges have deep structural underpinnings that are grounded in a sense of marginalisation and the loss of solidarities and belonging. The deterioration of citizenship is consequently an important starting point for seeking to understand the dimensions of the populist epoch.

The deterioration of citizenship

In contemporary political discourse, the concept of 'citizenship' has become associated with hard borders, migration restrictions, and simultaneous calls for both tightening access to and stripping 'undesirables' of citizenship. US President Donald Trump has sought to revoke birth right citizenship in the United States (Wagner et al. 2018), whilst in the United Kingdom the status of European Union (EU) citizens in the UK in the context of Brexit has become a point of central contention. The Australian government has sought to toughen citizenship requirements, including proof of competence in English, and to strip Australian-born Islamic State foreign fighters of their citizenship (Kainth 2018; Davidson & Remeikis 2019). Citizenship in contemporary political parlance has become synonymous with the consolidation of national identities. Yet it is only relatively recently that concepts such as 'cosmopolitan citizenship' achieved a level of popularity in academic discourse. Standing in strong contrast to contemporary definitions, cosmopolitanism derives from the Greek word 'kosmopolites' (citizen of the world) (Kleingeld & Brown 2014) and aims to challenge a perceived moral contradiction at the core of the modern state:

> The cosmopolitan argument is that world citizenship can be a powerful means of coaxing citizens away from the false supposition that the interests of fellow

citizens necessarily take priority over duties to the rest of the human race; it is a unique device for eliciting their support for global political institutions and sentiments which weaken the grip of exclusionary separate states.

(Linklater 1998: 24)

In the populist epoch, notions of a global community appear further away than ever. Recent developments with regards to the COVID-19 pandemic have revealed deep cleavages in international cooperation, even between supposedly friendly nations. Yet despite the rapid emergence of global populist regimes led by demagogic strongmen and subsequent challenges, the deterioration of citizenship has an evident longer lineage. To understand this, however, it is important to consider the sociological dimensions of citizenship and the difficulties inherent in any attempt to measure its decline.

There exist many forms of citizenship enacted across local, national, and international contexts, and direct comparison between them is difficult. Writing in an introduction to *The Handbook of Citizenship Studies*, Isin and Turner note the diversity of the field and the difficulty in pinning it down: 'To put it starkly, there is neither a singular way of engaging with citizenship studies nor a singular way of investigating its objects' (Isin & Turner 2002: 5). These two key figures in citizenship studies continue, noting that 'it is this discursive aspect that provides its vitality and liveliness, rather than an orthodox set of rules that govern conduct' (Isin & Turner 2002: 5). The handbook is instructive regarding the state of the field at the turn of the twenty-first century, with contributions on everything from more traditional liberal and republican citizenship through to sexual, multicultural, ecological, and, of course, cosmopolitan citizenship. These are not only difficult to compare but have very different potential forms of measurement in different contexts, often linked to the extent of their conceptual and theoretical development. Claims made here about the deterioration of citizenship rest on claims made by scholars in the field, typically based on a departure from classical conceptions of citizenship.

Amidst the body of scholarship on classical conceptions of citizenship and their evolution, Turner noted the threat to the welfare state resulting from monetarism, and sought, optimistically, to address this through a theoretical inquiry synthesising 'levels of analysis between the individual citizen, the organisation of social rights, and the institutional context of democracy' (1990: 190). However, in the context of significant global change, he wrote just over a decade later about the 'erosion of citizenship' (Turner 2001) and, most recently, that 'we are all denizens now' (Turner 2016). From a sociological perspective, Turner, drawing on Marshall's conception of rights and responsibilities, defines a citizen as:

a person who, by birth or naturalization, is resident in a territory where he or she has full rights of participation (legally, politically, socially, and culturally) and who has the right to a passport to move freely both internally and externally. As a consequence of these entitlements and privileges, a citizen is subject to certain obligations such as the payment of taxes and various other public duties that may include voting, military service, or jury service.

(Turner 2016: 682)

Turner distinguished between the traditional form of denizenship (a group of people permanently residing in a country though with limited and partial rights of citizenship) and what he terms 'Denizenship Type 2', which involves 'the erosion of social citizenship as citizens begin to resemble denizens or strangers in their own societies' as the world changes around them (2016: 679). If Turner's summation is correct, then this transition from full citizenship rights to only partial rights for those living in liberal democracies might be considered a significant deterioration both of citizenship and democracy. Other scholars go even further. Mackert (2017: 99) states that citizenship has unalterably changed:

> The modern institution of citizenship as we knew it no longer exists. In retrospect, it is obvious that neo-liberalism has profoundly transformed not only the global political economy, but also the power relations crystallised in national 'citizenship regimes'.
>
> (Mackert 2017: 99)

The challenges of measuring the deterioration of citizenship become even clearer. On the one hand, different forms of citizenship are said to be thriving, and the academic field of citizenship studies is continuously expanding; yet, on the other, some argue that citizenship is endangered, if not already extinct. Further, questions arise about the interplay of the economic conditions for citizenship. It is important to pin down precisely what form of citizenship is said to have deteriorated, for this is central to any attempt to understand factors that have created the pre-conditions for populism.

Traditional conceptions of citizenship: T.H. Marshall

T.H. Marshall's *Citizenship and Social Class* (1950) is considered by many to be the key historic reference point for traditional sociological notions of citizenship as they relate to England and the United Kingdom more broadly. The work also has been particularly influential in the Australian and New Zealand contexts, where classical conceptions of citizenship have been a core element of both nations' welfare states since the end of the Second World War. This work by Marshall is intimately linked to social welfare, Keynesian economics, and the role of trade unions in society; indeed, it commences by paying homage to Alfred Marshall, John Keynes's mentor. Traditional conceptions of citizenship and welfare may also be argued to characterise both the centrality of religious life in twentieth-century England and structural inequalities more generally (the source of most criticisms of Marshall and central to understanding the collapse of traditional citizenship). In understanding Marshall's traditional form of citizenship and its wider context and influences, we are able to go some way towards establishing a base for comparison with contemporary approaches to the structuring of societal rights and obligations as well as understanding the early origins of the new populism. As Moore noted:

> if there has been one central target for the New Right it has been the idea of citizenship. None has chosen to confront Marshall's work directly but the increasing extent to which Marshall has been discussed and footnoted in the last two decades is evidence enough of his influence.
>
> *(Moore 1991: vi)*

It would be wrong, however, to view Marshall's conception of citizenship as targeted only by the political right. As becomes evident below, Marshallian citizenship has been criticised by broadly left-aligned intellectuals on a number of grounds and stands in contradistinction to the pervasive identity politics that typify contemporary political life.

For Marshall, citizenship had three components: legal rights (*habeas corpus*), political rights (to vote), and social rights (to welfare, education, and health). Marshall regarded citizenship as a 'status, bestowed on those who are full members of a community', stating further that 'all who possess the status are equal with respect to the rights and duties with which the state is endowed' (Marshall 1950: 28–29). Whilst legal rights and political rights have, at least on paper, remained remarkably intact and even grown since the mid-twentieth century, social rights, including access to welfare, equitable education, and health, have regressed markedly.

Equality was an important dimension of Marshallian citizenship. Marshall sought to ensure that the market value of individuals was no longer determinant of their real income because of the provision, through state administration, of economic goods and services as a right (Barbalet 1993: 36). Marshall was effectively seeking to mitigate the most negative aspects of social class, including economic inequality and unequal access to opportunity that could lead to working class resentment and anger. Within this paradigm, government has an important – and interventionist – role to play. Marshall sought to influence the development of a collectivist social service that contributes to the development and maintenance of social welfare, provided that it did not undermine the operation of the free market (Pinker 1981: 12). Marshall's conception of welfare stood in very conscious contrast to Marxist and socialist perspectives, which viewed such provision of services as platitudes (Marshall 1950: 5–6).

Despite his seeking to distance himself from socialist perspectives, Marshall was favourably disposed toward trade unions. He framed labour rights as a fourth and separate form of citizenship in addition to legal, political, and social rights, claiming:

> the acceptance of collective bargaining was not simply a natural extension of civil rights; it represented the transfer of an important process from the political to the civil sphere of citizenship ... Trade unionism has therefore created

a secondary system of industrial citizenship parallel with and supplementary to the system of political citizenship.

(Marshall 1950: 44)

The concept of industrial citizenship has been the subject of considerable debate. Mundlak argues that the construction of a distinct group of rights by Marshall can be explained by their nature as 'process-oriented' rights. They do not secure end norms (the right to a minimum wage or welfare) but, rather like political rights, describe a process to ensure just outcomes (Mundlak 2007: 723). He argues that industrial rights of citizenship are 'active rights' requiring 'active participation by the citizenry to affect their community' (Mundlak 2007: 723). Marshall did allude, however, to what amounted to even then a subtle rebuke of remunerated (professional) trade union officials' lack of accountability (Marshall 1950: 45), a theme to which we will return shortly. As with social rights, the right to strike and to take industrial action in pursuit of a better economic bargain for members has been significantly altered since the time of Marshall.

Beveridge, Keynes, and Marshall: The centrality of state intervention

Marshall's citizenship was reliant on an ideal economic model of strong government and the provision of social services that would moderate the excesses of the free market. To this extent, Marshallian citizenship (and, in particular, social rights) may be understood as being enmeshed with economic developments leading to the formation of the welfare state. Writing at the peak of its influence, Asa Briggs defined the welfare state as 'a state in which organised power is deliberately used (through politics and administration) in an effort to modify the play of market forces in at least three directions' (Briggs 1961: 221). The first of these directions was to guarantee a minimum income irrespective of the market value of work or property; the second was to narrow insecurity by enabling individuals and families to meet 'social contingencies', such as illness or unemployment; and, finally, the third was to ensure that all citizens have access to the best standards of service provision available without reference to status or social class (Briggs 1961: 221).

A report by Sir William Beveridge (1942) titled *Social Insurance and Allied Services* sought to address both poverty and the characteristics believed to lead to poverty. Beveridge was a liberal with Fabian socialist links and a former Director of the London School of Economics and Political Science, which he left to relocate to Oxford. It is also important to consider, however, that Beveridge was influenced by Archbishop William Temple, the Anglican theologian and Archbishop of Canterbury (1942–44). Temple was a close friend of R.H. Tawney, Professor of Economic History at LSE, and became friends with William Beveridge through this relationship (Goldman 2019), even officiating at his marriage. It was Temple who would first use the phrase 'welfare state' in his book *Christianity and the Social Order* (1942), which called for universal access to health, education, housing, dignified conditions of work, and democratic representation. In the preface of the book, Temple acknowledged the intellectual contribution of John Maynard Keynes.

Beveridge's 1942 report is considered a key intellectual influence on the welfare state. It focused on universal access to education, a national insurance scheme, and the creation of the National Health Service (NHS). His subsequent book, *Full Employment in a Free Society* (1944), outlines the dimensions of the report:

> That Report takes Freedom from want as its aim, and sets out a plan for Social Security to achieve this aim. Want is defined as a lack of income to obtain the means of healthy subsistence – adequate food, shelter, clothing, and fuel. The Plan for Social Security is designed to secure, by a comprehensive scheme of social insurance, that every individual, on condition of working while he can and contributing from his earnings, shall have an income sufficient for the healthy subsistence of himself and his family, an income to keep him above want, when for any reason he cannot work and earn.
>
> *(Beveridge 1944: 1)*

The Beveridge Report's assertion of what Marshall termed 'social rights' was geared to a particular operation of the economy based on state intervention. It would accompany Keynesian economic approaches and become influential. A letter from Keynes to Beveridge in March 1942 makes this abundantly clear: 'Your general scheme leave[s] me in a state of wild enthusiasm ... I think it a vast constructive reform of real importance and I am relieved to find that it is so financially possible' (Keynes 1942).

A witness to the Great Depression, John Maynard Keynes challenged the neoclassical economic presumption that free markets provide full employment. In his 1936 work *The General Theory of Employment, Interest, and Money*, Keynes argued that the Great Depression had been caused by a drop in aggregate demand that could have been countered by increased government spending. He asserted that governments should actively intervene in the economy in order to stimulate employment and, where necessary, employ the unemployed on national infrastructure projects. Keynesian economics would ultimately assist in the development of the welfare state.

The work of Beveridge, Marshall, and Keynes defined social policy in postwar Britain. The underlying propositions of their work, grounded in the notion of an interventionist government and, in particular, social rights to welfare, also speak to a shared moral and ethical philosophical outlook. In this paradigm, a social and moral economy was fostered through the activities of an interventionist state (Harvey 2007a: 11). This reveals an important point for consideration and contrast with later neoliberal approaches to the management of the economy and social rights. The return to economic 'stimulus' spending in times of national crisis, including the COVID-19 pandemic, by governments to the right of the political spectrum demonstrates the continued relevance of the approach.

The underpinning influence of Christian values

The contributions of Beveridge, Keynes, and Marshall share a common, though not always overtly moral, imperative grounded in Christian values. As explored above, in formulating his conception of the 'welfare state', William Beveridge was influenced by his close friend Archbishop William Temple. Temple was influenced, in turn, by Keynes when writing *Christianity and the Social Order* (1942). Keynes reassured Temple that 'economics ... is a side of ethics' and urged him to more strongly assert the Church's right to make pronouncements on economics (Keynes 1941). Beveridge's 1942 report would be praised by Keynes, despite their history of fierce disagreement, and, in turn, it influenced his formulation of the welfare state. The small social and intellectual circle of these historically influential, yet often competing, scholars would become clear when Keynes attended the wedding of Beveridge, which was presided over by Temple in December 1942 (Marcuzzo 2010: 204).

There are a number of important similarities between Keynes and Marshall. Keynes, who had initially rejected religion but later reembraced it, has been viewed by some as adopting positions similar to the nineteenth-century Christian socialist movement, viewing religion as 'standing in opposition to a selfish and materialistic tendency' (Andrews 2017: 959). In a 1944 letter to Friedrich Hayek (with whom Keynes had long been in public debate) concerning Hayek's recently published book, *The Road to Serfdom*, Keynes, a former member of the Cambridge *Conversazione Society*, known colloquially as the 'Cambridge Apostles', emphasised the need for 'the restoration of right moral thinking':

> Moderate planning will be safe if those carrying it out are rightly oriented in their own minds and hearts to the moral issue. This is in fact already true of some of them. But the curse is that there is also an important section who could almost be said to want planning not in order to enjoy its fruits but because morally they hold ideas exactly the opposite of yours, and wish to serve not God but the devil. No, what we need is the restoration of right moral thinking – a return to proper moral values in our social philosophy.
>
> *(Keynes 1972)*

Marshall, who also passed through Cambridge, stated in his autobiographical outline that, in his youth at the Rugby School, he was a 'sincere and devout Christian' though had lost his faith by the end of his first year at Cambridge (Halsey 1984: 4). However, there is a hint of religious underpinning when Marshall states that 'welfare decisions ... are essentially altruistic and must draw on standards of value embodied in an autonomous ethical system' (Halsey 1984: 4), though as Halsey points out, Marshall is unable (or unwilling) to say 'how [those] ethical standards arise in a society or are recognised by its members' (Halsey 1984: 4). For Halsey, Marshall's transition from aristocracy and evangelical religion to supporter of the welfare state occurred through the medium of sociology and, as importantly, through the 'corpus of work in the moral sciences' in Cambridge from the middle of the nineteenth century. Haynes notes further that whilst Marshall would not attain the high scholarly stature or international influence of the Cambridge Apostles, of which Keynes was a key member, he nonetheless belonged to the same 'slightly wider circle of Trinity, Cambridge, and Bloomsbury' and this circle 'sought to define the nature and substance of an elevated secular civilization in its social and its professional forms' (Halsey 1984: 4).

This moral and ethical (and some may argue 'religious') dimension of the welfare state is particularly important, for, as we shall see, in competing visions of the role of government, there is no such place.

Marshall's social rights and the welfare state: Contrasts and similarities with the United States

Given the differences between policy approaches across the Atlantic, it is important to consider how Marshall was received in the United States. The Marshallian model of citizenship proved to be influential in North American sociology, where it was adopted by scholars, including Talcott Parsons (1965), to explore challenges of the social and political rights of African Americans. Mead, the key theorist behind the welfare to work reforms of the 1990s, notes that it is the political dimension of Marshallian citizenship that has most resonance in the United States, whereby equality is associated with equal citizenship rather than equality of wealth:

> There is evidence that, just as Marshall suggests, equal citizenship in America 'comforts' inequality. Americans are sufficiently satisfied with equal citizenship that social and economic inequality is seldom resented. Most people think equality is equal citizenship; they do not demand equal income or wealth. Status differences are usually ignored in politics provided they do not obtrude on how people are treated by government.
>
> *(Mead 1997: 199)*

The work of Judith Shklar (1990) is particularly resonant in outlining the dimensions of American citizenship. Shklar notes two primary forms of citizenship rights which fall broadly within the political and social rights outlined by Marshall: the right to vote and the right to work. These are bound together by the significance of social standing and were expanded upon in her Utah lectures:

> The significance of the two great emblems of public standing, the vote and the opportunity to earn, seems clearest to ... excluded men and women. They have regarded voting and earning as not just the ability to promote their interests and to make money but as the attributes of an American citizen. And people who are not granted these marks of civic dignity feel dishonored, not just powerless and poor.
>
> *(Shklar 1989: 388)*

Shklar seeks to make it clear that such a proposition does not undermine the role of unions in improving working life, but unions cannot prevent unemployment and the subsequent loss of social standing (Shklar 1990: 22). In this context, Shklar notes that whilst welfare may assist the recently unemployed as victims of 'social misfortune', long-term welfare dependence is to be viewed as 'to lose one's independence and to be treated as less than a full member of society. In effect, people who belong to the underclass are not quite citizens' (Shklar 1990: 22).

Fault lines in Marshallian citizenship

Despite the preoccupation of Marshallian citizenship with social rights and equitable outcomes through the provision of welfare, the extent to which such outcomes were to apply to all members of society has been called into considerable question by his critics. Revi (2014: 452), for example, notes that it fails to capture the perspectives of migrants, women, indigenous peoples, and cultural groups. Turner (1993: 8) notes that Marshall did not provide a causal explanation of how citizenship expands in either scope or to other social groups. These are important tensions and fault lines based on exclusion, particularly those related to the role of women as citizens, that exist to the present day. They are expressed in the identity-based politics that has become prevalent in recent decades.

In seeking to understand these fault lines in Marshall's conception of citizenship and how the collapse of the model has contributed to events almost 70 years later, it is important to consider the relationship in his thought of economy, gender, and citizenship.

Women in this citizenship framework were required to procreate and be subservient to the needs of the family, despite having been a vital element of the war effort. The aim of citizenship was to emancipate the working man, enabling them to become 'gentlemen' and to enjoy leisure time. Women's exclusion from citizenship was not unintentional. Indeed, it enabled, through operation of the home front, the potential for men to enjoy the rights extended to them (Fraser & Gordon 1992: 55). Revi argues that 'in this way, citizenship has been built on gender inequality' (2014: 459). In many respects, this conception of the gentleman was never anticipated to extend beyond that of men and locally born heterosexual British men at that. In this way, the Marshallian conception, like Athenian conceptions, is very much a product of the society in which it was built; in this case, post-war Britain. Combined with the state interventionist approaches on which it was founded, it ensured considerable prosperity in the decades after 1945. However, its simultaneous reliance on government economic intervention and the subordination of women to the domestic sphere in a world not yet touched by mass migration ensured that, when these circumstances were challenged, the Marshallian model would collapse.

From state intervention and the 'common good' to individualism

We may then understand the classical Marshallian conception of citizenship as being tied intimately with efforts to assist in the development of a middle class and to grant men a modicum of leisure time. Its success in doing so was tied to the success of the post-war economy, welfare state, and adoption of Keynesian economics, a bond solidified by the common intellectual moral and ethical concerns of both Marshall and Keynes. However, despite the apparent success of Keynesian programs, the logic of Keynesian economics and centralised governmental intervention in the economy, on which the Marshallian model of classical citizenship depended, was by no means uncontested. It would be this contest of ideas, ultimately won by those starkly opposed to Keynes and government intervention, that would shape the economic direction of Western governments and, consequently, conceptions of welfare, societal institutions, citizenship, and the notion of a 'common good'.

Mont Pèlerin Society and the Chicago School: The origins of neoliberal economics

Two individuals in particular would prove pivotal to undermining the prevalence of Keynesian economics and the welfare state, central dimensions of Marshallian citizenship. This would occur due to the simultaneous quality and rigor of their work and the ideological impetus that powered their ideas forward, leading to take up by key political advocates and leaders in the field of power.

These key figures were Austrian born Friedrich Hayek (1899–1992), the 'father of neoliberalism', and American Milton Friedman (1912–2006), a powerful proponent of the free market and monetarism. Both contributed to the formation of the classical liberal, anti-government-intervention, free-market think tank known as the *Mont Pèlerin Society* (Hayek passed the Presidency on to Friedman in the 1970s), and both worked together at the University of Chicago during a pivotal era in the formation of what we today term 'neoliberalism'. Other members of this intellectual cohort included Karl Popper and George Stigler. It is important to understand the rise to prominence of both Hayek and Friedman and the direct challenge they posed to Marshallian conceptions of citizenship.

Friedrich Hayek and *The Road to Serfdom*

Born into an extended family of Austrian scholars, economist Friedrich Hayek fought in the First World War as a young man before gaining doctorates at the University of Vienna in both law and political science in the early 1920s. He subsequently moved into economic advisory roles with the Austrian government. Hayek was born into a Catholic family yet remained non-practicing throughout his life. He moved to the London School of Economics (1931–1950), becoming a contemporary, and critic, of T.H. Marshall's work during his time there. Indeed, Marshall was the Head of the Social Sciences at LSE from 1939 to 1944, directly coinciding with Hayek's work on his highly influential *The Road to Serfdom* (1944). This book sought to cast a light on what Hayek believed to be totalitarian tendencies in Western democracies. He stated, 'many who think themselves infinitely superior to the aberrations of naziism, and sincerely hate all its manifestations, work at the same time for ideals whose realisation would lead straight to the abhorred tyranny' (Hayek 2014: 59). Friedman, who wrote the forward to the 50th anniversary edition of the book, argued that it constituted 'a sort of manifesto and a call to arms to prevent the accumulation of a totalitarian state' (Friedman 1994). Hayek transferred to the University of Chicago in 1950, a move prompted in part by the growing cluster of likeminded neoclassical liberal scholars gathering there at a time when such ideas were still marginalised within the academy. Hayek remained there during the Chicago School's critical formative years in the early 1960s.

Hayek was awarded the 1974 Nobel Prize in Economic Sciences (alongside Swedish economist Gunner Myrdal, who held alternative economic perspectives) for his work on the functional efficiency of different economic systems. He viewed the 'taut discipline of the market' as the thin line between abundance and starvation for the world's people. Drawing on his perspectives of the Second World War, Hayek stated:

> I believe that the main lesson which our generation has learnt is that we must find a new limit for the activities of government, a limit which leaves ample scope for sensible experimentation but which secures the freedom of the individual as the mainspring of all social and political activity.
>
> *(Hayek 2013: 194)*

In a similar vein, Hayek viewed trade unions as an impediment to the operation of the free market and, consequently, as undermining prosperity for workers. In a 1977 letter written to *The Times*, Hayek bemoaned what he considered the privileged position of the trade unions and asserted that '[t]here can indeed be little doubt to a detached observer that the privileges then granted to the trade unions have become the chief source of Britain's economic decline' (1977: 15).

Hayek's work became increasingly influential during the 1970s, resonating particularly strongly with a new breed of politicians from the right of the political spectrum, including British Prime Minister Margaret Thatcher (4 May 1979–28 November 1990). Thatcher, who was first exposed to Hayek's work whilst studying at Oxford in 1944, wrote, 'the most powerful critique of socialist planning and the socialist state which I read at this time [the late 1940s], and to which I have returned so often since [is] F.A. Hayek's *The Road to Serfdom*' (Thatcher 1995: 55). Hayek would become an advisor to Thatcher and a strong public supporter:

> It is Mrs Thatcher's great merit that she has broken the Keynesian immorality of 'in the long run we are all dead' and to have concentrated on the long run future of the country irrespective of possible effects on the electors ... Mrs Thatcher's courage makes her put the long run future of the country first.
>
> *(Hayek 1982: 13)*

The irony of this moral judgement aside, Hayek enjoyed a transatlantic appeal, and the American President Ronald Regan (20 January 1981–20 January 1989) was very familiar with and influenced by his works (Reagan 1983). According to former Speaker of the House Newt Gingrich, Reagan studied *The Road to Serfdom* extensively. Hayek was appointed a Companion of Honour in 1984 in the UK on the recommendation of Thatcher and was awarded the Presidential Medal of Freedom by President George Bush in 1991. His work was also influential amongst the quickly disintegrating Eastern bloc nations of Europe during the late 1980s, where his emphasis on economic freedom was particularly appealing.

Milton Friedman

Milton Friedman is considered of equivalent importance to Keynes in shaping twentieth-century economics and, as importantly, is his antithesis in economic thinking. Associated with the Chicago School from 1946 to 1977, Friedman was exposed to Keynesian thought in significant depth during his Fulbright Scholarship at Cambridge, where the economics faculty was deeply divided over Keynesian approaches.

Friedman argued that economic freedom was a necessary basis for political freedom. Writing in the *New York Review of Books*, noted economist Paul Krugman reflected:

> Keynesianism was a great reformation of economic thought. It was followed, inevitably, by a counter-reformation. A number of economists played important roles in the great revival of classical economics between 1950 and 2000, but none was as influential as Milton Friedman.
>
> *(Krugman 2007)*

His 1962 work, *Capitalism and Freedom*, outlined this thesis in depth and became a central pivot for the broadening of the neoliberal economic agenda to shape global politics.

Friedman won the Nobel Prize in Economic Sciences in 1976, just two years after his University of Chicago colleague Friedrich Hayek, for his research on consumption analysis, monetary history, and stabilization policy. A number of other Chicago School economists were elevated by Nobel Prizes and international accolades in subsequent decades, including George Stigler (1982), Ronald Coase (1991), and Gary Becker (1992). Friedman developed an extensive suite of policy alternatives to Keynesian economics grounded in monetarism (the incremental expansion of money supply rather than fiscal policies grounded in government intervention in the market). Policies he advocated included minimal taxation, the privatisation of government-owned State assets, and deregulation of the market.

If Hayek was a profound intellectual influence on the two most significant Western political leaders of the 1980s, Thatcher and Regan, Friedman was the key pivot in seeing neoliberal policies enacted by presidents and prime ministers alike:

'If by this stage Hayek was the benign philosopher king, Friedman was the frenetic man of business, jetting from lecture theatre to presidential suite, all but omnipresent on the op-ed pages and the tv screen' (Margaret Thatcher Foundation 2020).

Friedman wrote extensively on the Great Depression, describing the 1929–1933 period as 'the Great Contraction'. He argued that the Depression had been caused by an ordinary financial shock, the duration and seriousness of which were greatly increased by the subsequent contraction of the money supply caused by the misguided policies of the directors of the Federal Reserve.

His book and television series, *Free to Choose* (hosted with his wife Rose), extrapolated his free-market approach and gained national attention, including from President Ronald Reagan, to whom he would become a close advisor (whilst remaining formally outside the White House administration). Reagan labelled *Free to Choose* a 'survival kit for you, for our nation, and for freedom' (Friedman 1990). Friedman similarly inspired Margaret Thatcher's economic reforms and served as an advisor between 1979 and 1990. According to Thatcher, 'Milton Friedman revived the economics of liberty when it had been all but forgotten. He was an intellectual freedom fighter. Never was there a less dismal practitioner of a dismal science' (Thatcher 2006).

Friedman, like Hayek, was adamantly opposed to trade unions on the basis that they effectively monopolised higher wage growth:

> Trade unions were on the side of the angels and it was an automatic, conditioned reflex on the part of any intelligent well-meaning man that if you said trade union, you said 'good'. That's changed. And desirably it's changed. Why has it changed? Because the harms they have done – do – has become absolutely obvious and patent. But even the most innocent and naïve of well-meaning people may well have a warm feeling in his heart for labor, but he no longer makes the mistake of equating labor with labor unions.
>
> *(WPIX 1975)*

Friedman stood for a raft of policy measures commonly associated with neoliberal economics, including opposition to social security in favour of a negative income tax, support for private schools under the guise of 'school choice', and privatisation of the public sector. Indeed, Friedman considered profit making to be a key social responsibility for business (Friedman 1970). Friedman's work was influential amongst Catholic conservatives preoccupied with challenging socialist regimes in the developing world, including the 'Chicago Boys'.

The neoliberal attack on citizenship

The work of Hayek and Friedman extended well beyond monetarism and markets, providing an alternative paradigm to citizenship for the organisation of society. This project would come to be known as neoliberalism. Whilst there is a vast body of literature engaging with the concept, it is important here to broadly contemplate the dimensions of the neoliberal political project as understood within this work.

Neoliberalism is a catch-all term used in a variety of different contexts, however, it is most concisely articulated by Harvey, who considers that:

> Neoliberalism is a theory of political economic practices that proposes that human well-being can best be advanced by maximization of entrepreneurial freedoms within an institutional framework characterised by private property right rights, individual liberty, unencumbered market, and free trade. The role of the state is to create and preserve an institutional framework appropriate to such practices.
>
> *(Harvey 2007b: 22)*

If Marshallian citizenship was intertwined with Keynesian economics and grounded in a moral and ethical frame loosely (or otherwise) influenced by Christian principles, it is perhaps important to note that both Hayek and Friedman effectively rejected organised religion, describing themselves as agnostic. Friedman subscribed to evolutionary psychology, viewing morality as a product of natural selection that facilitates cooperation and collaboration. This corresponds with his perspective that the market acts as a form of financial natural selection or survival of the fittest.

Bourdieu has described neoliberalism as 'tending on the whole to favour severing the economy from social realities and thereby constructing, in reality, an economic system conforming to its description in pure theory' (1998: 610). Thompson considers neoliberalism to constitute the 'intensification of the influence and dominance of capital; it is the elevation of capitalism, as a mode of production, into an ethic, a set of political imperatives, and a cultural logic' (2005: 23). It is precisely this elevation of capitalism into an ethic that leads Harvey to describe neoliberalism as valuing market exchange as:

> an ethic in itself, capable of acting as a guide to all human action and substituting for all previously held ethical beliefs ... It holds that the social good will be maximized by maximizing the reach and frequency of market transactions, and it seeks to bring all human action into the domain of the market.
>
> *(Harvey 2007a: 3)*

To this extent, social relations governed by the rights and responsibilities of citizenship devolve into interactions governed only by the extent to which they serve the narrow self-interest of each individual. As Mackert and Turner note, 'around the globe, neo-liberal economics deeply affects both civil societies and the institution of citizenship through the intrusion of market principle into the private sphere' (Mackert & Turner 2017: 1).

Institutionalising neoliberalism through the political left

It is easy to neglect that prior to 9/11 and in the last decade of the twentieth century, the world was a very different place. Optimism girded by the fall of the

Berlin Wall in 1989 and rapid demise of the Soviet Union in 1991 signalled the apparent victory of Western liberal democracy. Political scientist Francis Fukuyama famously declared:

> What we may be witnessing is not just the end of the Cold War, or the passing of a particular period of post-war history, but the end of history as such: that is, the end point of mankind's ideological evolution and the universalization of Western 'liberal democracy' as the final form of human government. The 'end of history'.
>
> *(Fukuyama 1989: 1)*

This mood, for many, stretched for over a decade. Speaking in January 2000 at his eighth State of the Union Address, President of the United States Bill Clinton proclaimed 'We are fortunate to be alive at this moment in history. Never before has our nation enjoyed, at once, so much prosperity and social progress with so little internal crisis and so few external threats' (Clinton 2000).

In 1996 the Democratic Clinton Administration passed the *Welfare Reform Bill* and the *Personal Responsibility and Work Opportunity Reconciliation Act*. Clinton promised to 'end welfare as we know it', arguing that welfare dependency was a national crisis (Semeuls 2016). The new Act promoted 'personal responsibility' and stipulated that citizens could receive no more than five years of government benefits in their lifetime, although states could limit this to two years. The Act forced millions off welfare and into insecure, low-paid work with equally poor working conditions.

In 1998 British Labor Prime Minister Tony Blair co-authored a working paper with German Social-Democratic Chancellor Gerhard Schröder titled *Europe: The Third Way* (1998). The position paper radically redefined the approach of the European Political left, promoting 'self-help' and arguing that the 'safety net of entitlements' must be transformed into a 'springboard to social responsibility' (Blair & Schröder 1998: 10). This critical document included an outline of a model for creating a 'streamlined and modernised tax and benefits system', 'lowering the burden of tax and social security contributions on low paid jobs' expected of employers, and supporting the creation of individually owned small businesses as a 'viable route out of unemployment' (Blair & Schröder 1998: 11).

Less well known is that these direct attacks on the core dimensions of traditional citizenship were preceded by the Australian Labor Government, who instituted a Superannuation system in 1992, shifting the burden from the government to employers, who were required to make compulsory contributions to a fund tied directly to the free market. During the Hawke and Keating Labor governments (1983–1996), the Australian Labor Party transitioned from a 'top-down' welfare state system to what Paul Keating labelled a 'welfare model focused on the needs of each individual and which maximised choice', making the economy 'more efficient' in the process (Keating 1999). The subsequent Conservative government of

John Howard (1996–2007), for whom Thatcher was a personal inspiration, merely expanded these policies more aggressively.

More recently, governments from across the political spectrum have maintained a steady degradation of retirement, unemployment provision, social security, and welfare to the extent that contemporary programs, if they exist at all, would be barely recognisable to policy makers three decades ago. Notions of individual responsibility and choice, irrespective of social context, abound, and the aim of many programs is to make life for welfare recipients so unbearable and difficult that they do not bother to claim benefits. In May 2018 it was revealed that between July 2016 and June 2017, more than 33 million calls to Centrelink, the Australian welfare agency, went unanswered over the year prior (Dingwall 2018), which is particularly significant in a country with a population of just 25 million. Writing in the UK context, Fletcher and Wright (2017: 327) identify 'rising behavioural conditionality and the punitive turn', such as surveillance measures, the introduction of jobseeker's agreements and job search diaries, and criminalisation of those seen as exploiting the system. In the US context, Wacquant has written of the turn from welfare to workfare, reforms aimed primarily at the 'dispossessed and dependant' (2009: 59).

The impact of neoliberalism on citizenship

One way to measure the impact of neoliberalism on citizenship is to consider what scholars of citizenship were writing at the time. In 1992, for example, Ian Culpitt stated that 'political support for traditional welfare states is no longer an obvious feature of the public rhetoric of Western liberal democracies' (Culpitt 1992: 1). With explicit reference to the impact on citizenship, he commented: 'An essential aspect of this attack on the welfare state has been the complete rejection of those ideals of citizenship rights and obligations which were encapsulated in the political and social structures of welfare states' (Culpitt 1992: 1).

Writing almost a quarter of a century later, Turner claimed that 'the corrosion of the social, economic, political, and legal framework of citizenship offers a new slogan: "we are all denizens now"' (Turner 2016: 679). The notion that citizenship has deteriorated to such an extent that modern citizenship is equivalent to denizenship is, in historical terms, a profound leap and might rightfully be considered the cause of serious concern. However, to understand how we got to this point, it is important to explore the evolution from citizenship to what I term 'weak citizenship'.

Weak citizenship

The entitlement to welfare, public housing, education, affordable child care, work and retirement, secure pensions, and universal healthcare have been compromised, especially in the last three decades, by neoliberal economics and subsequent austerity policies (as much an ideological as an economic policy), individualisation, privatisation of public utilities, and marketisation (Barnes et al. 2018). In short, social citizenship is no longer an effective safety net against unemployment, underemployment, poor health, old age, and unaffordable housing. Individuals are now held responsible for their plight rather than large-scale structural changes brought about by technological change, structural transformations of the economy, or the negative consequences of outsourcing. Interestingly, in the context of the COVID-19 pandemic, countries have extended generous unemployment benefits to those who have lost their jobs as a direct result of the crisis, arguably because it is not their fault, compared to many already in the system who continue to be seen as a drain on the economy.

While social citizenship was originally tied to Keynesian economics and, in the United Kingdom, to the National Health Service on the basis of the Beveridge Report, these socio-economic assumptions have been swept aside. Critics of supply-side economics (a reduction on taxes overall) and trickle-down theory (a reduction in taxes on the rich resulting in greater wealth creation that filters downwards) have argued that inequality has increased and the global fiscal crisis dramatically demonstrated the dangers of aggressive deregulation (Calhoun & Derlugian 2011). Dieter Plehwe has gone so far as to assert that, in the context of austerity economics driven by neoliberalism, the 'present stage in the ongoing great transformation process has witnessed yet more welfare state retrenchment because of privatisation, cost-cutting, and even recalibrations dedicated to enhancing market coordination and individual responsibilities' (Plehwe 2017: 55). Most tellingly, he argues that 'remaining notions of social citizenship are thereby transformed into a neo-liberal alternative to the welfare state: secured market citizenship' (Plehwe 2017: 55). Margaret Somers has noted that, in the American context, whilst neoliberalism's moral reclassification of social security recipients has 'not yet achieved hegemony in American public opinion, it has nonetheless been remarkably successful with those who count among the political and economic elites' (Somers 2017: 90).

This (often implicit or hidden) transformation of citizenship rights has also been matched by an erosion of duties. If the Marshallian version of citizenship was based on a system of contributory rights, such as military service, the payment of taxes, familial care of the elderly, and volunteering, recent developments have demonstrated that this framework has largely disappeared, leaving only a vestige of the social model of citizenship – a 'weak citizenship' centred on the individual as economic actor. Individuals with economic power can readily move beyond the reach of the state and citizenship responsibilities. The 'Panama Papers', for example, represent almost 40 years of data leaked from Panamanian law firm Mossack Fonesca. They revealed the use of off-shore accounts by a wide array of wealthy and powerful actors, including billionaires, sports stars, celebrities, unelected government officials in developing countries, drug traffickers, and elected politicians, including the then Prime Minister of Iceland Sigmundur Davíð Gunnlaugsson (who resigned after the revelations) and then

British Prime Minister David Cameron (who did not resign). These revelations are widely considered only the 'tip of the iceberg' of tax avoidance by the wealthy and powerful (Trautman 2016).

If the institutions of global finance and tax avoidance have strengthened steadily in past decades, two key institutions, one representing 'industrial citizenship' and the other social and civic citizenship, have been hit particularly hard in the past half century. Trade unions have typically been a key point of reference for blue-collar working men (in particular) and acted as a base of intellectual leadership, providing both a protective mechanism against insecure and often dangerous work and a sense of solidarity and belonging. Churches have acted as a physical and community base for working people and provided moral guidance that framed responses to individual and larger societal struggles. As the following demonstrates, in the face of free market monetarism and consumerism grounded in identity politics, both have faced significant decline with repercussions for social cohesion and citizenship.

Trade unions

Trade unions have traditionally played an important role in advocating for working people (particularly men) and in offering intellectual leadership on key social issues. To view the trade union movement as a monolithic block would fail to recognise its significant intellectual diversity. The agendas and action plans of radical Marxist trade unions differ significantly from those proposed by Conservative Catholic-based trade unions, yet they often operate in the same city and, on some occasions, in the same workplaces. Irrespective of their differences, trade unions have historically offered members a sense of solidarity, support, and strength in bargaining for better pay and conditions. This form of industrial citizenship has long been threatened by economic globalisation and neoliberalism, enabling transnational corporations to relocate their operations to developing nations with weak citizenship rights and low pay (Gersuny 1994).

For working men, trade unions and their related institutions, including mechanics institutes, working men's clubs, and sporting teams, provided both an intellectual framing of the working-class predicament and a sense of working-class solidarity. At a time of increased casualisation alongside anti-trade union laws and sentiment, trade unions have been able to maintain membership in the public sector but declined in both influence and reach amongst the working classes in the private sector, falling to a small fraction of the workforce in the countries examined (Roose 2017). In 1960, a time often referred to as the 'golden age of capitalism' when Keynesian economics ruled supreme, trade union density was at or near its peak across the countries examined in this book. In the United Kingdom it stood at 40.5 per cent, in the United States at 30.9 per cent, and in Australia at 50.2 per cent (Organisation for Economic Co-Operation and Development 2019). By 2016 density had fallen to 23.7 per cent (UK), 10.3 per cent (US), and 14.6 per cent (Australia), constituting declines over the period 1960–2016 as a percentage of the workforce of 41.48 per cent (UK), 66.67 per cent (US), and 70.92 per cent (Australia). The drop in numbers decimated unions' operational budgets and their capacity to organise effectively.

Importantly, the most significant falls within the 1960–2016 period across the UK and US coincided with governments controlled by parties explicitly introducing neoliberal economic policies. The UK Thatcher Conservative government (1979–1990), as previously discussed, embraced neoliberalism and launched a full-scale attack against trade unions. Trade union density fell from a peak of 52.2 per cent in 1979 to 39.6 per cent in 1990 (24.14% drop), not only halting but reversing a period of sustained trade union growth. The single largest decline in trade unionism in the United States similarly occurred during the government of Ronald Regan (1981–1989), falling from 21 per cent density to 16.2 per cent (22.86% drop). In the Australian context, trade union density dropped 26.19 per cent in the five years of the centre-left Keating government (1991–1996), declining from 41 per cent of the workforce to 32 per cent. It declined even further under sustained attack from the Howard Conservative government (1996–2007), which continued to develop and expand Keating's neoliberal economic agenda, dropping 39.35 per cent in total number from 32 per cent to 18.8 per cent of the work force during this period, constituting a near fatal blow to the critical mass required for collective bargaining. Trade unions in the contemporary era now find their greatest areas of strength in the public services, education, and amongst white-collar workers (Gilfillan & McGann 2018). Manual labour is often contained in small, non-union businesses, a manifestation of neoliberal economics driving a wedge into the traditional labour party base. Perhaps, as a consequence, trade unions have demonstrated a tendency to immerse themselves in identity politics, which is more evident amongst the white-collar middle classes that fall outside of the unions' traditional remit. The move into identity politics alienates the unions from their traditional blue-collar base and workers, who may find it difficult to balance their conservative religious principles with trade union membership.

Labour-affiliated political parties

Despite centre-left parties adopting neoliberal economic policies, they have largely sought to protect their declining union bases. This, in turn, arguably had the effect of entrenching a select few unions in favourable positions to bargain and protect the rights of their members, whilst excluding many others. At the opposite end of the spectrum, trade union leaders have, from a Marxist perspective, often been accused of careerism and seeking personal political gain by climbing the ranks of a union before switching to an affiliated Labourist party (Van Tine 1973). In the UK and Australia, in particular, where Labour parties are formally linked to trade unions, the development of the 'professional politician' has had damaging consequences. Research by O'Grady on the prevalence of working-class politicians in the UK House of Commons reveals that just 8 per cent of the parliamentary Labour party in the 2010–2015 period was drawn from the working classes, compared to almost 30 per cent in the 1987–1992 period (O'Grady 2019: 547–548). The numbers were closer to 70 per cent in the 1920s (O'Grady 2019: 547–548).

Importantly, based on an analysis of speeches made in the House of Commons during the Blair Government, O'Grady found that while career politicians were more likely to adopt pragmatic policies designed to win elections, working class MPs adopted policy positions more favourable to working class people, including support for welfare. Careerist MPs lack not only socialisation, but affinity with working people:

> legislators who are former manual workers will form a long-lasting altruistic identification with other working-class people, raising their ideological support for policies that help them ... Careerist legislators lack these socialisation experiences. Instead, they go through different socialisation processes in their jobs. Having begun their working careers around campaigners, pollsters, party staff, and others who are invested in electoral success, they will come to view winning elections as an important goal in its own right, and an intrinsic part of their job. Having worked closely with the party leadership, loyalty will become more ingrained for them. And having been surrounded by people who are invested in politics as a career, they too will start to see it as a career with a structured trajectory like any other white-collar profession and will strive to reach high office.
>
> (O'Grady 2019: 550)

In a similar vein to neoliberalism, which strips economic decision-making of concerns about morality, retraction of trade unions and working people from Labour-affiliated political parties strips them of their working-class consciousness and concern for those facing the hard edge of neoliberalism. This is not a concern limited to the United Kingdom. Careerism is a significant problem in the United States and Australia. Carnes (2012) found that, whilst representation of women and racial minorities in the United States has risen significantly since the 1970s, the representation of the working class in Congress has decreased since the late 1970s and, similar to O'Grady's findings, working class experiences shape approaches to policies that benefit the working class (Carnes 2012: 10–11). In a study of Australian Labor party MPs' employment prior to entering parliament, Bramble and Kuhn (2007) found that by 2005 none of the Labor party's 88 federal parliamentary representatives had worked blue-collar jobs, whilst 19 (21.59%) had worked in white-collar or professional appointments, 14 had worked in business (15.91%), and 67 (76.14%) had worked for the Labor party or in a union. It becomes clear that there is little room for working-class men in the organised labour movement, resulting in organisations almost entirely deficient in first-hand job experience and full of careerists largely incapable of understanding those they claim to represent.

Religion and church

If trade unions once offered intellectual leadership and provided a sense of context, solidarity, and a framework for understanding members' position in society, then churches provided a sense of spiritual leadership, guidance, and community belonging. Morality remained central to the lived experiences of working men and scaffolded a sense of dignity and meaning in their work (Lamont 2000). Indeed, it was not unlikely that, historically, working class men were simultaneously members of a trade union and attended a local church on Sundays. The church sermon, or in multicultural societies the Jewish *Derasha* and Islamic *Khutbah*, address important moral topics. Aimed at laypeople, they are designed to act as reference points for everyday decision-making and to assist with navigating moral and ethical challenges. The minister, priest, rabbi, or imam is meant to serve as an accessible moral guide. Whilst an entire online world of access to religious sources and DIY religion has occurred since the development of the internet, relationships between working men, their families, and the local parish constituted important social bonds that in many ways held communities together, particularly in an era when the majority attended.

However, there has been a steady, bordering on terminal, decline in church attendance and membership, particularly across the traditionally largest denominations in the contexts studied in this book. This does not speak to cultural affiliation, however, it does provide important insights into formal religious institutions' reach into the daily lives of adherents. What follows below is a summation based on different national-level sources of church attendance over the past forty years.

UK

Paralleling the emergence of the Thatcher government and the adoption of a hardline, neoliberal economic approach twenty years later, total church attendance in Great Britain dropped from 11.8 per cent in 1980 to 7.6 per cent in 2000. By 2015 it had dropped to just 5 per cent, a total decline of 57.63 per cent as a percentage of the population. Looking specifically at England over the same period, the decline was most pronounced in the United Reformed (–82.42% as a percentage of the population), Catholic (–70.54%), Methodist (–67.02%), and Anglican (–51.84%) churches. By contrast, new churches (+121.33%) and Pentecostal churches (+34.78%) increased significantly in size during the same time period as a percentage of the population (British Academy 2005; Brierley 2006). Whilst no formal records are kept of attendance at synagogues and mosques, population growth suggests an exponential increase in Muslim communities in England and Wales (+509.95%), which is likely to equate to significantly increased mosque attendance.

United States

The United States, despite significantly higher average levels for church attendance, has also seen significant declines. Between 1992 (the commencement of the Gallup

Poll) and 2018, weekly church attendance in the United States dropped almost every year from 34 per cent in 1992 to 23 per cent in 2018 (−32.35% as a percentage of those surveyed). The category of 'never attending' increased in the same period from 14 per cent to 29 per cent (+107.14) (Gallup 2019). The slightly different measurement of church membership declined from 71 per cent in 1978 to just 50 per cent in 2018 (−29.58 per cent). Significantly, whilst 76 per cent of baby boomers (1946–64) identify as Christian, for millennials the figure stands at just 49 per cent (Pew Research 2019). No US government records are kept on the size of the American Muslim population; however, Pew Research Forum estimates an increase from 2.35 million Muslims in the US in 2007 to 3.45 million in 2017, an increase of 46.81 per cent (Pew Research 2017). This does not speak, however, to observance and regularity of mosque attendance. The number of Americans identifying as Jewish has increased by 15 per cent since 1957, however, due to population growth the number has declined as a percentage of the community. Approximately four million Americans identify as Jewish, though the number increases to 5.4 million if so-called 'secular Jews' are included (Pew Research 2013).

Australia

Australia, similarly to the United Kingdom and United States, has seen significant church decline over a prolonged period. A conservative estimate of decline is captured by the Australian National Church Life Survey (2017), associated with the Christian Research Association, which found that church attendance declined from 27 per cent of the population in 1980 to 16 per cent in 2016 (−23.28%). McCrindle Research (2019), by contrast, found that just 8 per cent of Australians attend church on a monthly basis. Australia is in the fortunate circumstance of capturing religion information over a prolonged period of time in its national census, which takes place every five years.

The Australian Census reveals that in 1981 the percentage of Australians identifying as Christian stood at 76.4 per cent, declining to 52.1 per cent by 2016 (−31.81 per cent as a percentage of the population). The drop was particularly pronounced amongst denominations, including the Anglican (−49.04), United (−54.88), and Presbyterian (47.73%) churches. The Catholic Church minimised its losses through large-scale immigration from Catholic communities across Asia (−13.08%) (ABS 1981; ABS 2016). Judaism remained consistent on 0.4 per cent throughout the 1981–2016 period. Contrastingly, Pentecostals grew significantly in adherents (120%). Other religions also grew significantly, coinciding with the introduction of multiculturalism into Australia as official policy in 1974. In 1980, Muslims constituted just 0.5 per cent of the overall population, whilst in 2016 their numbers had grown to 2.6 per cent (+420%). The number of Buddhists grew as a percentage of the population from 0.2 per cent to 2.4 per cent (+1100%).

Reasons for decline

The reasons for decline in both church membership and attendance are highly politicised. Those to the left of the political spectrum blame slow-moving, conservative institutions stuck in dogmatic and archaic ways of thinking and, thus, unable to communicate with potential younger members. Those to the right of the spectrum blame the supposed liberalisation of the church and rejection of tradition, such as the Second Vatican Council (Vatican II), which occurred between October 1962 and December 1965. This Council focused on moving beyond dogmatism toward church renewal, including focusing on ecumenism (development of Christian unity), developing respect for non-Christians, and allowing the use of local languages for Mass (rather than Latin). Whilst beyond the scope of this book, these changes can be said to have created a significant and long-lasting gulf between the conservative and liberal arms of the Catholic Church, which is contested to this day between the leadership of Pope Francis, a liberal, and leading members of the American Catholic Church with links to leading demagogic populist and conspirator, Steve Bannon. Conservatives across the Christian churches blame the liberal turn for everything from gay marriage and LGBTIQ rights to the legalisation of abortion and the decline of the nuclear family. In contrast to liberals and conservatives, secularists in particular point out, on one hand, the significant advances in science education challenging central notions of Christianity, such as creationism, and, on the other, the immeasurable damage inflicted on children and communities by child sexual abuse committed through religious institutions on a global and as yet not fully comprehensible scale.

Conservative arms of the major Christian churches, noting their seemingly terminal decline, have adopted the mindset of the embattled minority. A central feature of this loss of privilege and power has been to embrace the language and activism of the disenfranchised, appealing to the fundamental human right of freedom of religion. Far from the genocide and cultural destruction of religious minorities in developing countries, which such principles were framed to shield against, religious conservatives across Western nations seek to use these principles as a sword to attack disenfranchised groups in society that have obtained the rights of citizenship, including women, LGBTIQ members of the community, and non-Christian minorities. As Woodhead compellingly asserts in relation to the Church of England:

> Religion flourishes when it is enmeshed with the lives of those it serves and dies when it no longer connects. Societal churches depend on a healthy relationship with their societies, even when there is mutual criticism. But in England, after the 1980s, the increasingly stretched ties between the two snapped. Church and society spun off in different orbits. The gulf is now so profound that, despite residual constitutional ties, the chance of reconciliation is virtually zero.
>
> *(Woodhead 2016)*

The decline in Christianity may well have been greater but for the often highly religious Christian immigrants from the developing world who have replaced declining white congregations and, most tellingly, priests and ministers in the seminaries. Many, such as African bishops in the United Kingdom or Asian priests in Australia, have brought with them a strong conservatism pervasive in their homelands that may further divide local religious congregations. Growth in Pentecostal and Evangelical movements, by contrast, has been on the rise. Prosperity Gospel teaching, which emphasises individual responsibility and the centrality of wealth as a sign of god's favour, is aligned with neoliberal economic principles, suggesting that we might do well to look beyond the culture war that has been fought inside Christian churches for decades and examine more broadly the causes of religious decline.

The ascendancy of amorality

It is argued here that, much as trade unions have suffered as a direct result of the implementation of neoliberal economic policies that changed workplaces and undermined workers' bargaining power, neoliberal economics have fundamentally undermined the preconditions necessary for the mainstreaming of religious values central to the success of the Christian church and the filling of pews on Sundays. While Keynesian economics and the notion of the welfare state were grounded in Christian socialist moral principles found amongst young intellectuals at Oxford, Cambridge, and even the London School of Economics, amongst other established institutions, they would eventually hit their limit in a rapidly globalising world economy.

Neoliberal economics, as has been discussed, is devoid of morality. Harvey describes it as 'an ethic in itself, capable of acting as a guide to all human action and substituting for all previously held ethical beliefs' (Harvey 2007a: 3). This stands in stark contrast to the subtle, yet no less present, Christian moral and ethical concerns infused in the work of Beveridge, Keynes, and Marshall. The impact of neoliberal economics on everything from political institutions to the development of popular culture and new technologies delivered on a global scale would, over several decades, fundamentally shift and degrade the place of traditionalist Christian institutions. Whereas older generations and new migrants not yet fully immersed in wider society may hold on to religious institutions, the institutions themselves may retain only a small core of dedicated churchgoers. Neoliberal attacks on workers' rights and conditions (as an impediment to the free operation the market) combined with successive generations of politicians across the political spectrum not only embracing neoliberal economic reform, but straitjacketing unions through legislative action has resulted in a massive imbalance in the power of employers over workers' ability to define their own destinies. The insecurities and displacement of neoliberalism were exacerbated by the 2009 global financial crisis (Vieten & Poynting 2016: 535), whilst the true impact of the COVID-19 pandemic, including a likely global recession and increased inequality, remains to be seen. With the ongoing decline of citizenship and other key societal institutions, including trade unions, political parties, and churches, the vacuum created will likely grow larger and there will be more room for demagogues to use populist tactics to exploit. Indeed, the wide-sweeping powers conceded to governments by populations to deal with the pandemic will very likely be used to extend the power of demagogues and are unlikely to be fully retracted.

The following chapter looks more closely at the role of declining religion (and, in particular, Christianity) in the context of the new wave of global populism, asserting that in a context defined by existential struggle for survival, religious actors are far from being hostages to the populists. Rather, they are very often active participants seeking to exploit social divisions to invigorate and grow their base.

References

ABS (Australian Bureau of Statistics). (1981). Census of Housing and Population. Canberra: Australian Bureau of Statistics.

ABS (Australian Bureau of Statistics). (2016). Census of Housing and Population. Canberra: Australian Bureau of Statistics.

Alvaredo, F., Chancel, L., Piketty, T., Saez, E., & Zucman, G. (2018). *World Inequality Report 2018*. World Inequality Lab.

Andrews, D. (2017). Keynes and Christian Socialism: Religion and the Economic Problem. *The European Journal of the History of Economic Thought*, 24 (4), 958–977.

Barbalet, J.M. (1993). Citizenship, Class Inequality, and Resentment. In B.S. Turner (Ed.), *Citizenship and Social Theory* (pp. 36–57). London: Sage.

Barnes, T., Humphrys, E., & Pusey, M. (2018). From Economic Rationalism to Global Neoliberalism?: Marking 25 Years Since Economic Rationalism in Canberra. *Journal of Sociology*, 54 (1), 3–11.

Beveridge, W. (1942). *Social Insurance and Allied Services: Report by Sir William Beveridge*. London: Her Majesty's Stationery Office.

Beveridge, W. (1944). *Full Employment in a Free Society: A Report by Lord Beveridge*. London: George Allen & Unwin Ltd.

Blair, T. & Schröder, G. (1998). *Europe: A Third Way/Die Neue Mitte*. Johannesburg: Friedrich Ebert Foundation.

Bourdieu, P. (1998). The Essence of Neoliberalism. *Le Monde diplomatique*. December. Retrieved from https://mondediplo.com/1998/12/08bourdieu.

Bramble, T. & Kuhn, R. (2007). *The Transformation of the Australian Labor Party*. Canberra: Australian National University Research Publications.

Brierley, P. (2006). *Pulling Out of the Nosedive. A Contemporary Picture of Churchgoing: What the 2005 English Church Census Reveals*. London: Christian Research.

Briggs, A. (1961). The Welfare State in Historical Perspective. *European Journal of Sociology/Archives Européennes de Sociologie*, 2 (2), 221–258.

British Academy. (2005). The 2005 English Church Census. *British Religion in Numbers*. Retrieved from http://www.brin.ac.uk/figures/findingsfromtheenglishchurchcensus2005.

Calhoun, C. & Derlugian, G. (Eds.). (2011). *Business as Usual: The Roots of the Global Financial Meltdown*. New York: NYU Press.

Carnes, N. (2012). Does the Numerical Underrepresentation of the Working Cass in Congress Matter? *Legislative Studies Quarterly*, 37 (1), 5–34.

Clinton, B. (2000). State of The Union Address. Speech given in US Congress, Washington, DC, 27 January. *C-SPAN*. Retrieved from https://www.c-span.org/video/?154326-1/2000-state-union-address.

Culpitt. I. (1992). *Welfare and Citizenship: Beyond the Crisis of the Welfare State*. London: Sage.

Davidson, H. & Remeikis, A. (2019). Neil Prakash 'Not a Fiji Citizen': Dutton Move to Strip Australian Citizenship in Doubt. *The Guardian*, 2 January.

Dingwall, D. (2018). More than 33 Million Centrelink Calls Unanswered as DHS Denies Staffing Problem. *The Age*, 7 March.

Fletcher, D.R. & Wright, S. (2018). A Hand Up or a Slap Down?: Criminalising Benefit Claimants in Britain via Strategies of Surveillance, Sanctions, and Deterrence. *Critical Social Policy*, 38 (2), 323–344.

Fraser, N. & Gordon, L. (1992). *Beyond Contract-verses-Charity, Toward Participation and Provision On the Concept of Social Citizenship*. CSST Working Paper 76 (May). Ann Arbor, MI: University of Michigan.

Friedman, M. (1970). The Social Responsibility of Business is to Increase Its Profits. *The New York Times Magazine*, 13 September.

Friedman, M. (1990). Volume 3: Freedom and Prosperity. *Free to Choose*. Television program. Retrieved from https://miltonfriedman.hoover.org/objects/57797/volume-3-freedom–prosperity.

Friedman, M. (1994). C-Span Interview: 50th Anniversary Edition of F.A. Hayek's Road to Serfdom. Television interview. *C-Span*. 20 November. Retrieved from https://www.c-span.org/video/?61272-1/milton-friedman-road-serfdom.

Fukuyama, F. (1989). The End of History? *The National Interest*, 16 (Summer), 3–18.

Gallup. (2019). Religion. *Gallup*. Retrieved from https://news.gallup.com/poll/1690/religion.aspx.

Gersuny, C. (1994). Industrial Rights: A Neglected Facet of Citizenship Theory. *Economic and Industrial Democracy*, 15 (2), 211–226.

Gilfillan, G. & McGann, C. (2018). *Trends in Union Membership in Australia*. Canberra: Australian National Parliamentary Library.

Goldman, L. (2019). Founding the Welfare State: Beveridge, Tawney, and Temple. In L. Goldman (Ed.), *Welfare and Social Policy in Britain Since 1870: Essays in Honour of Jose Harris*. Oxford: Oxford Scholarship Online. doi:10.1093/oso/9780198833048.003.0003.

Halsey, A.H. (1984). T.H. Marshall: Past and Present 1893–1981: President of the British Sociological Association 1964–1969. *Sociology*, 18 (1), 1–18.

Harvey, D. (2007a). *A Brief History of Neoliberalism*. Oxford: Oxford University Press.

Harvey, D. (2007b). Neoliberalism as Creative Destruction. *The Annals of the American Academy of Political and Social Science*, 610 (1), 21–44.

Hayek, F.A. (1977). Trade Union Immunity Under the Law. *The Times*, 21 July, p. 15.

Hayek, F.A. (1982). Thatcher's Economics. *The Times*, 1 July, p. 13.

Hayek, F.A. (2007). *The Road to Serfdom*. In B. Caldwell (Ed.), *The Collected Works of F.A. Hayek, Vol. 2: The Road to Serfdom*. Chicago, IL: University of Chicago Press.

Hayek, F.A. (2013). The Decline of the Rule of Law. In B. Caldwell (Ed.), *The Collected Works of F.A. Hayek, Vol. 15: The Market and Other Orders* (pp. 178–194). Chicago, IL: University of Chicago Press.

Isin, E.F. & Turner, B.S. (2002). Citizenship Studies: An Introduction. In E.F. Isin & B.S. Turner (Eds.), *Handbook of Citizenship Studies* (pp. 1–10). London: Sage.

Kainth, S. (2018). Government's Proposed Citizenship Changes Face New Challenge from Greens. *Special Broadcasting Service*, 28 December.

Keating, P. (1999). The Labor Government 1983–1996: Speech at the University of New South Wales. 19 March.

Keynes, J.M. (1941). Letter to William Temple (3 December).
Keynes, J.M. (1942). Letter to William Beveridge (17 March).
Keynes, J.M. (1972). *The Selected Writings of John Maynard Keynes*. Cambridge: Cambridge University Press.
Kleingeld, P. & Brown, E. (2014). Cosmopolitanism. In E.N. Zalta (Ed.), *The Stanford Encyclopedia of Philosophy* (Fall Edition). Stanford, CA: The Metaphysics Research Lab, Stanford University. Retrieved from https://stanford.library.sydney.edu.au/archives/fall2014/entries/cosmopolitanism.
Krugman, P. (2007). Who was Milton Friedman? *The New York Review of Books*, 15 February.
Lamont, M. (2000). *The Dignity of Working Men: Morality and the Boundaries of Race, Class, and Immigration*. Cambridge, MA: Harvard University Press.
Linklater, A. (1998). Cosmopolitan Citizenship. *Citizenship Studies*, 2 (1), 23–41.
Mackert, J. (2017). Why We Need a New Political Economy of Citizenship: Neo-liberalism, the Bank Crisis, and the 'Panama Papers'. In J. Mackert & B.S. Turner (Eds.), *The Transformation of Citizenship: Political Economy* (pp. 99–117). London: Routledge.
Mackert, J. & Turner, B.S. (2017). Introduction: A Political Economy of Citizenship. In J. Mackert & B.S. Turner (Eds.), *The Transformation of Citizenship: Political Economy* (pp. 1–13). London: Routledge.
Marcuzzo, M.C. (2010). In R.E. Backhouse & T. Nishizawa (Eds.), *No Wealth but Life: Welfare Economics and the Welfare State in Britain, 1880–1945* (pp. 189–206). Cambridge: Cambridge University Press.
Margaret Thatcher Foundation. (2020). Thatcher, Hayek, and Friedman. *Margaret Thatcher Foundation*. Retrieved on 20 January 2020 from https://www.margaretthatcher.org/archive/Hayek.asp.
Marshall, T.H. (1950). *Citizenship and Social Class*. Cambridge: Cambridge University Press.
McCrindle Research. (2019). *Faith and Giving in Australia: Exploring Generosity and Giving Habits of Australian Churchgoers*. Macquarie Park, NSW: Baptist Financial Services. Retrieved from https://www.bfs.org.au/faith-giving-in-australia-research.
Mead, L. (1997). Citizenship and Social Policy: T.H. Marshall and Poverty. *Social Philosophy and Poverty*, 14 (2), 197–230.
Moore, R. (1991). Forward. In T.H. Marshall & T. Bottomore (Eds.), *Citizenship and Social Class* (pp. vi). London: Pluto Press.
Mundlak, G. (2007). Industrial Citizenship, Social Citizenship, Corporate Citizenship: I Just Want My Wages. *Theoretical Inquiries in Law*, 8 (2), 719–748.
National Church Life Survey. (2017). NCLS Study Finds Decline in Attendance at Religious Services has Slowed. *NCLS*. Retrieved from http://www.ncls.org.au/research/religious-service-attendance.
O'Grady, T. (2019). Careerists versus Coal-Miners: Welfare Reforms and the Substantive Representation of Social Groups in the British Labour Party. *Comparative Political Studies*, 52 (4) 544–578.
Organisation for Economic Co-Operation and Development. (2019). OECD.Stat: Trade Union Density. *OECD*. Retrievable from https://stats.oecd.org/Index.aspx?DataSetCode=TUD#.
Parsons, T. (1965). Full Citizenship for the Negro American? A Sociological Problem. *Daedalus*, 1009–1054.
Pew Research. (2013). How many Jews are there in the United States? *Pew Research Centre*, 2 October.

Pew Research. (2017). U.S. Muslims Concerned About Their Place in Society, but Continue to Believe in the American Dream: Findings from Research Center's 2017 Survey of U.S. Muslims. *Pew Research Centre*, 26 July.

Pew Research. (2019). In U.S., Decline of Christianity Continues at Rapid Pace. *Pew Research Forum*, October 17.

Pinker, R. (1981). Introduction. In T.H. Marshall (Ed.), *The Right to Welfare and Other Essays* (pp. 1–28). London: Heinemann Educational Books.

Plehwe, D. (2017). Varieties of Austerity Capitalism and the Rise of Secured Market Citizenship: The Neo-Liberal Quest against Social Citizenship. In J. Mackert & B.S. Turner (Eds.), *The Transformation of Citizenship, Vol. 1: Political Economy* (pp. 55–75). London: Routledge.

Reagan, R. (1983). Presidential Diary Entry, 17 November.

Revi, B. (2014). T.H. Marshall and His Critics: Reappraising 'Social Citizenship' in the Twenty-First Century. *Citizenship Studies*, 18 (3–4), 452–464.

Roose, J.M. (2017). Citizenship, Masculinities, and Political Populism: Preliminary Considerations in the Context of Contemporary Social Challenges. In J. Mackert & B.S. Turner (Eds.), *The Transformation of Citizenship, Vol. 3: Struggle, Resistance, and Violence* (pp. 56–76). London: Routledge.

Semeuls, A. (2016). The End of Welfare as We Know It. *The Atlantic*, 1 April. Retrieved from https://www.theatlantic.com/business/archive/2016/04/the-end-of-welfare-as-we-know-it/476322.

Shklar, J.N. (1989). *American Citizenship: The Quest for Inclusion* (The Tanner Lectures on Human Values). Delivered at the University of Utah, 1–2 May.

Shklar, J.N. (1990). *American Citizenship: The Quest for Inclusion*. Cambridge, MA: Harvard University Press.

Somers, M.R. (2017). How Grandpa Became a Welfare Queen: Social Insurance, the Economization of Citizenship and a New Political Economy of Moral Worth. In J. Mackert & B.S. Turner (Eds.), *Populism and the Crisis of Democracy* (pp. 76–98). Oxon: Routledge.

Temple, W. (1942). *Christianity and the Social Order*. London: SCM Press.

Thatcher, M. (1995). *The Path to Power*. London: Harper Collins.

Thatcher, M. (2006). Statement on the Death of Milton Friedman ('an intellectual freedom fighter'). *Margaret Thatcher Foundation*, 17 November. Retrieved from 20 August 2019 from https://www.margaretthatcher.org/document/110883.

Thompson M.J. (2005). Review of *A Brief History of Neoliberalism*. *Democratiya* 3 (Winter), 22–27.

Trautman, L.J. (2016). Following the Money: Lessons from the Panama Papers: Part 1: Tip of the Iceberg. *Penn State Law Rev.*, 121 (3), 807–873.

Turner, B.S. (1990). Outline of a Theory of Citizenship. *Sociology*, 24 (2), 189–217.

Turner, B.S. (1993). Contemporary Problems in the Theory of Citizenship. In B.S. Turner (Ed.), *Citizenship and Social Theory* (pp. 1–18). London: Sage.

Turner, B.S. (2001). The Erosion of Citizenship. *The British Journal of Sociology*, 52 (2), 189–209.

Turner, B.S. (2016). 'We are all Denizens now': On the Erosion of Citizenship. *Citizenship Studies*, 20 (6–7), 679–692.

Van Tine, W.R. (1973). *The Making of the Labor Bureaucrat: Union Leadership in the United States, 1870–1920*. Cambridge, MA: University of Massachusetts Press.

Vieten, U.M. & Poynting. S. (2016). Contemporary Far-Right Racist Populism in Europe. *Journal of Intercultural Studies*, 37 (6), 533–540.

Wacquant, L. (2009). *Punishing the Poor: The Neoliberal Government of Social Insecurity*. Durham, NC: Duke University Press.

Wagner, J., Dawsey, J., & Sonmez, F. (2018). Trump Vows Executive Order to End Birthright Citizenship, a Move Most Legal Experts Say Would Run Afoul of the Constitution. *The Washington Post*, 30 October.

Woodhead, L. (2016). How the Church of England Lost the English People. *ABC Religion and Ethics*, 8 November. Retrieved from https://www.abc.net.au/religion/how-the-church-of-england-lost-the-english-people/10096376.

WPIX. (1975). Milton Friedman: Living Within Our Means. Television interview. *Richard Heffner's Open Mind*, 7 December. Retrieved from https://www.thirteen.org/openmind-archive/public-affairs/living-within-our-means.

3
RELIGION AND POPULISM

Introduction: Has religion been 'hijacked'?

This book so far has sought to demonstrate that the decline of citizenship, the welfare state, and key social institutions caused by the enactment of amoral neoliberal economic and social policies has created an intellectual and moral vacuum ripe for exploitation by those employing populist tactics. The reasons for this vacuum are many. On the one hand, it may be attributed to the emergence of neoliberal economic doctrines fundamentally opposed to traditional conceptions of citizenship grounded in state interventionism and religious principles, such as the common good. On the other, a combination of naked self-interest, institutional nepotism, and corruption of guiding principles have also played a key role in undermining popular support for the previously pivotal social institutions that provided intellectual and moral leadership for the working and, increasingly, the middle classes.

This chapter now turns to an important corollary of the first thesis by addressing the notion, which has become popular in some academic quarters, that religion has been 'hijacked' by populists in the name of identity politics, leaving organised religion largely external to contemporary developments. This chapter focuses in particular upon continental Europe, which is at the epicentre of the argument. Consideration of the issue in the United States, United Kingdom, and Australia will follow in individual chapters. It is necessary to consider some historical perspectives to contextualise present events; this requires occasionally moving across centuries, in comparison to many contemporary works that focus on spans of decades.

It is first important to provide a brief overview of what I mean by 'religion'. Christian Joppke (2015) notes that the concept of 'religion' as a set of beliefs that exists distinct from the state stems from the European Wars of Religion in the sixteenth and seventeenth centuries and Hobbes's *Leviathan*. As a result of this era and the secularisation of Europe, religion has become a category of analysis rather than deeply held 'true' faith. Faith is recognised within this book as a propelling force, and one in which intense personal and collective energy may be directed and indeed accumulated, very often with a focus on the common good. However, here I am particularly concerned with the social dimension of religion and, in particular, textualist claims to possession of the 'truth' to the exclusion of other actors.

I draw here upon Joppke's historical and institutional perspective of religion as structuring principle on the one hand and as actor and claim maker in secularised settings on the other. As structuring principle, religion in its various faith and denominational manifestations has shaped our language, institutions, political frameworks, and conception of morality more than any other organising frame. It remains embedded in our daily lives, even within secular societies, however, it is regulated to prevent *religious actors* from steering our political institutions or competing for primacy with the State. This is precisely because religion, grounded in faith that one possesses universal truth, is an incontrovertible claim maker. From benefitting from tax exemptions on the basis of charitable status to seeking exemptions from discrimination laws, religion and, in particular in the Western context, Christianity and Islam are claim makers that mobilise collective identity to seek to achieve economic, political, and social outcomes that reflect their principles.

The most important early work to develop the thesis that religion has been hijacked is the edited collection by Marzouki, McDonnell, and Roy (2016). The collection cumulatively argues that, for populists (broadly defined), religion is more about 'belonging' than 'belief' and is deployed to identify the local Christian in-group and Muslim out-group. It is asserted that Church elites typically condemn the instrumentalisation of religion for these purposes. Marzouki and McDonnell separately argue that '[w]e are … faced with the increasing exploitation of religion in political discourse by both mainstream politicians and right-wing populists to express belonging rather than believing. To defend the territory of Christendom rather than the values of Christianity' (Marzouki & McDonnell 2018). Roy asserts that this hijacking has occurred 'due to the Church's lack of credibility and clarity' (2018). Yet it extends well beyond this.

It is argued here that, whilst some groups do embrace an empty and rhetorical form of Christian identity, organised religion is an important ingredient of the contemporary global populist surge. Attempts to exonerate organised religion and religious leadership from responsibility for the demonisation of other faiths show a startling lack of understanding about how the theological framing of truth amongst fundamentalist textualist elements of organised religion shapes highly energised and often hostile responses to other faiths that have everything to do with 'religion'. Furthermore, far from being passive actors, organised mainstream religion (be it through denominational leaders, factional figureheads, or publicly aligned politicians) is actively competing for political status and power, pursuing religious exemptions from secular laws, and *taking sides*, be it with the 'establishment' or the new demagogues, in their efforts to achieve survivability or, contrastingly, growth.

In order to establish this, the chapter addresses four interrelated guiding questions. First, how do theologically based claims to truth result in hostility toward other faiths? Second, where do different contemporary mainstream religious actors stand in relation to the new demagogues – do they seek to mobilise them for political gain or reject them outright? Third, are different Christian denominations pursuing different political strategies or theological justifications and why? Fourth, how does the religion's standing in relation to the State, power, and authority shape these strategies?

Textualism and theological claims to truth

Possession of a unique claim to 'truth', that is, an understanding and unique relationship with God or a supreme deity, is an essential component of most, if not all, religions. Indeed, the most significant and indeed 'proudest claim' of any theological proposition is to be *true* (Corbett 1983: 134). For some deeply pious faith holders, the claim to truth leads to a journey of discovery and attempts to reconcile this with other faith traditions through interfaith work or ecumenicalism. For many others, the claim to unique possession of truth defines the boundary of religious community. Those who use truth claims to demarcate community are identified throughout this book as 'textualists' or 'fundamentalists'. Daniel Lasker has noted that the 'Jewish-Christian debate is as old as Christianity when immediately after the crucifixion, the first Christians, who were themselves Jews, began spreading the good news of the messianic redemption among other Jews' (Lasker 2003). The first anti-Jewish comments followed soon after from the Apostle Paul, leading other Christian missionaries to 'compose a number of polemical treatises to try to convince themselves and others of the truth of this new religion' (Lasker 2003).

Historically, challenges to truth claims by perceived imposters (and all that they meant politically) have been dealt with through violent means, whether via symbolic repudiations using powerful language or conquest. Writing in Book 1 of *Summa Contra Gentiles* (Book on the Truth of the Catholic Faith against the Error of the Unbelievers) in 1259 (in between the seventh and eighth Crusades), St. Thomas Aquinas addressed the growth of Islam and critiqued the claims to divine truth of the Prophet Muhammad:

> Mohammed seduced the people by promises of carnal pleasure to which the concupiscence of the flesh urges us. His teaching also contained precepts that were in conformity with his promises, and he gave free rein to carnal pleasure. In all this, as is not unexpected; he was obeyed by carnal men. As for proofs of the truth of his doctrine, he brought forward only such as could be grasped by the natural ability of anyone with a very modest wisdom. Indeed, the truths that he taught he mingled with many fables and with doctrines of the greatest falsity.
>
> *(Aquinas 1259: Book 1)*

Aquinas argued further that 'no wise men, men trained in things divine and human, believed in him from the beginning' (Aquinas 1259: Book 1). Similarly, though from the opposite side of the religious divide, approximately four decades after Aquinas and two decades after the ninth Crusade, Islamic theologian Ibn Taymiyyah wrote *The Correct Response to Those who Have Corrupted the Deen [Religion] of the Messiah*, accusing Christians of corrupting the scriptures and, consequently, requiring their punishment:

> Christians do not have a reliable authentic transmission from Christ concerning the exact wordings of the Bible or a reliable transmission for most of their religious laws. This is also applicable to the Jews who do not have authentic transmissions for the wordings of the Torah or the prophecies of their prophets. On the other hand, Muslims have authentic, clear chains of transmitters for the Qur'an and the Sunnah, which contain facts known to non-specialised as well as specialised people.
> *(Ibn Taymiyyah c.1293–1321: 147–148)*

Importantly, Ibn Taymiyyah set clear boundaries around believers and disbelievers:

> It is an acknowledged fact in Islam that the Jews are wrong doers, disbelievers, transgressors and deserve the torment and punishment of Allah. It is also a known fact that the Christians are wrongdoers, transgressors, disbelievers and deserve the torment and punishment of Allah.
> *(Ibn Taymiyyah c.1293–1321: 169)*

Importantly, as even a cursory examination reveals, St. Thomas Aquinas and Ibn Taymiyyah continue to influence the development and practice of conservative Catholic and Sunni Islamic doctrine and law to the current day.

Europe

A prolonged break in religious hostilities occurred between the fourteenth and sixteenth centuries, though it did not last. The European Wars of Religion, fought by a combination of volunteers, mercenaries, and professional standing armies, commenced at the time of the Protestant Reformation in 1517 and did not end until the Peace of Westphalia (1648).

German professor of moral theology Martin Luther (1483–1546) sought to challenge the perceived deviation of the Catholic Church from fundamental tenants of Christianity, such as its sale of 'indulgences' to reduce the need for purification from sin in purgatory before believers entered heaven (a practice ceased by the Catholic Church in 1567). In contrast to the Catholic reliance on scripture and tradition, Luther asserted the centrality of text, arguing that the Bible is the only source of revelation and faith in God alone is the path to salvation. In a tract titled *Against Catholicism* (1535) he railed:

> The chief cause that I fell out with the pope was this: the pope boasted that he was the head of the Church, and condemned all that would not be under his power and authority; for he said, although Christ be the head of the Church, yet, notwithstanding, there must be a corporal head of the Church upon earth. With this I could have been content, had he but taught the gospel pure and clear, and not introduced human inventions and lies in its stead. Further, he took upon him power, rule, and authority over the Christian Church, and over the Holy Scriptures, the Word of God; no man must presume to expound the Scriptures, but only he, and according to his ridiculous conceits; so that he made himself lord over the Church, proclaiming her at the same time a powerful mother, and empress over the Scriptures, to which we must yield and be obedient; this was not to be endured. They who, against God's Word, boast of the Church's authority, are mere idiots. The Pope attributes more power to the Church, which is begotten and born, than to the Word, which has begotten, conceived, and born the Church.
>
> *(Luther 1907: 119)*

Luther's work and activism were fundamental to the dissolution of the Catholic Church's authority across continental Europe, leading indirectly to the birth of Anglicanism and the Church of England. Luther was excommunicated from the Catholic Church in 1521, though his theology and actions resulted in divisions in Christianity that exist to this day. Contemporary political commentators have made comparisons between Luther's hostility to the Catholic Church as an institution ruling over Europe, his use of vitriolic slurs and crude language, and his use of the printing press to spread his message and contemporary British hostility to the European Union and the use of social media to spread contemporary populist messages (Feffer 2014; Stanford 2017; Massing 2018). Similar resonances may equally be found in the tactics used by President Donald Trump (Berlinerblau 2019).

Importantly, despite his primary focus on resisting the papacy and his initial support for the Turks (Muslims) as a thorn in the side of the Catholic Church, Luther was forced to turn his attention to the military campaign of the Ottoman Turks in Europe. Luther viewed the siege as an 'apocalyptic threat' foretold in the eschatological prophecies in scripture (Francisco 2016), though he urged resistance based almost entirely on secular protection of lands and people rather than a religious crusade against the Muslims. Grafton claims further that Luther, who never engaged with Muslim scholars, adopted a primarily theological rejection of Islam (Grafton 2017: 682). Luther states in *On the War Against the Turk* (1529):

> I have some pieces of Mohammed's Koran which might be called in German a book of sermons or doctrines of the kind that we call pope's decretals. When I have time, I must put it into German so that every man may see what a foul and shameful book it is. In the first place, he praises Christ and Mary very much as those who alone were without sin, and yet he believes nothing more of Christ than that he is a holy prophet, like Jeremiah or Jonah, and denies that he is

God's Son and true God. Besides, he does not believe that Christ is the Savior of the world, who died for our sins, but that He preached to His own time, and completed His work before His death, just like any other prophet.

On the other hand, he praises and exalts himself highly and boasts that he has talked with God and the angels, and that since Christ's office of prophet is now complete, it has been commanded to him to bring the world to his faith and if the world is not willing, to compel it or punish it with the sword; and there is much glorification of the sword in it. Therefore, the Turks think their Mohammed much higher and greater than Christ, for the office of Christ has ended and Mohammed's office is still in force.

(Luther 1529: 27–28)

Not satisfied with denouncing Islam and Catholicism, in 1543, after unsuccessful attempts to convert European Jews, Luther wrote an extensive, 65,000-word treatise denouncing Judaism titled *On the Jews and their Lies*. Luther commenced with theologically based denunciations of Judaism that simultaneously posited the Jewish people as being set on the destruction of Christians. According to a version published by the Christian Nationalist Crusade of Los Angeles in 1948:

They are real liars and bloodhounds who have not only continually perverted and falsified all of Scripture with their mendacious glosses from the beginning until the present day. Their heart's most ardent sighing and yearning and hoping is set on the day on which they can deal with us Gentiles as they did with the Gentiles in Persia at the time of Esther. Oh, how fond they are of the book of Esther, which is so beautifully attuned to their bloodthirsty, vengeful, murderous yearning and hope.

(Luther 1948: 17)

Throughout the tract Luther continuously incited extreme animosity and violence toward the Jewish people. Whilst this could be understood as part of a continuum in the evolution of medieval anti-Semitism, the depth of the animosity was such that the work was used, albeit problematically, in National Socialist propaganda 400 years later (Edwards 1983). Luther referred variously to Jews as 'whores', 'rogues', 'sluts', and as being 'full of malice, greed, envy, hatred toward one another, pride, usury, conceit, and curses against us Gentiles' (Luther 1948: 20). In Part 11 of the Treatise, Luther gave his 'sincere advice' in the form of a seven-point plan for the Jews' treatment, including setting fire to synagogues and schools, razing and destroying their houses, taking their prayer books and Talmudic writing, forbidding Rabbis from teaching (on pain of loss of limb or death), removing safe conduct on the highways (travel), stripping them of their wealth, and forcing them to manual labour. It is not difficult, despite the four-century gap in time, to see stark similarities between this particular work and the program of persecution carried out by National Socialist Germany, albeit under the rubric of race rather than religion.

From old world to new

The European colonisation of the United States commenced in earnest in the sixteenth century, with religion playing a significant and well-documented role in the establishment of a number of the original thirteen colonies. For example, the English Puritans, a group that believed that the Church of England had not fully and sufficiently stripped itself of Roman Catholic doctrine, settled at Plymouth in 1620, whilst others settled at Massachusetts Bay (1629) and further along the East Coast in subsequent decades. Other states with religious origins include Pennsylvania (Quakers), Maryland (English Catholics), and Virginia (Anglicans).

Doctrinal differences in the early era of settlement resulted in the formation of new colonies on the East Coast of the United States. Roger Williams, a graduate of the University of Cambridge and former apprentice to Sir Edward Coke (arguably amongst Britain's greatest jurists), for example, was expelled from the Massachusetts Bay Colony in 1635 for his criticisms of the colony's failure to completely separate from the Church of England and its failure to properly purchase land from local Narragansett people. Williams, amongst others, was a firm advocate of the separation of church and state, a notion grounded in the Protestant principle that asserts the right of private judgement in biblical interpretation (Miller 2012). Upon his return to England, Williams wrote *The Bloudy Tenent of Persecution for Cause of Conscience* (1644), a treatise attacking religious and political intolerance in Britain and America that proved influential with scholars in England, including John Locke.

Nicholas Miller argues that Protestant principles played a significant role in religious disestablishment in the American context. Of particular interest is Miller's exposition of the synergistic intellectual cooperation between two giants of religious toleration, William Penn and John Locke, who were contemporaries at Christ Church Oxford (founded by King Henry VIII):

> The story of Penn and Locke provides key insights into the early roots of American church/state thought. It reveals how strands of dissenting Protestant principles, both directly and through their shaping of moderate Enlightenment views, influenced American commitments to disestablishment. It was a paradigm embraced, as we shall see, as fully by many biblically committed, religious people as by advocates of the Enlightenment. And this common embrace came about, significantly, because many religious believers viewed this new church/state framework as more heavily indebted to Protestant religious ideas than to the Enlightenment.
>
> *(Miller 2012: 53–54)*

William Penn, whose early work on religious tolerance influenced Locke, founded a Quaker colony at Philadelphia in the State of Pennsylvania, which was named after his father. Locke wrote several key texts of classical liberalism that set out the intellectual groundwork for the Enlightenment. In *A Letter Concerning Toleration*

(1689a), Locke outlines the basis for mutual understanding between religions on the grounds that human beings cannot assess truth claims, applying the concept to 'Mahometans', pagans, and Christians alike. In the context of well over a thousand years of theological rivalry and intolerance, this tract proved to be a particularly compelling break with the past and served as a key and, arguably, 'unequalled' foundation for the principle of the separation of church and state, referred to centuries later as secularism (Kateb 2009). Locke's *Two Treatises on Government* (1689b), which outlines the necessity of gaining the consent of the governed, is another key work. His theory of social contract was particularly influential amongst Americans seeking to overthrow the English during the American Revolution (1775–1783) because it argued that the people have the right to replace their leaders.

Locke's works influenced the American *Declaration of Independence* (1776) and elements of the *Constitution of the United States of America* (1788). The *Virginia Statue for Religious Freedom*, authored by Thomas Jefferson (influenced by Locke), drafted in 1777, and enacted in 1786, disestablished the Church of England and guaranteed religious freedom for peoples of all denominations and faiths (Jefferson 1777).

Other leading thinkers and political actors, such as American founding father James Madison; Irishman Edmund Burke; and Frenchman Alexis de Tocqueville, author of *Democracy in America* (1835), maintained that the protection of individual rights, toleration, and limited government 'derived support' for Christian faith institutions ensured that religion was 'most secure in a free society' (Berkowitz 2019). The religious freedoms established in the United States would prove to be a pivotal break with the old world and a Europe divided on religious grounds. Furthermore, it created a fertile terrain for the emergence of new Christian denominations, many grounded to varying extents in Protestant theological bases. Many of these new groups faced their own forms of discrimination as they developed. However, ultimately, the American judicial system affirmed the right to freedom of religion and, in many ways, shaped developments in Europe, Australia, and internationally.

Contemporary secularism

Historically, exclusivist theologically based claims to religious truth have led to extremist religious and political discourse, which seeks to undermine challengers to the divine right to claim possession of God's truth, and, very often, to violence. As much as some may argue otherwise, theologically based claims do not stand apart from state matters of worldly political authority, particularly when states are closely aligned with particular faith perspectives.

Secularism promised to keep the state apart from the competition for claims to divine truth and the state-based rewards that accompany successful parties. It consequently stands in constant tension with religion as 'faith', understood here as a theologically driven, experiential moral framework, which at its fullest extent demands full adherence with the precepts of the faith both in the private and public spheres. As Calhoun, Juergensmeyer, and VanAntwerpen argue,

However one defines secularity and secularism ... it involves religion. It is the absence of it, the control over it, the equal treatment of its various forms, or its replacement by the social values common to a secular way of life.

(Calhoun et al. 2011: 5)

Secularism has been adopted in different forms in diverse national contexts. More plural, multicultural societies accept a faith-based presence in the public sphere, allocate resources to religious groups (provided they conform to laws and secular standards), and in some instances even allow faith-based courts and tribunals some autonomy to determine faith-based precepts in family and inheritance law (though others reject this dimension vehemently). Other secular laïcité societies adopt what has been described as a more 'militant' posture, rigorously legislating and enforcing a strict division between private religious practice and conformity with a preconceived national identity in public space.

As with any doctrinal approach to complex social issues, secular fundamentalists ultimately emerged. In Western contexts many such staunch secularists, particularly from the 1930s onwards, were influenced by Marxism, which in its own fundamentalist strain rejected religion entirely as an 'opiate of the masses' that deadened any revolutionary impulse (Marx 1843). This has resulted in seemingly paradoxical developments in Western contexts. The political left (influenced by Marxism) joins with Muslim communities in denouncing 'Islamophobia' whilst simultaneously attacking the place of Christian prayer in national parliaments. The far right, who have traditionally opposed LGBTIQ rights and feminism, attack Muslim migration on the grounds that Muslims oppose liberal values of toleration, yet they stand in close proximity to Muslims on issues related to the centrality of the family to society and reproductive rights.

Secularism has never been enacted in a pure form – precisely because there is no 'one' secularism. In cannot be and to some extent was never intended to be enacted in a uniform manner. It is important to return to the fact that the separation of church and state was advocated for by European and American Christians who had witnessed and, indeed, participated first-hand in the life and death struggles that occur when two competing claims to religious truth come head to head. (Of course, many instances of peaceful coexistence across religions in many other contexts exist throughout history). Whilst there was a concern with ensuring religious tolerance across faiths, there also was arguably a concern with developing doctrinal and denominational tolerance in societies that had been torn apart by claims as to who could call themselves the 'true' Christians. The only way to ensure the possibility of human flourishing, peace, and prosperity, much less to forge a new or stronger nation, was to separate religious claim making from the operation of the state. This approach, emphasising freedom of religion and, thus, freedom from the imposition of truth claims or persecution by others, is reflected in leading human rights instruments, including Section 18 of the Universal Declaration of Human Rights, which asserts the human right 'to freedom of thought, conscience, and religion' (United Nations 1948).

The evolution of secularism and its discontents

It has become popular in scholarship on religion to question the ongoing relevance of secularism as an organisational principle for the governance of society. For example, Jürgen Habermas, widely credited with framing the concept of the 'post-secular', argued that Western culture is deeply rooted in Judeo-Christian values and that 'secular citizens must be open to religious influence' (2008: 17). This is particularly so amongst scholars of faith. Critiques often frame secularism loosely and as an abstract concept. From a Catholic perspective, for example, José Casanova argued over twenty-five years ago in *Public Religions in the Modern World* that 'religious traditions throughout the world are refusing to accept the marginal and privatized role which theories of modernity as well as theories of secularization had reserved for them' (1994: 5). He was arguing, in effect, that the deprivatisation of religion was a relatively new and irreversible global trend (Casanova 2009). In his 2007 work, *A Secular Age*, Catholic philosopher Charles Taylor argued that, despite the predominance of secularism, 'our age is far from settling into comfortable unbelief' (2007: 227). According to Taylor, in a world defined by the individual pursuit of happiness and embedded in consumer culture, people are increasingly reengaging with faith and spiritual life. In an associated argument, Catholic theologian William Cavanaugh (2009) asserted a 'myth of religious violence', arguing that secular constructions of religion ascribe certain characteristics to it, including irrationality and a propensity to violence, and secularism, not religion, is a cause of neocolonial violence. Protestant theologian and sociologist Peter Berger, similar to his Catholic counterparts, stated that 'the assumption that we live in a secularized world is false' and that 'the world … is as furiously religious as it ever was' (Berger 1999: 2).

Islamic scholars of religion have been similarly critical of secularism. Talal Asad, for example, argues that the secular sphere is defined not by tolerance and rationality, but by myth, violence, and the inequitable distribution of power, and he goes so far as to assert that a religious community should be able to enter political debate 'on its own terms' (Asad 2003: 185). Assad's position is a form of semi-cloaked advocacy that has become increasingly common in contemporary scholarship. Secularism is represented as irredeemable and the re-emergence of religion into public life irrepressible. Yet, as Christopher Brittain argues, this raises important questions:

> Asad wants, it would appear, to refashion secular public debate in democratic societies, *and* to advocate that the voices of religious adherents marginalized by liberal secularism be included in public debates *as* religious adherents. Religion, in other words, is to be de-privatized. But if such a process is not to be reduced to a re-assertion of universal authority and orthodoxy on the part of a religious community, then it is difficult to understand how Asad could imagine anything other than the very secular state whose assumptions he so thoroughly rejects.
>
> *(Brittain 2005: 154)*

Saba Mahmood argues in the Muslim majority context of Egypt that secularism exacerbates religious tension and inequality through relegating religious matters to the family, a site of patriarchy, and through privileging majority norms (Mahmood 2015). In doing so, Mahmood echoes Asad's critique, though in a Muslim majority context. This is criticised by Joppke, amongst others, who asserts that the problems stem not from secularism but from too little of it (2017: 579). Others, including Bhargava (2011: 92–113), have come to the defence of secularism, arguing that it is necessary to look beyond doctrinal versions of Western secularism to other contexts where it has been implemented with an eye to local context. It is in locations such as India, Bhargava argues, that secularism is seen not as acting against religion, but 'against religious homogenisation and institutionalised religious domination' (2011: 92). He argues that viewing these as such entails the conclusion 'that we still do not possess a reasonable, moral and ethical alternative to secularism. Secularism remains our best bet to help us deal with ever-deepening religious diversity and the problems endemic to it' (Bhargava 2011: 92).

There can be no doubt that we live in an increasingly religious world. In 2015, the Pew Research Center released a highly influential report titled *The Future of World Religions: Population Growth Projections 2010–2050* (Pew Research 2015). The report projected that, driven by high fertility rates in developing countries, the percentage of the population who identify with a religion is growing rapidly. As importantly, it notes that the religious profile of entire geographic areas is changing, with Islam projected to equal Christianity in numbers of adherents globally by 2050 and anticipated to become the world's numerically largest religion by 2070. Whilst non-religion (including atheism) will grow in real terms, it will decline as a percentage of the world's population. It is clear that, over the medium to long term, religion is remerging as an increasingly influential actor shaping local and global politics, economies, laws, the environment, conflicts, and solidarities.

Whilst a well-educated minority elite of religious actors conduct ecumenical and interfaith work aimed at promoting mutual respect and understanding – important work vital to the secular compact – for many more distrust of other religions has grown, including among lay people who do not actively attend a church, mosque, or other place of worship but who may still feel closely bonded to the religious dimension of their identities. A continuing study by Pew Research demonstrates that between 2007 and 2016 governments worldwide increasingly acted to restrict religious freedoms, favoured certain religious groups, and limited certain religious activities (Pew Research Center 2018). Examples include the mass internment and cultural genocide of Uighur Muslims by the Chinese government (Fallon 2019) and the French state's treatment of Muslim women. However, in the same period, the percentage of countries with 'high' or 'very high' levels of social hostilities involving religion rose from 20 per cent in 2007 to a peak of 33 per cent in 2012 before dropping back to 27 per cent in 2017 (Kishi 2018). Recent developments, such as the emergence of the Islamic State movement and their genocide of the Yazidi populations of Iraq, the crackdown on LGBTIQ activists and Jehovah's witnesses in Russia inspired by the Eastern Orthodox Church, the genocide of Muslims in Myanmar by militant Buddhists, and the targeting of Christian minorities in the Middle East and Indonesia, reveal that religion and the pursuit of earthly power are inextricably linked.

Religious claims to universal truth are now occurring in a world where key institutions of liberal democracy have receded and religious literacy, which is the ability to not only understand basic, factual information about religion, but to critically engage with texts and truth, poses a serious challenge. The vacuum that has enabled populist narratives to emerge and reach into lounge rooms and bedrooms across secular societies has seen religion inextricably and actively fused to contemporary political agendas, and (some) religious actors have sought to exploit societal fault lines. To this extent, the spiritual compensator theory developed by Stark and Bainbridge (1985), with some modification, has continued relevance.

Framed within the rational choice model of understanding religion, Bainbridge and Stark's spiritual compensator theory was originally developed in the context of new religious movements (Robbins & Lucas 2007). In the absence of earthly rewards (beyond communal belonging), adherents to new religious movements accepted compensators, such as the promise of rewards in the afterlife. For Stark and Bainbridge, traditional religion declines in the absence of compelling compensators. Catholicism and Anglicanism appear to falter in providing adherents, the majority of whom work for a living, not only spiritual, but earthly compensators. This is particularly the case in comparison with Pentecostal and other evangelical churches, which offer a direct connection to God and a prosperity gospel that fuses the urge for afterlife and earthly rewards (wealth). The flip side of spiritual compensator theory and its framing of religion, however, is the role of elites, who utilise religion solely for earthly rewards, including status, wealth, and power. In some ways, this is central to the notion that religion has been 'hijacked'. Powerful actors are cloaking themselves in religion to further a political cause. It is argued here, however, that religious actors have not been hijacked in this process. Many, particularly amongst those experiencing (or frightened of experiencing) membership decline and a subsequent loss of societal status and privilege, are actively exploiting religious fault lines, particularly in relation to the emergence of the political right. Such behaviour also has parallels with how religion may be viewed through Bourdieu's theory of practice (Roose 2016). Here, different religious actors bring different forms of capital to bear on an uneven playing field to compete for key stakes (*enjeu*). In this case the stakes of the game are recognition from the state, adherents, and, ultimately, power both on earth and, in the eyes of those with power, in the hereafter. Such approaches may be criticised by theologians as instrumentalist, however, the very existence of the Vatican City State and its status in international affairs, including the negotiation of agreements, most recently with China, demonstrates the very worldly orientation of the Church.

Contemporary religious actors and the new demagogues

For political science scholars making the claim that religion has been hijacked, it makes good sense to look to the leaders of key religious institutions as they stand today, particularly those that possess a liberal outlook. The head of the Catholic Church, Pope Francis, is presumed to speak for the world's one billion Catholics. The Archbishop of Canterbury, Justin Welby, similarly speaks for the world's Anglicans. Other denominations and faiths have individual leaders (almost universally men) who not only lead the institutions of the faith, but also represent the religion in public life. Importantly, however, very few of these leaders, including the Pope (College of Cardinals) and Archbishop of Canterbury (Crown Appointments Commission and Prime Minister) are elected by laypeople, and women do not play any significant role (Woodhead 2016).

The younger the denomination, the more devolved their authority becomes. Baptist churches, for example, are fully autonomous and elect their own leadership. Nonetheless, authority over the actions and activities of churches or Imams – and their claims to possession of a universal truth – remains concentrated in the hands of a select few. In a world defined by the securitisation of religion and the policing of acceptable speech, it is advantageous for many such religious leaders to represent themselves as 'mainstream' in contrast to an extremist, religiously oriented fringe. It should thus come as no surprise that these deeply hierarchical institutions stand in opposition to movements that both contest the allocation of resources within the institution and challenge religious and political orthodoxy and claims as to what represents true practice consistent with the faith. It is pertinent here to focus, in particular, on the world's largest and most powerful religious institution, the Roman Catholic Church.

Denominational differences: Contestations within contemporary Catholicism

Internal theological and political cleavages within religions and denominations often involve significant animosity, although those on each side seek the same reward, legitimacy, and opportunity to lead the institution in the direction they wish it to go. This is particularly the case where authority is not devolved. To understand the theological and factional (political) contestations in the contemporary Catholic Church, one most only look to the current and former Pontiffs, who share the historically unusual position of living at the same time. The early retirement of Joseph Ratzinger, Pope Benedict XVI, in 2012 was the first resignation by a sitting Pope since 1415. Ratzinger took the pontifical name of Benedict (the blessed) after two individuals who had influenced his life's work: Pope Benedict XV, who was Pope from 1914 to 1922 (during the First World War and its immediate aftermath), and St. Benedict of Nursia, founder of the Benedictine Order monasteries and highly influential in the spread of Christianity across Europe (Benedict XVI: 2005).

Notwithstanding his achievements in authoring accessible, substantive, and vivid homilies and encyclicals on topics including love, the virtue of hope, and charity (Imbelli 2013), Pope Benedict was defined in the eyes of many Catholics and non-Catholics alike by his Regensburg address, delivered on 12 September 2006, five years and a day after the 9/11 attacks. Ostensibly a 'masterclass' on faith and reason (Lamb 2017), the lecture turned quickly to a dialogue between the 'erudite' Byzantine Emperor, Manuel II Palaiologos [Eastern Orthodox tradition Christian], and an 'educated Persian' [Muslim of the Ottoman Caliphate] on the 'subject of Christianity and Islam, and the truth of both' that is believed to have occurred during the siege of Constantinople between 1394 and 1402.

Referring specifically to the topic of violence, Pope Benedict pointed to a 'startling brusqueness' exhibited by Emperor Manuel II Palaiologos in his comments on Islam. Addressing the matter of the relationship between religion and violence, Benedict quoted the Emperor: 'Show me just what Mohammed brought that was new, and there you will find things only evil and inhuman, such as his command to spread by the sword the faith he preached' (Benedict XVI 2006).

Pope Benedict continued, contrasting what he argued was the Christian tradition on non-violence grounded in Greek philosophy and rationality with a transcendent and irrational Muslim god:

> The decisive statement in this argument against violent conversion is this: not to act in accordance with reason is contrary to God's nature. The editor, Theodore Khoury, observes: For the emperor, as a Byzantine shaped by Greek philosophy, this statement is self-evident. But for Muslim teaching, God is absolutely transcendent. His will is not bound up with any of our categories, even that of rationality. Here Khoury quotes a work of the noted French Islamist R. Arnaldez, who points out that Ibn Hazm went so far as to state that God is not bound even by his own word, and that nothing would oblige him to reveal the truth to us. Were it God's will, we would even have to practise idolatry.
>
> *(Benedict XVI 2006)*

The speech provoked an almost binary response between the Muslim world and secular European nations. Muslim leaders condemned the Pope and demanded a retraction. The Iranian government declared the Pontiff's remarks were 'the latest link' in the 'chain of conspiracy against Islam' (Fisher 2006a), whilst Tayyip Erdogan, the Prime Minister of Turkey, declared the remarks to be 'erroneous, ugly, and unfortunate' and demanded an apology (Hirst 2006). Western European nations, by contrast, largely supported the Pontiff. Chancellor of Germany Angela Merkel stated that the Pope had been 'misunderstood' (Paulick 2006), while the Interior Minister of Switzerland declared the speech 'intelligent and necessary' (SWI 2006). A former prime minister of Spain rejected calls for the Pope to apologise and asked why Muslims had not apologised for the occupation of Spain, while José Manuel Durão Barroso, the President of the European Union

Commission, labelled the criticism 'completely unacceptable' and stated that 'we must defend our values' (Al Jazeera 2006).

In the aftermath, Pope Benedict issued a footnote to the address, which stated that he was, in effect, paraphrasing earlier dialogue and regretted certain passages of his address that sounded offensive and that may 'offend[ed] the sensibilities of the Muslim faithful' (Fisher 2006b). The reference to 'brusqueness' was interpreted by many as implying support for the blunt language used, and later the official transcript of the speech was edited to state 'a brusqueness that we find unacceptable' (Magister 2006). Benedict's conservative followers viewed the apology as a necessary political step, yet remained satisfied that the argument had been made. With the emergence of the Islamic State movement, Benedict's supporters, such as conservative Canadian theologian Fr. Raymond de Souza, argued that 'Regensburg was not so much the work of a professor or even a pope … It was the work of a prophet' (Gibson 2014). Speaking in an address ten years after the Regensburg Lecture, Cardinal Müller, a Prefect of the Doctrine of the Faith, argued that 'political and religious authorities in Islamic countries [must understand] how the so-called Sword Verses in the Qu'ran can be reconciled with the basic right of freedom of religion', framing the lecture as a key moment in Christian-Islamic dialogue and asserting the need for reason: 'The intention here is not one of retrenchment or negative criticism, but of broadening our concept of reason and its application' (Pongratz-Lippit 2016).

The Regensburg address was, at best, a misguided attempt at developing a dialogue between Christianity and Islam over the rejection of religious violence. Benedict would later state:

> These in fact were a quotation from a medieval text, which do not in any way express my personal thought. I hope this serves to appease hearts and to clarify the true meaning of my address, which in its totality was and is an invitation to frank and sincere dialogue, with mutual respect.
>
> (BBC 2013)

Yet to view the language used as accidental would be to dramatically underestimate both the intellectual capacity and orientation of Pope Benedict, who very much viewed Europe as Christian and sought to position himself as a defender of Europe's Christian identity.

Importantly, given the thesis that populists 'hijack' religion, it is worth considering the manner in which this speech, amongst many other statements from the leader of the world's Catholic population, directly inspired (and was not appropriated by) the new populists. When the key right-wing populist and provocateur, Milo Yiannopoulos, was asked in an interview for the Michigan-based *Church Militant* website who was his role model in the Catholic Church, living or dead, he stated:

> Pope Benedict XVI is still the wisest and most erudite man in Europe, though I'm sure he doesn't deserve to have me hung around his neck as an admirer.

He was also brave enough to declare publicly that Islam's irrationalism is one of the world's great problems.

(*Church Militant* 2017)

The alignment of fundamentalist Catholicism and populism in North America

Upon his resignation Pope Benedict was replaced by Jorge Mario Bergoglio, who became the first Jesuit pope and adopted the name 'Francis' after St. Francis of Assisi, known for his care of the poor. This election would prove to be a pivotal turn away from a hard-line, conservative theology toward one slightly more open to progressive theological positions, such as admitting remarried Catholics to communion and committing earnestly to interfaith dialogue. In 2013, just a week into his position as Pope, Francis called for more of such dialogues, particularly with Islam (Povoledo 2013), and expressed support for migration, arguing the 'need for Europe to rediscover its capacity to integrate' (Taylor 2016).

Amongst many sweeping reforms and realignments made to reflect his approach, Pope Francis replaced Cardinal Müller, a committed anti-Islamic theologian and the Vatican's doctrinal head, with a Spanish Jesuit and removed arch-conservative US Cardinal Raymond Burke as a Vatican Supreme Court Justice. Given the significant theological and political shifts that have occurred since Pope Francis took on the role, it is no surprise that he has made powerful enemies, both within the Church and beyond. In 2017, for example, 62 critics of Pope Francis within the Church signed a 'Filial Correction' concerning Pope Francis's exhortation on remarriage and communion. Many of Pope Francis's critics appear to come from the United States. Following the 2017 'correction', critics led by Cardinal Burke and Steve Bannon, a former Trump advisor deeply embedded in far-right populist circles worldwide, particularly in Europe, accused Pope Francis of public actions that indicated a 'rejection of the truths of the faith' and 'the canonical delict of heresy' (National Catholic Register 2019). In other words, the more liberal theological orientation of Pope Francis stood in contrast to their hard-line fundamentalist approach, prompting the critics to commence political activism outside of the institutions of Vatican power. The first and most powerful weapon in their arsenal was to attack the Pope for denying 'divinely revealed truth'.

Cardinal Burke had extensive links with the Dignitatis Humanae Institute, a right-wing aligned Catholic Institute formed by British Conservative Benjamin Harnwell as a 'direct response to a growing secularist intolerance to Christians of all confessions that has led to a myriad of attacks on human dignity' (Dignitatis Humanae 2019). The Institute has close links with a key figure in global populism, Steve Bannon. Whilst Cardinal Burke served as President of its Advisory Board for a number of years and met with Bannon 'on occasion to discuss Catholic social teaching regarding certain political questions', he ultimately resigned from the Institute, criticising Bannon's statements regarding the continence of priests and a video project aimed at exposing homosexuality in the Vatican (Catholic News Service 2019). Despite the irreconcilability of Cardinal Burke's theological differences with Bannon, the two have a high level of political overlap. Burke stated at a May 2019 conference in Rome:

> To resist large-scale Muslim immigration in my judgement is to be responsible. [Islam] believes itself destined to rule the world. You don't have to be a rocket scientist to see what has happened in Europe ... Muslims have said that they are able today to accomplish what they were not able to accomplish in the past with armaments because Christians no longer are ready to defend their faith, what they believe; they are no longer ready to defend the moral law. [Limiting] large-scale Muslim immigration is in fact, as far as I'm concerned, a responsible exercise of one's patriotism.
>
> *(Duncan 2019)*

In an interview with the *Eternal Word Television Network* also in May 2019, Cardinal Burke stated 'with regard to this whole question of populism' that 'patriotism is in fact part of the natural moral law' (Matt 2019).

The United States has become a particularly powerful centre of fundamentalist Catholicism. Non-profits such as the Napa Institute, Legatus, and the Acton Institute are examples of Catholic 'renewal' organisations that simultaneously promote religious liberty and propose libertarian economic approaches grounded in neoliberal free-market principles fused with fundamentalist theological principles (Roberts 2019). The Knights of the Republic Order seeks to '[r]estore the prestige and power Holy Mother Church and Christendom' through the capacity of the American constitutional republic (Knights of the Republic 2019), whilst the Knights of Columbus define themselves as 'Catholic Men building a bridge back to faith' with principles of 'charity, unity, fraternity, and patriotism' (Knights of Columbus 2020). The latter organisation had almost two million members and over $2.2 billion in revenue in 2015 (Roberts 2015). As a 'fraternal' organisation, the Knights of Columbus does not feature women amongst its highly paid office holders. Much of its revenue is donated to charity. However, as Roberts observes, these charities are Catholic not-for-profits and think tanks that push a hard-line Catholic fundamentalist political agenda, which has been taken up by populist politicians. One commentator named the Knights of Columbus 'the cash cow of the Catholic Right' (Silk 2017).

The United States has also given rise to hard-line Catholic media organisations, such as Church Militant, a media organisation that positions itself as a 'Christian militia' that 'does battle against sin, the devil, and the demonic "rulers of the darkness of this world, against spiritual wickedness in high places" (Ephesians 6:12)' (Church Militant 2019).

Whilst Cardinal Burke has been the most high-profile critic of Pope Francis, there are many more senior members of the Catholic clergy who have responded negatively to the Pope's progressive, moderate, and arguably more liberal theology. Nonetheless, the political manoeuvring undertaken by Burke speaks to the relationship between populism and religion.

On a number of occasions, Cardinal Burke met with Matteo Salvini, a staunch critic of Pope Francis, Federal Secretary of the far-right Lega Nord (Northern League), Minister of the Interior, and Deputy Prime Minister of Italy (1 June 2018–5 September 2019). Whilst the extent of their conversation is not known, the very act of meeting carried immense symbolic significance. Salvini never met with Pope Francis during his tenure and was refused a papal blessing by the Pontiff in May 2019. Criticised by a Catholic newspaper for publicly displaying a rosary during an election event, Salvini responded, 'My pope is Benedict' (Kirchgaessner 2018). Salvini also rejected Pope Francis's call for forgiveness for those closing the door to refugees and asked, 'How many refugees are there in the Vatican?' (AFP 2015).

The alignment of fundamentalist Catholicism and populism in North America and Europe

In contrast to the Pope's rejection of the Lega Nord approach to immigration and refugees in Italy, the Catholic Church has worked closely with the ruling populist Law and Justice Party in Poland, whose name is biblically derived from Psalm 33:5. Speaking in the lead up to the European Parliamentary elections, the Chairman of the party, Jarosław Kaczyński, launched an attack on members of the LGBTIQ movement, painting them as an existential threat:

> We are dealing with a direct attack on the family and children – the sexualisation of children, that entire LBGT movement, gender ... This is imported, but they today actually threaten our identity, our nation, its continuation, and therefore the Polish state.
>
> *(Davies 2019)*

In July 2019, the Law and Justice Party declared major Polish cities 'LGBTIQ-free zones', suggesting that any public identification as lesbian, gay, bisexual, or transgender would result in violent consequences.

Far from calling for toleration or criticising such measures as transgressions of human rights, Marek Jędraszewski, the Archbishop of Krakow and a friend of Pope John Paul II throughout his life, compared activism for LGBTIQ human rights to a virus, with the logical conclusion that it must be eradicated. In an interview with Australian television he stated:

> This time it's not a red plague, but a rainbow plague. An ideology that wants to subjugate us is a threat to our hearts and minds. It is a great threat, so we need to defend ourselves like against any other plague.
>
> *(Australian Broadcasting Corporation 2020)*

Jędraszewski further stated the ideal end goal was the repatriation of the Polish nation within the umbrella of the Catholic Church:

From the very beginning, the history of the Polish state and Polish nation were connected with the history of Christianity. Hence this special role with these three elements: Christianity, nation, and state were so tightly connected, they were almost inseparable.

(Australian Broadcasting Corporation 2020)

The Law and Justice Party made it illegal to accuse the 'Polish nation' of active participation and complicity in the Holocaust, though international pressure forced it to back down from the imposition of prison sentences (Sobczak 2018). Raising the spectre of far-right hate speech, Kaczyński used language reminiscent of National Socialist propaganda when he stated at a 2015 political rally that Poland may have to resettle 100,000 Muslim refugees who 'carry all sorts of parasites and protozoa, which ... while not dangerous in the organisms of these people, could be dangerous here' (Cienski 2015). The talk of LGBTIQ and Muslims as viruses has significant implications. As Anderson notes, 'metaphors matter':

> they are at their most effective when they are surreptitious and uncontested, not when they are applauded or called out, but when they pass unremarked into our language. That is, when they shift from simile to metaphor suggesting the horror lurking beneath reason.
>
> *(Anderson 2017: 15)*

Whilst disagreements between the Bishops and Law and Justice Party officials do occur, they have not disrupted the close relationship for any prolonged period of time. Jesuit priest Stanisław Obirek argued that the Law and Justice Party has 'shaken hands with fundamentalist Catholicism' and, further, that 'it was only through the submissiveness of all political parties towards the church that we ended up with the political situation we have in Poland today' (Prange 2017).

In Hungary, another European nation that has elected right-wing populist government, almost 40 per cent of the population are Catholic. László Kiss-Rigó, the Bishop of Szeged, an area which Muslim migrants have predominantly entered since 2006, commented: 'Europe can ignore or deny or struggle against its own identity and its Christian roots. But by doing so the society commits suicide ... and the more migrants that come, the more Christian values will be watered down' (Walker 2019).

The same Bishop later explicitly stated the support of at least some bishops for right-wing populism:

> We are very happy that there are a few politicians like Orbán and Trump who really represent those values which we Christians believe to be important ... I don't think he [Orbán] will be canonised in the Catholic Church but this is not the point. After the attempted dictatorship of nihilism, manipulated by the PC-talkers, his personality is a refreshing one.
>
> *(Walker 2019)*

Viktor Orbán, the Fidesz party right-wing populist Prime Minister of Hungary since 2010, has actively sought to assert the Christian identity of Hungary and Europe: 'Those arriving have been raised in another religion and represent a radically different culture. Most of them are not Christians, but Muslims … This is an important question, because Europe and European identity is rooted in Christianity' (Mackey 2015).

This is not to say that other Catholic bishops and other denominations, such as the Lutherans, have not sought to assist Muslim refugees. However, there is certainly no unified church response to Muslims that makes it possible to assert a clear delineation between populist and religious leaders. Such patterns have been observed in other contexts, including Australia, where the Catholic Church has embraced a right-wing, hard-line conservative political agenda on domestic matters, such the status of LGBTIQ members of the community, divorce, and the right to discriminate in employment. Yet, simultaneously, the Church called for an end to the 'intolerable' treatment of refugees on Nauru and Manus Island, where Australia imprisons those who enter Australian waters by boat (Coleridge 2018).

Textualist Catholicism, as articulated by Pope Benedict and other key figures, frames Christianity as inherently rational (compared to an 'irrational' Islam) and as the only faith grounded in God's truth. Europe is a key domain of Christianity, and its status is considered to face an existential threat from Muslim migration and liberal progressivism. Grounded in a strong sense of history dating back to conflicts with the Muslim world many centuries ago, fundamentalist Catholicism is often more publicly critical of what they might frame as the enemy within (progressive Catholics including the current Pope) than they are of the Muslim world. Whilst some populists, such as Steve Bannon, have actively intervened in and worked with Church figures to further a populist agenda, other theologically illiterate far-right populists align with the political identarian and historic dimension of conservative Catholicism. At the overt level, religion is not being hijacked. Rather, it is actively aligning with political power to seek to challenge the status quo. At a more subtle level, a marriage of convenience between desired political outcomes has developed. In either case, religion has not been 'hijacked'.

Islam in Europe

The flip side of the debate about Christendom and European identity is the notion that religion has been hijacked in the context of Islam. The presence of Islam in European contexts has caused considerable anxiety amongst Christian leaders and politicians for many hundreds of years. Whilst secular policies have played a significant part in mediating the extent of anti-Muslim hostility across Europe, this has changed markedly in past decades. The emergence of Islamist movements across the Muslim world, the *Satanic Verses* controversy in the 1980s, the first Gulf War in 1994, and the September 11 attacks in 2001 have led to Islam once again being represented as an existential threat to 'Christian' Europe. The past twenty years have been defined by the 'war on terror'. Terror attacks by Salafi jihadists and the securitisation of Muslim communities have served as two sides to the same coin, polarising public sentiment and having often detrimental impacts on Muslims across Western contexts. Negative sentiments have combined with significant increases in the size of Muslim populations across Europe, exacerbated in recent years by the arrival of hundreds of thousands of asylum seekers fleeing the Syrian civil war. High Muslim fertility rates, Muslim migration, and a concomitant decline in the non-Muslim European population have raised fears amongst a conglomeration of right-wing politicians, conservative Christians, and pseudo intellectuals alike of a significant shift in the composition of Europe.

Modelling by the Pew Research Forum (2017), for example, demonstrates that if European nations were to collectively adopt a zero-migration policy between 2016 and 2050, Muslim populations would increase from 4.95 per cent of the 2016 European population to 7.43 per cent by 2050. Whereas, if European nations were to adopt or continue high migration policies, the Muslim population would increase to 14.04 per cent of the population over a period of 35 years, with significantly greater demographic change likely by the end of the twenty-first century.

The securitisation of Muslim communities has led, on the one hand, to greater efforts to develop links between faith communities through interfaith work, but, on the other, a hardening of Muslim identity, particularly amongst second- and subsequent-generation Western Muslims, who, in response to social pressure, have been noted to engage more substantively with their faith and embrace it as a public identity (Roose 2016). The notion of 'political Islam' – Muslims as a 'fifth column' determined to change the social and political structures of the West – has a particularly strong current in far-right populist discourse. It is thus important to understand the dimensions of political Islam in seeking to address the issue.

Building on Habermas's conception of the public sphere, Nilüfer Göle frames the movement of Islam into the public sphere of European societies and the challenges that this poses:

> The public domain becomes the privileged site for the manifestations of globalised Islam in Europe. The search for the public visibility of religion triggers public controversies in different national contexts and across borders. Islam participates in the formation of a transnational European public, but in confrontation with the norms and moral of European secular modernity.
>
> (Göle 2015: 42–43)

Political Islam may be understood as a broad category of analysis for the description of Islamic activism in the public sphere. The term was first developed in the 1970s by political scientists examining the seemingly rapid rise to power of Islamic political movements across the Muslim world. It is now utilised across the social scientific disciplinary spectrum in an often *ad hoc* and all-encompassing manner bereft of context. In its contemporary usage, political Islam has become conflated with Islamism, a textualist political ideology aimed at ridding Islam of its 'cultural baggage' and returning to the word of God and practices of the Prophet Muhammad (Roose 2017).

As within Christianity, considerable sectarian and political divisions have emerged with Islam since the death of the Prophet Muhammad. The primary theological division in Islam is the split between Sunni and Shiite Muslims, which is based on who should succeed the Prophet after his death (Sunni Muslims believing the community of Muslims should determine his successor; a smaller group of Shiite Muslims believing a family member should succeed him). The primary political division in Islam in Western contexts remains that between moderates and Islamists. Importantly, the division in Western contexts can be intra-sectarian, with moderates and Islamists both being largely Sunni in origin. Whereas moderate Muslims largely draw inspiration from other Western Muslim scholars and seek to reconcile often competing value statements common to many religions and neoliberal economics, Islamists derive inspiration primarily from historic sources, such as the aforementioned Ibn Taymiyyah, and from Salafi doctrine. Islamists emphasise a return to 'true' Islamic practice emanating from Saudi Arabia and the Middle East.

Under secular governments, treatment of moderates and Islamists often differs. Moderate Muslims who publicly profess support for the State may receive grants or funding, access to politicians and other decision makers, and praise. Islamist groups emphasising resistance are surveilled, pressured, and coerced; governments devise legislation to target their movements and associations purporting to act to prevent potential attacks. In contrast to secular governments, populist governments make no such distinctions. All Muslims are represented as a potential fifth column that collectively seeks to undermine society and pave the way for the implementation of Sharia, be it through higher birth rates or violence. Muslim populists, by contrast, position themselves as saviours of the *Ummah* and Islamic values in the face of a corrupted West at war with Islam. In many instances, they turn on intra-Islamic opponents with ferocious rhetoric or, in the Muslim world, violence. Textualists in Islam, as in Christianity, make truth claims and aggressively assert them both internally and externally in public space.

Politics and religion

The first question raised in this chapter related to how theologically based claims to truth result in hostility to other faiths. Theological claims to exclusive possession of divine truth have historically incited what we would term 'populist' approaches from figureheads and adherents alike. This is particularly the case amongst fundamentalist religious sects and movements seeking to usurp the power of established figureheads.

In their outright rejection of alternate theological and intellectual positions, highly emotive attacks upon ruling elites, imagined community based on exclusivist characteristics, and association with the powerless and marginalised, religion and what we now term populism, have long gone hand in hand. Indeed, religion has evolved and adapted over time precisely because of these characteristics. Without the populist fervour of Luther and his Protestant Reformation, for example, Europe and the wider world would be entirely different. In the contemporary era, those excluded from the formal mechanisms of power, be they within Christianity or Islam, have sought to mobilise their followers, build links with allies, and deploy an array of tactics to gain political power using whatever means at their disposal here on earth. Notwithstanding the interfaith and ecumenical work undertaken by some religious actors, theological claims to possession of an exclusive truth unobtainable to others sets religious actors apart morally, politically, and, more often than not, physically.

The second question raised related to the issue of where contemporary mainstream religious actors stand in relation to the new demagogues and whether they are actively engaged in attempts to mobilise adherents or whether they reject them. The issue is tied in with the fourth question to be addressed, which is, How does their standing in relation to the state, power, and authority shape political strategies? To this extent, DeHanas and Shterin made the important point that 'the multifaceted roles of religion in populism should prompt us to abandon any naïve assumptions that religion is merely an empowering force, or that when it does empower it will work for the social good' (2018: 183).

One pattern, however, appears to be evident. Where a religion or denomination is in the ascendancy; has state support or funding of its subsidiary organisations, such as schools and hospitals; has a sizeable following; and is protected by anti-discrimination legislation, it has little interest in rocking the political boat or mobilising for change, which often results in subtly (or occasionally vigorously) worded condemnations of populist politics and actors. This is not to exclude the factional ruptures that exist within various faiths between conservative and progressive adherents, which in many ways are as old the religion themselves. Those with less political capital, yet who are no less convinced of the veracity of their claim to universal truth, consistently challenge established powers and will actively side with forces outside the religion, if necessary, to further their chances of gaining the ascendancy.

The third question is focused on whether different denominations are pursuing different political strategies or theological justifications and why. The core (cumulative) argument of the 'religion as hijacked' perspective is that Christianity in Europe has been appropriated (and, indeed, held hostage) by populists to develop anti-Islam and anti-Muslim narratives, and the faith and theological dimensions of Christianity remain largely abstracted from populist identity politics. However, as Forlenza (2018) argues, this deprives those drawn to populist narratives who actively identify as Christian of the possibility that they may experience the emotions of fear, anger, and resentment related to the notion of an existential threat to their faith and identity, no matter how imaginary the threat might be. The argument also fails to engage with denominational differences (and competition) and the broader political manoeuvring of Christian churches across Europe and the United States as they engage with or challenge populist leaders and movements to enhance their social and political standing. The political and solidaristic dimensions of religion thus tend to be dismissed as illegitimate (Morieson, 2017).

The wider social and political context is important. Pentecostals in the United States have aligned almost entirely with demagogic populist figurehead Trump. However, in the United Kingdom, Pentecostals largely voted against leaving the European Union (Woodhead & Smith 2018). Baptists can range from highly progressive to fundamentalist and deeply polarising depending entirely on geography, leadership, and membership. The Catholic Church in Poland has aligned with the Law and Justice Party, and Catholic Bishops support measures taken against Muslim migration in Hungary and Italy. Pope Francis is at the opposite end of the political spectrum to his predecessor, who actively antagonised relationships with the Muslim world. He simultaneously decries populist demagogues and battles the American Cardinals ideologically aligned with them.

The Catholicists

There is a large and growing body of scholarship on the relationship between Islam and politics. Yet, due to the secular context in which the Christian churches operate, similar scholarship on fundamentalist Catholicism has often missed the mark. I propose here the term 'Catholicist' to describe the intractable relationship between those Catholics who proclaim exclusive ownership of divine 'truth' and their political actions in the public sphere to change the world in their image. This is a political ideology centred on the attainment of power on earth. The *-ist* suffix denotes unerring and dogmatic adherence to Catholic doctrine over and above state laws.

Catholicists, like Islamists, seek a return to the past, an imagined golden era of Catholicism in which enemies were subordinated and, globally, Church and nation-state were inextricably intertwined. They perceive the secular state as illegitimate and immoral. Like Islamists, Catholicists seek to shut down free and open debate, rely on undermining the faith credentials of their opposition, and view them as apostates. Framed in this manner, fundamentalist Catholicism may be viewed as a political ideology at ease with the new populism and willing to work with demagogic leaders, particularly where they are in power, to develop control over the state apparatus.

Conclusion

Secularism and conceptions of citizenship based on toleration (not necessarily celebration or even support) of difference have long moderated religious conflict. However, in the context of the 'post-secular turn', populism emphasising identity politics, and a loss of status, fundamentalist religion has thrived and grown emboldened, in part through promotion of a project to reclaim 'lost' power and status,. It has, in turn, gained strength through the emergence of populist actors. Historically and to this day, religion and populism developed hand in hand. Only a recalibrated and inclusive secularism, like citizenship, has the capacity to tame textualism.

References

AFP. (2015). Salvini Snubs Pope's Call to 'Forgive' over Migrants. *The Local.it*, 17 June. Retrieved from https://www.thelocal.it/20150617/salvini-rejects-popes-forgiveness-over-migrants.

Al Jazeera. (2006). EU official Criticizes Muslim Fury. *Al Jazeera*, 25 September. Retrieved from https://www.aljazeera.com/archive/2006/09/20084915578900616.html.

Anderson, B. (2017). The Politics of Pests: Immigration and the Invasive Other. *Social Research: An International Quarterly*, 84 (1), 7–28.

Aquinas, St.Thomas. (1259 [1975]). *Summa Contra Gentiles, Book 1: God*. Translated by A.C. Pegis. Notre Dame, IN: University of Notre Dame.

Asad, T. (2003). *Formations of the Secular: Christianity, Islam, and Modernity*. Stanford, CA: Stanford University Press.

Australian Broadcasting Corporation. (2020). A New Crusade. Television program. *Foreign Correspondent*, 28 April.

BBC. (2013). Pope Benedict XVI in His Own Words. *BBC News*, 11 February. Retrieved from https://www.bbc.co.uk/news/world-europe-21417767.

Benedict XVI. (2005). General Audience: Reflection on the Name Chosen: Benedict XVI. Transcript of lecture delivered at the Vatican. 27 April.

Benedict XVI. (2006). Faith, Reason, and the University: Memories and Reflections. Transcript of lecture delivered at Aula Magna of the University of Regensburg. 12 September.

Berger, P.L. (Ed.). (1999). *The Desecularization of the World: Resurgent Religion and World Politics*. Washington, DC: Ethics and Public Policy Center.

Berkowitz, P. (2019). Recovering the Christian Foundations of Human Rights. *RealClear Politics*, 20 April. Retrieved from https://www.realclearpolitics.com/articles/2019/04/20/recovering_the_christian_foundations_of_human_rights__140109.html.

Berlinerblau, J. (2019). Donald J. Trump, the White Evangelicals, and Martin Luther: A Hypothesis. *Interpretation: A Journal of Bible and Theology*, 73 (1), 18–30.

Bhargava, R. (2011). Rehabilitating Secularism. In C. Calhoun, M. Juergensmeyer, & J. VanAntwerpen (Eds.), *Rethinking Secularism* (pp. 92–113). Oxford: Oxford University Press.

Brittain, C.C. (2005). The 'Secular' as a Tragic Category: On Talal Asad, Religion, and Representation. *Method & Theory in the Study of Religion*, 17 (2), 149–165.

Calhoun, C., Juergensmeyer, M., & VanAntwerpen, J. (Eds.). (2011). *Rethinking Secularism*. Oxford: Oxford University Press.

Casanova, J. (1994). *Public Religions in the Modern World*. Chicago, IL: University of Chicago Press.

Casanova, J. (2009). *Public Religions Revisited*. Religion Revisited International Conference. Heinrich Böll Foundation & United Nations Institute for Social Development, Berlin, Germany, 5–6 June.

Catholic News Service. (2019). Cardinal Burke Cuts Ties with Institute, Citing its Alignment with Bannon. *National Catholic Reporter*, 25 June. Retrieved on 10 September 2019 from: https://www.ncronline.org/news/quick-reads/cardinal-burke-cuts-ties-institute-citing-its-alignment-bannon.

Cavanaugh, W.T. (2009). *The Myth of Religious Violence: Secular Ideology and the Roots of Modern Conflict*. New York: Oxford University Press.

Church Militant. (2017). The Catholic Magazine Interview with Milo They Refuse to Print. *Church Militant.com*. Retrieved from: https://www.churchmilitant.com/news/article/the-catholic-magazine-interview-with-milo-they-refuse-to-print.

Church Militant. (2019). Mission. *Church Militant.com*. Retrieved from: https://www.churchmilitant.com/mission.

Cienski, J. (2015). Migrants Carry 'Parasites and Protozoa', Warns Polish Opposition Leader. *Politico*, 14 October. Retrieved from https://www.politico.eu/article/migrants-asylum-poland-kaczynski-election.

Coleridge, M. (2018). *Statement from ACBC President Mark Coleridge*. Australian Catholic Bishops Conference. Retrieved from http://www.ACBC%20Statement%20on%20Refugees%20and%20Asylum-Seekers.pdf.

Corbett, T. (1983). Criteria for Theological Truth. *Irish Theological Quarterly*, 50 (2–4), 134–150.

Davies, C. (2019). Woman Arrested in Warsaw over Posters of Virgin Mary with Rainbow Halo. *The Guardian*, 7 May.

De Tocqueville, A. (1835 [2000]). *Democracy in America*. Translated by H.C. Mansfield & D. Winthrop. Chicago, IL: University of Chicago Press.

DeHanas, D.N. & Shterin, M. (2018). Religion and the Rise of Populism. *Religion, State and Society*, 46 (3), 177–185.

Dignitatis Humanae. (2019). About the Institute. *Dignitatis Humanae*. Retrieved from http://www.dignitatishumanae.com/index.php/about-us/about-the-institute.

Duncan, R. (2019). Cardinal Burke: Limiting Muslim Immigration is Patriotic. *Catholic Herald*, 20 May.

Edwards, M., Jr. (1983). Martin Luther and the Jews: Is There a Holocaust Connection? *Shofar*, 1 (4), 14–16.

Fallon, J.E. (2019). China's Crime against Uyghurs is a Form of Genocide. *Fourth World Journal*, 18 (1).

Feffer, J. (2014). Europe's Populist Reformation. *HuffPost*, 12 August.

Fisher, I. (2006a). Many Muslims Say Pope's Apology is Inadequate. *The New York Times*, September 18.

Fisher, I. (2006b). Vatican Says Pope Benedict Regrets Offending Muslims. *The New York Times*, 17 September.

Forlenza, R. (2018). 'Abendland in Christian hands': Religion and Populism in Contemporary European Politics. In G. Fitzl, J. Mackert, & B.S. Turner (Eds.), *Populism and the Crisis of Democracy Volume 3: Migration, Gender, and Religion* (pp. 133–149). London: Routledge.

Francisco, A.S. (2016). Martin Luther, Islam, and the Ottoman Turks. *Oxford Research Encyclopaedia of Religion*.

Gibson, D. (2014). Regensburg Redux: Was Pope Benedict XVI Right about Islam? *National Catholic Reporter*, 11 September. Retrieved from https://www.ncronline.org/news/world/regensburg-redux-was-pope-benedict-xvi-right-about-islam.

Göle, N. (2015). *Islam and Secularity: The Future of Europe's Public Sphere*. Durham, NC: Duke University Press.

Grafton, D.D. (2017). Martin Luther's Sources on the Turk and Islam in the Midst of the Fear of Ottoman Imperialism. *The Muslim World*, 107 (4), 665–683.

Habermas, J. (2008). Notes on Post-Secular Society. *New Perspectives Quarterly*, 25 (4), 17–29.

Hirst, M. (2006). Pope Must Withdraw His Ugly Remarks. *The Telegraph*, 17 September.

Ibn Taymiyyah. (c.1239–1321). *Answering Those Who Altered the Religion of Jesus Christ*. Edited by Ash-Shahhat Ahmad At-Tahhan. Umm al-Qura: Banyan Translating Services. Retrieved from https://books.google.com.au/books?id=u0p_KY1GCoAC&pg=PA147&lpg=PA147&dq=Christians+do+not+have+a+reliable+authentic+transmission+from+Christ+concerning+the+exact+wordings+of+the+Bible+or+a+reliable+transmission+

for+most+of+their+religious+laws.+This+is+also+applicable+to+the+Jews+who+do+not+have+authentic+transmissions+for+the+wordings+of+the+Torah+or+the+prophecies+of+their+prophets.&source=bl&ots=m2tT7IMf2B&sig=ACfU3U2qN03wXmCK3nLn-37EqpdVnXS4fw&hl=en&sa=X&ved=2ahUKEwj0vK7evo3rAhWOaCsKHa90DKQQ6AEwA3oECAsQAQ#v=onepage&q&f=false.

Imbelli, R. (2013). Lasting Impressions: The Legacy of Pope Benedict XVI. *U.S. Catholic*, 7 March.

Jefferson, T. (1777). *Virginia Statute for Religious Freedom*.

Joppke, C. (2015). *The Secular State Under Siege: Religion and Politics in Europe and America*. Cambridge: Polity.

Joppke, C. (2017). Blaming Secularism: Saba Mahmood – Religious Difference in a Secular Age: A Minority Report (Princeton NJ, Princeton University Press 2016). *European Journal of Sociology*, 58 (3), 577–589.

Kateb, G. (2009). Locke and the Political Origins of Secularism. *Social Research*, 76 (4), 1001–1034.

Kirchgaessner, S. (2018). Salvini Meets Cardinal Burke, Staunch Critic of Pope Francis. *The Guardian*, 17 June.

Kishi, K. (2018). *Key Findings on the Global Rise in Religious Restrictions*. Washington, DC: Pew Research Centre.

Knights of Columbus. (2020). *Knights of Columbus Website*. Retrieved from http://www.kofc.org/un/index.html.

Knights of the Republic. (2019). *Knights of the Republic: Eqvites Res PvBlica Website*. Retrieved from https://www.knightsrepublic.com/about-us.E

Lamb, C. (2017). Francis and Benedict: Two Popes, Two Divergent Approaches to Islam. *National Catholic Reporter*, 3 May. Retrieved from https://www.ncronline.org/news/vatican/francis-and-benedict-two-popes-two-divergent-approaches-islam.

Lasker, D. (2003). Competing Claims for Truth: Medieval Judaism and Christianity in Conflict. Boston College, 6 February. Retrieved from https://www.bc.edu/content/dam/files/research_sites/cjl/texts/cjrelations/resources/articles/lasker.htm.

Locke, J. (1689a [2013]). *A Letter Concerning Toleration*. Buffalo, NY: Prometheus Books.

Locke, J. (1689b [1993]). *Two Treatises on Government*. Edited by J.W. Yolton. London: Everyman.

Luther, M. (1529 [1967]). On War against the Turk. In J. Pelikan (Ed.), *Luther's Works*, vol. 46 (pp. 161–205). Philadelphia, PA: Fortress Press.

Luther. M. (1907). Against Catholicism. In O.J. Thatcher (Ed.), *The Library of Original Sources: Volume V: 9th to 16th Century* (pp. 119–126). Milwaukee: University Research Extension Co.

Luther, M. (1948). *The Jews and Their Lies*. Los Angeles, CA: Christian Nationalist Crusade.

Mackey, R. (2015). Hungarian Leader Rebuked for Saying Muslim Migrants Must be Blocked 'to Keep Europe Christian'. *The New York Times*, 3 September.

Magister, S. (2006). 'A brusqueness that we find unacceptable...': All the modifications introduced by Benedict XVI into the definitive version of his September 12, 2006 Lecture at the University of Regensburg. *L'Espresso*. 12 October. Retrieved from http://chiesa.espresso.repubblica.it/articolo/88645%26eng%3Dy.html?refresh_ce.

Mahmood, S. (2015). *Religious Difference in a Secular Age: A Minority Report*. Princeton, NJ: Princeton University Press.

Marzouki, N. & McDonnell, D. (2018). 'Us' and the 'Other': How Populists Continue to Hijack Religion. *Populism and Religion Blog: London School of Economics*, 15 October. Retrieved on 22 October 2015 from https://blogs.lse.ac.uk/religionglobalsociety/2018/10/us-and-the-other-how-populists-continue-to-hijack-religion.

Marzouki, N., McDonnell, D., & Roy, O. (Eds.). (2016). *Saving the People: How Populists Hijack Religion*. London: Hurst and Co.

Massing, M. (2018). Luther vs. Erasmus: When Populism First Eclipsed the Liberal Elite. *New York Review of Books*, 20 February.

Matt, M.J. (2019). Burke Defends Populism, Trump's Wall against Francis Attack. *The Remnant*, 31 May.

Miller, N. (2012). *The Religious Roots of the First Amendment: Dissenting Protestants and the Separation of Church and State*. Oxford: Oxford University Press.

Morieson, N. (2017). Are Contemporary Populist Movements Hijacking Religion? *Journal of Religious and Political Practice*, 3 (1–2), 88–95.

National Catholic Register. (2019). Open letter to the Bishops of the Catholic Church (Easter). *National Catholic Register*. Retrieved from https://www.ncregister.com/images/uploads/open-letter.pdf.

Paulick, J. (2006). Pope's Notorious Regensburg Talk Named Speech of the Year. *Deutsche Welle*, 19 December. Retrieved from https://www.dw.com/en/popes-notorious-regensburg-talk-named-speech-of-the-year/a-2283274.

Pew Research. (2015). *Future of World Religions*. Washington, DC: Pew Research Center.

Pew Research Center. (2018). *Global Uptick in Government Restrictions on Religion in 2016*. *Pew Research Forum*, 21 June.

Pew Research Forum. (2017). Europe's Growing Muslim Population. *Pew Research Forum*, 29 November.

Pongratz-Lippit, C. (2016). Benedict's Regensburg Address was 'Prophetic' says German Cardinal. *The Tablet: The International Catholic News Weekly*, 15 September. Retrieved from https://www.thetablet.co.uk/news/6131/benedict-s-regensburg-address-was-prophetic-says-german-cardinal.

Povoledo, E. (2013). Pope Appeals for More Interreligious Dialogue. *The New York Times*, 22 March.

Prange, A. (2017). How the Catholic Church Ties in to Poland's Judicial Reform. *Deutsche Welle*, 24 July. Retrieved from https://p.dw.com/p/2h2Ep.

Robbins, T. & Lucas, P.C. (2007). From 'Cults' to New Religious Movements: Coherence, Definition, and Conceptual Framing in the Study of New Religious Movements. In J.A. Beckford & J. Demerath (Eds.), *The SAGE Handbook of the Sociology of Religion* (pp. 227–247). Thousand Oaks, CA: Sage.

Roberts, T. (2019). The Rise of the Catholic Right. *Sojourners*, March. Retrieved from https://sojo.net/magazine/march-2019/rise-catholic-right.

Roose, J.M. (2016). *Political Islam and Masculinity: Muslim Men in the West*. New York: Palgrave.

Roose, J.M. (2017). Political Islam. In B.S. Turner (Ed.), *Wiley Blackwell Encyclopedia of Social Theory*. Hoboken, NJ: Wiley Blackwell. doi:10.1002/9781118430873.est0277.

Roy, O. (2018). 'A Kitsch Christianity': Populists Gather Support while Traditional Religiosity Declines. *LSE Populism and Religion Series*, 22 October. Retrieved from https://blogs.lse.ac.uk/religionglobalsociety/2018/10/a-kitsch-christianity-populists-gather-support-while-traditional-religiosity-declines.

Silk, M. (2017). Knights of Columbus, Cash Cow of the Catholic Right. *Religion News Service*, 16 May. Retrieved from https://religionnews.com/2017/05/16/knights-of-columbus-cash-cow-of-the-catholic-right.

Sobczak, P. (2018). Poland Backs Down on Holocaust Law, Moves to End Jail Terms. *Reuters*, 27 June.

Stanford, P. (2017). Five Centuries On, Martin Luther Should be Feted as a Hero of Liberty and Free Speech. *The Guardian*, 19 March.

Stark, R. & Bainbridge, W.S. (1985). *The Future of Religion: Secularization, Revival, and Cult Formation*. Berkeley, CA: University of California Press.
SWI. (2006). Couchepin Backs Pope's Islam Comments. *SWI: swissinfo.ch*, 17 September. Retrieved from https://www.swissinfo.ch/eng/couchepin-backs-pope-s-islam-comments/5450510.
Taylor, C. (2007). *A Secular Age*. Cambridge, MA: The Belknap Press of Harvard University Press.
Taylor, F. (2016). Pope Francis: Christianity and Islam Must Integrate in Europe. *Christian Today*, 17 May. Retrieved from https://www.christiantoday.com.au/news/pope-francis-christianity-and-islam-must-integrate-in-europe.html.
United Nations. (1948). Resolution 217/3: Universal Declaration of Human Rights (10 December 1948). *United Nations*. Retrieved from https://www.un.org/en/universal-declaration-human-rights.
Walker, S. (2019). Orbán Deploys Christianity with a Twist to Tighten Grip in Hungary. *The Guardian*, 14 July.
Williams, R. (1644 [2018]). *The Bloudy Tenent of Persecution for Cause of Conscience Discussed: And Mr. Cotton's Letter Examined and Answered*. London: Forgotten Books.
Woodhead, L. (2016). How the Church of England Lost the English People. *ABC Religion and Ethics*, 8 November. Retrieved from https://www.abc.net.au/religion/how-the-church-of-england-lost-the-english-people/10096376.
Woodhead, L. & Smith, G. (2018). Religion and Brexit: Populism and the Church of England. *Religion, State, and Society*, 46 (3), 206–223.

4
MALE SUPREMACISM

Introduction

The third thesis explored in this book requires an exploration of how displays of populist hyper-masculinity, irrespective of the local context, are indicative of deep-seated social injury and wounded masculine pride. In framing masculinity, it argues that alienation of and anxiety amongst working and, increasingly, middle-class men are key contributors to new populist movements, resulting in misogyny and resentment toward women amongst a small, though potentially increasing, segment of the community. This is reflected in the political discourse of the new demagogues. The chapter commences by outlining contemporary scholarly approaches to the intersection of masculinity and the new populism, followed by an exploration of the role played by anxiety and alienation in shaping the attraction to new populist movements. I then explore contemporary developments, focusing in particular upon the emergence of targeted political violence directed towards women on the basis of gender. I develop the concept of ideological masculinity, which may go some way to explaining the phenomenon of male supremacism, and explore important clues as to its prevalence in the wider community.

Masculinity and the new populism

The concept of masculinity, understood here as 'the social construction of what it is to be a man' (Kimmel & Bridges 2011), invites us to view actors who have been cast in the public imagination as inherently malevolent and fanatical as both human and subject to social processes. It enables reflexivity and removal from pre-formed opinions, such as embedded narratives about 'radicalisation', in order to address deeper-seated factors, such as emotional drivers. Importantly, the concept of masculinity also enables us to explore why the conception of 'what it is to be a man' might be different amongst those attracted to the populist groups compared to the wider community in which they are situated.

In the context of the populist epoch, policy makers, scholars, and commentators alike have scrambled to make sense of why men are joining or affiliating with groups that express anti-social political messages grounded in ethno-nationalism, religious extremism, and radical social change as well as whether they are likely to lead to violence. As Anderlini makes clear, the 'control, co-option, coercion, and subjugation of women are central features of VE [violent extremist] movements today' (2018: 28).

It is important to look at what we already know and where we might start to conceptualise developments. Raewyn Connell's conception of hegemonic masculinity suggests a relationship between masculinity (as power) and ideology (Duerst-Lahti 2008: 159), and her scholarship is arguably the 'central reference point for many, if not most, writers on men and masculinity' (Wetherell & Edley 1998: 156). Connell's *Masculinities* exposits the concept of hegemonic masculinity, an ideal type of masculinity dominant in any given society. Drawn from the Gramscian analysis of class relations, which refers to the 'cultural dynamic by which a group claims and sustains a leading position in social life', hegemonic masculinity explores how 'one form of masculinity is culturally exalted' at any one point in time (Connell 2005: 77). Connell states that hegemonic masculinity can be 'defined as the configuration of gender practice which embodies the currently accepted answer to the problem of the legitimacy of patriarchy' (Connell 2005: 77). In a re-evaluation of the text ten years after its initial publication, Connell and Messerschmitt differentiated between hegemonic and subordinated masculinities. Hegemonic masculinity 'embodied the currently most honoured way of being a man, it required all other men to position themselves in relation to it, and it ideologically legitimated the global subordination of women to men' (Connell & Messerschmidt 2005: 832).

Despite the salience of concepts, masculinities are often overlooked in attempts to understand the attraction of men to far-right movements (Lewis et al. 2017). Capturing this sentiment, populism scholar Cas Mudde asserted recently 'it is time we take masculinity more seriously in discussions of the far-right and right-wing politics' (2018). Standing argues that young white men in situations of precarious employment are readily mobilised by 'neo-fascist messages' of the kind increasingly played out in major cities (Standing 2011: 250, Peucker & Smith 2019). Yet since it is clear that not all precariously employed young men are led to the far-right, that cannot be a complete explanation. Kelly (2017) proposes that far-right affiliation represents 'reactionary rehabilitation' for 'white' masculinity at a time when the certainties of historical patriarchy are being challenged.

Michael Kimmel asserts that it is not possible to understand violent extremist movements without analysing gender and understanding how masculinity is 'deeply and intimately enmeshed' in participants' experience (Kimmel 2018: 9). He argues for the existence of a gendered political psychology of extremism grounded in a sense of 'aggrieved entitlement' and masculine compensation for what is lost (Kimmel 2018: 10). The notion of 'aggrieved entitlement' is problematic and essentialist. It overlooks how class, race, religion, and sexuality (amongst other contributing factors) shape the attraction to violent extremism. However, the sense of shame and humiliation is significant. Vieten and Poynting conclude that, '[t]riggered by processes of globalisation and Europeanisation, "status loss" and the fear of it, is what draws increasingly larger scales of populations, in particular, of male and working-class background, to far-right populism' (Vieten & Poynting 2016: 537). Galston argues that the right-wing populist agenda resonates especially with 'less-educated citizens' who feel threatened by technological changes in a post-industrial and 'more knowledge intensive economy' as they feel 'denigrated and devalued' in the face of the emerging well-educated, meritocratic urban elite that 'dominates government, the bureaucracy, the media, and major metropolitan areas.'(Galston 2018: 23).

The concept of 'meritocracy' is a particularly important component of citizenship. As previously discussed, Shklar talks in the American context about the 'two great emblems of public standing' – the 'right to vote' and the 'opportunity to earn' – as marks of civic dignity (Shklar 1989: 388; Shklar 1990: 3), whilst for Mead, equal citizenship in America 'comforts' inequality (Mead 1997: 199). For generations a core element of the dignity of work has been the notion that hard work (earning) results in an upward social trajectory and, by contrast, poor work, laziness, or ineptitude lead to negative consequences and downward social trajectories. Littler (2017: 8) argues that meritocracy should be 'unpacked as an ideologically charged discourse' that simultaneously serves as a social system 'based around the idea that individuals are responsible for working hard to activate their talent' and serving as an 'ideological discourse' that 'uphold particular power dynamics' (Littler 2017: 9):

> The dominant meaning of meritocracy in circulation today might therefore be broadly characterised as a potent blend of an essentialised and exclusionary notion of 'talent', competitive individualism, and the need for social mobility. Neoliberal meritocracy promotes the idea of individualistic, competitive success, symbolised by the ladder of opportunity.
>
> *(Littler 2017: 8)*

When this neoliberal form of meritocracy frames our understanding of work and reward (or lack thereof), wealth inequalities are 'naturalised' in mainstream political discourse and media as indicative of hard work and talent rather than any deep-seated structural inequality. Those who have been at the coalface of industrial change and lost the most, including their public standing as citizens through having been brutally 'expelled' from the economy (Sassen 2014), and those whose children have witnessed and been directly impacted by such change are the first to have to carve out a new place without the dignity and belonging that comes with being a member of a solidaristic work-based community.

The successful transition to employment is 'a key element of the establishment of an acceptable version of manhood' (McDowell 2003: 58) across the contexts discussed in this book. Hegemonic working-class masculinities grounded in roles represented as 'heroic, with punishing physical labour that involved different degrees of manual skills and bodily toughness' (Ward 2013: 4) have been undermined. In the context of neoliberalism and the 'new economy', they have been subordinated to masculinities equipped with the requisite cultural capital and bodily dispositions to achieve in a world where manual labour is less valued, particularly in the absence of the valorisation of the 'working-class man' by blue-collar unions.

Alienation and anxiety: Structural contributions

Anger, anomie, anxiety, and alienation undermine traditional working-class notions of masculinity bound up in self-reliance, strength, and the ability to provide for one's family (Standing 2011).

It very often these alienated working men (or sons of working men) who form the base of contemporary populist movements whose narratives promote empowerment, honour, belonging, and, most ominously, revenge. The experience of working- and lower-middle-class masculinities is grounded in real-world struggle defined by alienation from labour, anxiety due to the precarious nature of their work, anger due to downward social trajectories, and anomie based in a deficit of moral guidance and social bonds (Standing 2011). One need only look at the crowds at many populist events or online propaganda videos for groups, such as the Islamic State, to see that such men form the base of support for the new demagogues, a representation also supported by numerous statistical sources (Tyson & Maniam 2016; Shanahan 2019; Statista 2016). Many of these men demonstrate hyper-masculinities that belie their subordinate status. They are driven by humiliation, social injury, a lack of respect and recognition, and a perceived stripping of honour and dignity. Hage (2011) refers to this process as 'misinterpellation', the process of shattering that occurs when society's promise that hard work will result in upward social mobility is found to be false. The process of misinterpellation is central to increased receptibility to populist narratives. A sense of victimhood functions to provide an alternate source of meaning defined in opposition to a blameworthy 'other' and a sense of upward social and spiritual mobility through action. In plain language, those joining these groups transform from 'zero' to 'hero' and gain an instant sense of belonging.

Barbalet claims that it is 'through emotions that actors are engaged by others and through their emotions that they alter their relations with them' (Barbalet 1993: 133). He argues further that subjection to arbitrary power, punishment where there should be reward, and frustrated attempts to satisfy needs are likely to evoke strong emotions including depression, fear, and anger. The current political context has evolved over a period of sustained economic and political pressure as well as degradation of social status. With the stripping of honour and dignity from work, we are witnessing the death of working class stoicism, which emphasises endurance, self-control, and inner strength, and its replacement with a what Campbell and Manning (2014) frame as a culture of victimhood, where aggrieved parties highlight their identity as victims and emphasise their innocent suffering at the hands of a privileged and blameworthy elite. Paradoxically, the collapse of working-class masculine stoicism parallels increased displays of physical hyper-masculinity.

Middle-class resentment

To frame this only as a working-class problem, however, misses an important dimension of the issue. In a period when male-dominated employment in manufacturing, agriculture, and mining has been contracting, women have entered the white collar professions en masse. With a suite of hard-won protections relating to childbirth and child care, combined with delayed fertility by older women, they have held down positions that in previous generations would have been impossible. Although there is a glass ceiling in many professional occupations, men are forced to compete for jobs previously regarded as their inherited birthright, and mediocrity is no longer tolerated (Besley et al. 2017a; Besley et al. 2017b). Men who do not perform at the requisite standard are increasingly expelled into short-term contract work (Besley et al. 2017a; Besley et al. 2017b). For many more young men, this form of work is all that they have known.

No fault divorce in the United States, Australia, and a multitude of other Western countries enables women to leave unhappy marriages. Legislators and courts alike have become increasingly attuned to enforcing child support payments and requiring salaried divorced men to continue to economically support their children through to adulthood by taking funds directly from their wages. This even looks likely to emerge in the United Kingdom as well with the introduction of a relevant bill in Parliament in early 2020. These developments, which are commonly understood to have provided a semblance of balance in the power relations between the sexes, are seen by some men impacted by them as a root cause of resentment and incivility.

In addition to class, an obvious dimension of the problem appears, on the surface at least, to be related to race. Much has been written on 'white privilege' and the emergence of 'white populism'. Sally Robinson argued compelling at the turn of the century that white men have been 'conflated with normativity in the American social lexicon' and have not been understood as 'practicing identity politics because they are visible in political terms, even as they benefit from the invisibility of their own racial and gender specificity' (Robinson 2000: 2). For Robinson, anxiety over loss of this privilege 'competes with a desire to forge a collective identity around claims of victimisation'

> in order for white masculinity to negotiate its position within the field of identity politics, white men must claim a symbolic disenfranchisement, must

compete with others for cultural authority bestowed upon the authentically disempowered, the visibly wounded.

(Robinson 2000: 7 & 12)

The intersection of white masculinity and social class may well lead to different forms of political practice. For white working-class men, it may well lead to anger, to seeking out the collective, and to participation in hyper-masculine political rallies and groups. For white-collar men a perceived sense of victimisation may lead to expressions of a more pernicious form of slander, professional undermining, and vindictive behaviour in anonymous online forums, which require not only access to computers, but a generally high level of online literacy.

To ground contemporary developments only on white masculinity, however, would risk overlooking a significant multicultural dimension of the emergence of contemporary populism. To this extent, Nira Yuval-Davis has written of the autochthonic politics of the far-right, where the claim 'I was here before you' can be applied in any situation. A flexible concept, it 'combines elements of naturalisation of belonging with vagueness as to what constitutes the essence of belonging' (Yuval-Davis 2019: 73). This may go some way to explaining recent diversity in the far-right and the emergence of far-right Jewish and gay activists, both traditionally reviled by the far-right. Many of the most militantly Christian, anti-Muslim, and anti-secular activists in Western contexts come from Christian minorities in the developing world, including Africa and South Asia.

The new demagogic strongmen

In this context defined by anger, anxiety, and anomie, a new class of global strongmen emerged from the margins of the political establishment: Donald Trump in the United States (2016–), Nigel Farage in the United Kingdom, Viktor Orbán in Hungary (2010–), Recep Tayyip Erdoğan in Turkey (2014–), Narendra Modi in India (2014–), Rodrigo Duterte in the Philippines (2016–), and Jair Bolsonaro in Brazil (2019–), to name but a few. These demagogic figures have sought to appeal directly to men, and to do so they employed misogynistic, divisive language as a core element of their communications.

Trump attracted primarily male support. A December 2015 poll conducted by the *Washington Post* and ABC News during the Republican primaries found that Trump's supporters were primarily male (47% of Republican voters) rather than female (28% of overall Republican voters) (Ross 2016). Importantly, 50 per cent of Trump supporters had incomes under $50,000 a year, and less than one in three (29%) possessed a college degree (Ross 2016). Exit poll data from the time of the election indicated that race played a decisive role, with 62 per cent of white men voting for Trump and 52 per cent of white women (CNN 2016). The election was just eight years after the sub-prime housing disasters that triggered the global financial crisis and decimated the assets of large swathes of lower-income Americans. Trump successfully captured a sizeable segment of white working-class men who felt alienated, angry, and resentful about their marginalisation in political debate.

Trump's appeal to men at the margins was based in his simultaneous focus on economic growth at any cost (discussed in Chapter 6) and his hyper-masculinist posturing. Whilst campaigning for president, tapes emerged of Donald Trump boasting openly that 'when you're a star, they let you do it. You can do anything … Grab 'em by the pussy. You can do anything' (New York Times 2016). His comments were described by Nigel Farage, the UKIP interim leader and key Brexit protagonist, as 'ugly' but excusable as 'alpha male boasting' (Martinez 2016).

Gender politics were less visible in the vote to leave the European Union, yet they remained important. Nigel Farage, speaking after posing on a tank at the Heywood Tank Museum in Lancashire, admitted the party was 'blokeish' and had a 'women problem' (McSmith 2014). Farage admitted further:

> The problem with female voters and UKIP is that, over the last 5 to 10 years, at times, on a very bad day, we've looked a bit blokeish, a bit like a rugby club on a day out and I'm probably the most guilty person of all … The pub and everything else. It's true, it was a very male dominated party in every aspect.
> *(McSmith 2014)*

He added, 'What do you want me to do? Go sell flowers?' (McSmith 2014). A breakdown of the Brexit vote would reveal that 45 per cent of men chose to remain compared to 55 per cent of male voters who chose to leave the European Union. This is compared to the 51 per cent of women who voted to remain compared to 49 per cent who voted to leave the EU (Statista 2016). A study by Green and Shorrocks, which drew on the British Election Study Internet Panel, found that the impact of gender and gender-equality-related economic and social change had not only been overlooked, perceived discrimination against men (found particularly in older working men) was a 'significant predicator in voting Leave at the EU Referendum':

> This perhaps indicates that men who hold gender-based resentments may be a group that becomes particularly frustrated over delays and compromises in the Brexit process as it continues. More broadly, the results also suggest that there is a significant minority of men who may vote in British elections on the basis of anger and resentment about the unfair treatment of men in society.
> *(Green & Shorrocks 2019)*

An examination of the emergence of Trump, the 'Brexit' vote, and the electoral momentum of populist parties appears to confirm that Western Liberal democracies, particularly those in the 'Anglosphere', have in some way, shape, or form given rise to a population of men who feel disenfranchised and who are alienated, resentful, and angry.

This is not limited, however, to white working-class or professional men. During the 2014–16 period, the messaging of self-proclaimed Islamic State Caliph Abu Bakr al-Baghdadi, relayed in English to Western Muslims through a sophisticated propaganda apparatus, resulted in approximately 6,000 Western foreign fighters, out of approximately 15,000 total foreign fighters, joining the Islamic State movement (Briggs & Silverman 2014: 9). The vast majority were men (see Chapter 7).

It is clear that a proportion of men in Western contexts are attracted to the messaging of the new demagogues, resulting in global changes to the political landscape as the new demagogues achieve political and, in the case of the Islamic State, military success. Arguably, there is little particularly new about the use of fear and hatred for political mobilisation. Indeed, parallels between such leaders often lead to simplistic comparisons between demagogues from different historical epochs. It is important to consider more closely the issue of masculinity and, in particular, new formations of masculinity that have to some extent developed, grown, and evolved in parallel with the rise of the new demagogues.

It is my argument that these amorphous groups, which are difficult to physically pin down, operate primarily online, yet with real world consequences. The politicisation and weaponisation of masculinity are at the base of what I term 'ideological masculinity', which centres on the reassertion of men's control of the public and private domains, and which uses physical, verbal, and symbolic violence to achieve its ends. As will be demonstrated in subsequent chapters, anti-women attitudes do not emerge from interviews with blue-collar men in working-class towns, indicating they lie elsewhere. The following examines ideological masculinity on a graduated scale from established pillars of gender inequality and prejudice through to the new anti-women activism, anti-women violence, and anti-women terrorism.

Evangelical men's movements

The centrality of manhood to traditionalist conservative religion is not a new development. Men have long been posited as the head of the household, the leader of prayer, the earner of a salary, and the representative of the family in public life. In the same context, women have long been confined to the domestic sphere. Movements seeking equal rights for women, such as feminism, have been viewed with hostility. What is of particular interest here, however, is the renewed hostility toward feminism and women's rights and an accompanying willingness to engage with political actors who demonstrate behaviour traditionally antithetical to Christianity. Whilst the appeal of Donald Trump will be explored in detail in Chapter 6, it is worth considering the work of Kristin du Mez, who demonstrates how, beginning in the 1970s and over several generations, a cohort of authors and faith leaders in the evangelical movement began to frame Christianity and Jesus in hyper-masculine terms:

> Trump appeared at a moment when evangelicals feel increasingly beleaguered, even persecuted. Issues related to gender – from the cultural sea change on gay

marriage to transgender bathroom laws to the Hyde Amendment and the contraceptive mandate – are at the centre of their perceived victimisation.

(Du Mez 2017)

The domination of organised religion by men, whether it is labelled 'patriarchy' or 'male supremacist' (I gravitate toward the latter), is grounded in an understanding of inherent gender inequality as reflecting God's 'truth'. Such inequality and beliefs are likely to be particularly pronounced in the practices of fundamentalists, whether Catholicists or Islamists. Both refuse to contemplate the notion that women might lead prayer or become imams or priests, as if women are spiritually or physically deficient and bereft. Whilst demonstrating the natural ease of fit between hypermasculine demagogic strongmen and fundamentalist religion, it is not a new development. It may be understood as an established pillar of gender inequality. To understand the formation of new pillars of contemporary hegemonic and what I term 'ideological masculinity' centred on the control of women under threat of violence, we must look to the Alt-Right, Manosphere, and Incel movements.

The 'alt-right' and spin-off groups

The self-proclaimed 'alternative' or 'alt' right originated primarily in the United States before spreading globally. It represents a new trajectory in far-right politics. The term was originally coined by far-right activist Richard Spenser. Those self-identifying as 'alt-right' assert a particularly vitriolic form of white identarian politics that emphasises both white supremacy and seeks to vigorously attack the political left.

Seeking to differentiate themselves from traditional representations of the far-right, such as ultra-masculinist, tattooed, neo-Nazi skinheads, the 'alt-right' have simultaneously developed an online and physical presence by using passive aggression, sarcasm, and meme culture and by adopting a more refined version of far-right masculinity that can still translate relatively easily to extreme violence.

Evidence of the violent possibilities of the alt-right was demonstrated at the August 2017 'Unite the Right' Rally in Charlottesville, Virginia. Organised to symbolise resistance to the removal of Confederate monuments, the protest resulted in clashes with counterprotesters that left dozens injured. One far-right activist drove his car into a group of counterprotesters, killing activist Heather Heyer. Other groups broadly associated with the alt-right have also captured international attention. The 'Proud Boys', formed by Vice Media co-founder Gavin McInnes, were initially situated within the broad definition of alt-right before adopting what McInnes labelled 'Western chauvinism' (as opposed to concern primarily with race) and distancing themselves from the 'alt-right' label. Posited as a men-only drinking club, the group has an initiation process referred to as obtaining 'four degrees'. It includes a loyalty oath stating pride in being a 'Western chauvinist', a beating by fellow club members, a tattoo and an agreement not to masturbate, and, finally, participation in a fight 'for the cause'. Members wear yellow-trimmed black Fred

Perry polo shirts. They sport what have been referred to as 'fashy' (short for fascist) 'high and tight' haircuts. The group's website stipulates that members of all religions and races can join, though not women, confirming a deeper-seated dislike of women.

McInnes stated on his YouTube program: 'Maybe the reason I'm sexist is because women are dumb. No, I'm just kidding, ladies. But you do tend to not thrive in certain areas – like writing' (McInnes 2017). McInnes, like many others actively asserts that women's roles are defined by their genetic predispositions, a position that conveniently returns the sphere of paid employment back to men:

> Women are forced to pretend to be men. They're feigning this toughness. They're miserable. Study after study has shown that feminism has made women less happy. They're not happy in the work force, for the most part. I would guess 7 percent [of women] like not having kids, they want to be CEOs, they like staying at the office all night working on a proposal, and all power to them. But by enforcing that as the norm, you're pulling these women away from what they naturally want to do, and you're making them miserable.
>
> *(Huffington Post 2013)*

In a follow-up interview stemming from controversy over his remarks, McInnes asserted that having children 'made me religious', and he became 'a God-fearing Catholic because of the miracle of life' (May 2013). McInnes is a member of the Knights of Columbus, the Catholic fraternal order discussed in Chapter 3 that plays a significant role in funding fundamentalist, right-wing Catholic think tanks. Demonstrating further the crossover between the alt-right, related groups such as the Proud Boys, religiosity, and the Manosphere, McInnes stated in a 2015 interview that 'women earn less in America because they choose to', they are 'less ambitious', and the gender pay gap is 'sort of God's way – this is nature's way – of saying women should be at home with the kids' (Mazza 2015).

The Proud Boys actively advocate for political violence against their opponents, particularly those to the left of the political spectrum. After one such act of violence, a street brawl in New York, McInnes commented, 'I want violence, I want punching in the face. I'm disappointed in Trump supporters for not punching enough' (Daily News Editorial Board 2018). In a 2017 episode of the 'Gavin McInnes Show', he said, 'We will kill you. That's the Proud Boys in a nutshell. We will kill you. We look nice, we seem soft, we have boys in our name … we will assassinate you' (McInnes 2017). The Proud Boys group was designated as a hate group by the Southern Poverty Law Center, and it attracted considerable scrutiny form law enforcement in the United States. However, numerous international affiliates have been formed, including in Australia, New Zealand, Canada, and the United Kingdom.

Whilst the relationship between the amorphous, primarily on-line grouping known as the alt-right and formal religion is, at best, ambiguous, the shared emphasis upon 'reclaiming' masculinity from political correctness and feminism is clear cut. Like many sub-cultures before them, the alt-right and those that have branched off from it have developed a specific vocabulary designed to vilify perceived opponents whilst further solidifying the link between them. In an examination of this linguistic development, the central role of anxiety, alienation, anomie and their intersection with masculinity come to the fore. Terms such as 'Chad' (a pejorative word for handsome men who are sexually successful with women) and 'cuck' (a shortened form of 'cuckold', a man whose wife has cheated on him, used to describe weakness and emasculation) provide powerful insight into the extent to which masculinity is a key element of the self-definition of the alt-right. The concept of the 'red pill', derived from the film *The Matrix*, refers to taking a pill than enables users to see the truth about society, including the apparent emasculation of men.

Contemporary literature does not adequately delve into the largely under-explored dimension of animosity in the new populism, which extends beyond hatred of foreigners and, in particular, Muslims. Hatred and/or deep-seated resentment of women is pervasive throughout populist political discourse, from alt-right backyard sheds to presidential and prime ministerial dining rooms. Masculinity, in this context, has become a political identity in and of itself. It intersects with key populist messages targeted at supporters. It is linked to alienation of and anxiety amongst working-class men and, increasingly, middle-class and white-collar men. Understanding this dimension of populism enables us to connect the dots to identify what has contributed to the strength of populism in the world at this particular point in time, linking to the same political agenda the rise of textualism and hard-line fundamentalist religion and hatred and resentment of women.

The 'manosphere': Men Going their Own Way (MGTOW)

One individual or group (it is not clear) launched the *MGTOW: Men Going Their Own Way* website as a way of cohering the movement. The site is significant in size and scope, containing several million individual contributions and an active, up-to-date discussion forum. It is instructive to quote at some length from the website's definition of the 'manosphere', which ties to key themes prevalent in this chapter:

> Play or be played: That's the world the vast majority of men wake up to in the present day. For these young men, it's not a philosophy or an attitude; it's reality.
> The companies they work for demand loyalty, but will fire them or lay them off without a second thought if profits dip one tenth of one percent.
> (MGTOW 2020)

The definition moves seamlessly from precarious work grounded in the neoliberal economy to a complaint about women, depicting them as materialistic, superficial, and demanding:

The women they encounter demand attention, loyalty, resources, and undue privilege, while offering very little in return. The natural hypergamous nature that once served them well in their quest to secure the best possible mate is now a sustained lifestyle bringing an endless pursuit of bigger and better. The average young woman today is less concerned about the number of quality men who would commit to her than she is about the number of men who retweet a photo of her breasts.

(MGTOW 2020)

Religion in the 'manosphere' is a facet of life, however churches are not fundamentalist enough to subordinate women:

Young men today attend churches with pastors who demand they '*man up*' and support the church and its female parishioners, but that same church does nothing to cultivate an environment that encourages feminine strength. Sunday after Sunday they listen as the same Bible used to preemptively absolve women of all past, current, and future transgressions is used to condemn men.

(MGTOW 2020)

Women are represented as controlling, deceptive, and exempt from the unsatisfying life that the reader is invited to identify with:

They have best friends from childhood who disappear six months after the wedding, because the new bride doesn't want her hubby hanging out with single losers.

They have to pick up the tab for dad's dinner, because his [sic] going broke trying to support mom, her new live-in boyfriend, and a 12 year old he's not certain is even his. The young man watches as middle-management dad making $70k per year tries to crank the engine in his 11 year old car to no avail, and then has to give him a ride back to his apartment on the seedy side of town. The young man shudders as he realises the father who 'did the right thing' by sacrificing his life for his family can fit everything he owns into a 580 sq. ft. apartment with plenty of room to spare.

The young man has finally learned that men and women share the same inherent character flaws, but not the same consequences. He has sinned, and he has paid dearly. She has sinned, and she has been exalted.

(MGTOW 2020)

In summary, the member of the manosphere is righteous, rational, and a victim of forces bent on his subordination. By linking with others, he gains a solidaristic bond denied to him in other areas of life and forges his own destiny:

He doesn't hate his corporation; he hates the system. He doesn't hate God; he hates what the church does in God's name. He doesn't hate women; he hates the unforgiving female support machine. He doesn't hate feminists or White Knights; he hates navigating the environment they create.

That's why there's a Manosphere, and that's why it's growing.

(MGTOW 2020)

In addition to developing a reasonably cohesive narrative of victimhood and promoting hatred of women, by definition the MGTOW movement also implies avoiding participation in conventional or violent political activity. Other elements of the men's rights movement, however, do not do so.

Incitement to physical violence

The scale of the manosphere, for some, has proven relatively profitable. Speaking via videoconference at the 2018 International Conference on Men's issues in London, Paul Elam, the founder of *A Voice for Men*, a key for-profit men's rights website and one of the highest profile 'men's rights' groups in the world, claimed:

> We've become part of a philosophy that opposes longstanding and intense social programming to ignore men's issues in the name of forever putting women and all other groups first. The ideas we embrace are healthy, functional, and corrective to social problems, yet are viewed by the general population as pathological and even dangerous.
>
> *(Elam 2018)*

Elam framed men's rights activists as victims of a society intent on belittling them:

> Thanks in part to the fake news media, we've been labelled as haters, even though our work demonstrates that we are in fact rejecting hatred and hateful ideology. That's life for MRA's and more broadly red pill people, and its often marked by loneliness, isolation, and varying degrees of frustration.
>
> *(Elam 2018)*

In contrast to his depiction of his group as peaceful, Elam previously advocated violence against women, proclaiming a 'Bash a Violent Bitch Month' for male survivors of domestic violence, albeit in the name of satire (a common tactic used by alt-right actors to bypass criticism and laws):

> I don't mean subdue them, or deliver an open handed pop on the face to get them to settle down. I mean literally to grab them by the hair and smack their face against the wall till the smugness of beating on someone because you know they won't fight back drains from their nose with a few million red corpuscles. And then make them clean up the mess … To all the men out there that decided to say 'damn the consequences', and fight back, you are heroes to the cause of equality; true feminists. And you are the honorary Kings

of Bash a Violent Bitch Month. You are living proof of just how hollow 'don't fuck with us', rings from the mouths of bullies and hypocrites. And then make them clean up the mess.

(Elam 2010)

Gavin McInnes, previously discussed, also advocated violence against women:

This woman, yes, I'm advocating violence against women, this woman, should be punched in the face. It shouldn't be by a man. Maybe by another woman. Maybe her twin sister should just punch her in the face. Or maybe mace her.

(McInnes 2016)

Whether satire or otherwise, the incitement to violence against women is clear and not unusual. In the manosphere, it also extends to sexual violence.

Incitement to sexual violence

The 'neomasculinity' of Daryush 'Roosh V' Valizadeh valorises traditional sex roles, the nuclear family, a binary sex model, and an understanding of women as being programmed to seek the 'highest possible value male' (2015a). Valizadeh asserts that patriarchy was a 'superior societal system that catered to the innate abilities of the sexes and provided them with roles that not only furthered their own abilities and interests but that of civilization as a whole' (2015a). His social Darwinist depiction of the 'sexual marketplace' has proved particularly resonant with his followers, emphasising as it does that women are programmed to seek 'high value males' and that in the context of the modern dating market (now as 'fluid as the job market'), that men at the top can attract many females whilst those at the bottom 'struggle to attract even one' (Valizadeh 2015a).

Valizadeh argues that 'neomasculinity' is 'a superior ideological alternative for men who reject the poison pills prescribed by the modern political and cultural elite' (2015a). Given the seriousness with which Valizadeh has developed his ideology of neomasculinity, it is worth considering both his repeated guidance on 'negging' (treating women with no respect in order to keep them interested) and his argument for the legalisation of rape if it takes place on private property. In 'How to Stop Rape', labelled a 'satirical thought experiment', he asserts:

Consent is now achieved when she passes underneath the room's door frame, because she knows that that man can legally do anything he wants to her when it comes to sex. Bad encounters are sure to occur, but these can be learning experiences for the poorly trained woman so she can better identify in the future the type of good man who will treat her like the delicate flower that she believes she is.

(Valizadeh 2015b)

Valizadeh was subsequently banned from a number of countries, including the United Kingdom and Australia. However, his website and books remain freely available.

In 2019, Valizadeh very publicly joined the Armenian Apostolic Church, stating that 'God' was the final pill (Burton 2019a). He has since embraced chastity, and many of his former blog posts can no longer be found. At first instance this may appear to signal a rejection of his former work. However, as theologian Tara Burton notes, religion offers an alternate source of meaning lacking in such men's daily lives:

> The conversion of Roosh V highlights another, even more vital, truth about the anti-feminist and alt-right movements: They already function as quasi-religions. These movements gain adherents precisely because they tap into young men's existential hunger for the kind of things that also underpin religious observance.
>
> *(Burton 2019a)*

The 'manosphere' is clearly defined by a deep-seated resentment of women and the advances made in women's rights. Marriage, increasingly unobtainable to working men (Lichter et al. 2019), is represented as a form of modern-day slavery designed to trap men in a sexless financial trap. In other words, they 'don't want it even if they could have it'. Women and, in particular, feminists are blamed for subverting the natural order of male power and for making themselves sexually unavailable. To gain access to women, men must manipulate them into compliance or 'train women' through legalised sanctions, such as rape for promiscuity, and by ensuring that men are at the top of the 'value chain'.

Anxiety, anomie, and alienation from wider society are clearly evident in the primarily online sphere of men's rights advocacy and the collective assortment of sub-species of misogynistic activists. Rather than engaging with the structural factors shaping the 'expulsion' of working people from the global economy, gender has become the key defining feature and lens through which these activists form their worldview. Protagonists frame this variously as their 'philosophy' or 'ideology', a key point which I will return to later. They give members a 'meaningful account of why the world is the way it is' and 'provide them with a sense of purpose and the possibility of sainthood. They offer a sense of community' (Burton 2019b).

Utilising violent and hateful language firmly situated in depictions of victimhood and having shed all dignity and honour, these groups are largely an online phenomenon. In recent years the online community has changed with the evolution of the 'involuntary celibate' or 'incel' subculture from a relatively benign subculture based on sharing stories about the inability to find sexual partners to a radicalised outlook that advocates a range of measures, including online deception, killing women on the basis that they deny sex, and violence against those men who are successfully 'accessing them'.

Incels: Graduation to terrorist violence

'Incels' (involuntary celibates) are broadly self-defined as those that have not had sex for more than six months, despite a desire to do so. The term was first coined in 1993 by a Canadian university student who founded the group 'Alana's Involuntary Celibacy Project' to capture the experiences of those who had not experienced a relationship or intimacy for an extended period of time (Kassam 2018). In the online environment, 'incel' evolved from a community of mutual support to one based on mutual debasement and self-loathing, which was particularly active on message board sites, such as *4chan* and *Reddit*. In November 2017, *Reddit* banned the r/incels subreddit discussion page, which at the time had up to 40,000 members.

The incel movement (broadly defined), is in some ways a logical outgrowth of the 'manosphere'. Incels embody the angst, alienation, and self-flagellation of men who not only consider themselves to be emasculated by the rejection of women, they feel anger, rage, and a desire for revenge against those perceived to be holding them back. The subculture developed its own neologisms, such as 'heightcel' (a man rejected by women due to his height) and 'ethnicel' (a man excluded on the basis of ethnicity), amongst many others.

Even a cursory examination of online forums finds many examples of incels bemoaning their association with violent attacks. Indeed, many may be happy to remain anonymous in online forums. However, others branch out into attacks on women, whether online or the real world, ranging from deception to terror attacks. In the case of violent incels, the goal of terrorist actions is less about the restoration of lost masculinity and more about the nihilistic and misogynistic destruction of women and the men who have enjoyed access to women.

In a manifesto written before committing a violent attack on his housemates and a female sorority house in Isla Vista, California, Elliot Rodger claimed he was seeking a day of retribution against men who have 'pleasurable sex lives' and a 'war on women', which would 'punish all females for the crime of depriving me of sex', in order to 'deliver a devastating blow that will shake all of them to the core of their wicked hearts' (Rodger 2014). It is important to consider that, in the manifesto, Rodger disclosed that he was seeing both a psychiatrist and a counsellor. Speculation remains strong about whether he suffered from a mental illness. In the attack Rodger killed six people and injured fourteen others before killing himself.

Rodger's manifesto explained his planned 'day of retribution':

> Women don't care about me at all. They won't even design to tell me why they've mistreated me. This just shows how evil and sadistic they are. Oh well, they will realise the gravity of their crimes when I slaughter them all on the Day of Retribution. How dare they reject a magnificent gentleman like me!
>
> *(Rodger 2014)*

Whilst the majority of the manifesto was about Rodger's personal hatred of women and the men with access to them, he also outlined a program for the extermination of women and the 'ultimate and perfect ideology of how a fair world work', wherein sexuality and women would not exist:

> In order to completely abolish sex, women themselves would have to be abolished. All women must be quarantined like the plague that they are, so that they can be used in a manner that actually benefits a civilised society. In order to carry this out, there must be a new and powerful type of government, under the control of one divine ruler, such as myself. The ruler that establishes this new order would have complete control over every aspect of society, in order to direct it towards a good and pure place. At the disposal of this government, there needs to be a highly trained army of fanatically loyal troops, in order to enforce such revolutionary laws.
>
> *(Rodger 2014)*

Women in this world would be 'quarantined' and 'deliberately starved to death', with a 'few women spared' for 'the sake reproduction'. Such a state of affairs – a 'pure world' – would enable men to 'expand' their intelligence and 'advance the human race to a state of perfect civilisation'.

Subsequent violent actors have cited Rodger's 2014 attack as an inspiration. In 2018 in Toronto, Alex Minassian, who killed ten people with his van and injured 16 more, referred to 'overthrowing' promiscuous attractive men (the 'Chads') and women (the 'Stacey's') (Beauchamp 2018). In Tallahassee, Florida, 40-year-old Scott Beierle posted videos online, including 'The Rebirth of My Misogynism' and 'The American Whore' in which he discussed the crucifixion of promiscuous women, before he attacked a yoga studio, shot and killed two women, injured four other women and a man, and killed himself (Beierle 2018). In May 2020, a Toronto 17-year-old became the first person charged with terrorism in an attack allegedly motivated by the incel movement (Toronto Police 2020).

Political violence against women: The most worrying development of all?

Reports of sexual and physical violence against women in Western contexts are increasing. In Australia, for example, intimate partner violence is the greatest health risk factor for women between the ages of 25 and 44, and reported rates of sexual assault have been climbing nationally for the past five years (AIHW 2019). Reports are increasing in wealthy global cities in particular, such as London, Paris, Toronto, and New York. Some have attributed increased reporting to the success of the #MeToo movement, though in the absence of quality data, it alone cannot explain what is occurring.

Globally, international institutions have identified violence against women as a 'global pandemic' (World Bank 2019), as 'one of the most widespread, persistent, and devastating human rights violations in our world today' (United Nations 2019), and as a major public health problem (World Health Organisation 2017).

Such definitions draw on epidemiological terminology, as though such violence is an illness that can be directly treated through controlled interventions. In this context, factors such as poverty, lack of education, and even natural disaster are considered key contributors to physical and sexual violence against women and, increasingly, they inform where governments direct both domestic resources and foreign aid aimed at improving women's rights.

However, for this analysis to be complete, a question must be asked: Why are rates of violence increasing in places where poverty is lower, rates of education are higher, and women are more engaged in public life than ever before? I argue that a new paradigm, 'ideological masculinity', is required for understanding the increase in violence against women in Western contexts (in particular) and its links with demagoguery, masculinity, religion, and the new populism.

Hatred and resentment of women: An evolution

This new paradigm is geared toward gaining an understanding of ideological masculinity as a virulent, increasingly potent form of violent extremism, which requires intervention by the state. However, before addressing the paradigm, it is important to outline some obvious, yet not always overtly recognised, facts. Hatred of and prejudice toward women extends well beyond the current populist epoch and deep into history. What I believe is different in the contemporary context, however, is the relatively recent phenomena that have emerged online. Increasingly, real world acts are linked directly to the emergence of the new demagogues, social media, and online forums alongside the discernible shift in the economy from traditionally male roles to roles that are favourable to women's participation – and success – en masse.

The new demagogues appeal to a sense of loss of status and power amongst their support bases, which is echoed in the manosphere and amongst religious conservatives (often they are intertwined). The simultaneous growth of the alt-right and manosphere, the reinvigoration of hard-line religious fundamentalists, and the emergence of newer phenomena, including incels, has been accompanied by anti-women movements seeking the (re)subordination of women as a desirable and urgent goal in and of itself. In this context, masculinity becomes ideological, and violence to enact it is framed as being both desirable and necessary.

Conceptualising anti-women activism

Feminist scholars have developed a toolbox of terms for understanding the relationship between violence and power. The noun 'femicide' is used to describe the 'killing of a woman or girl, in particular by a man and on account of her gender' (Oxford Dictionary 2015). Caputi and Russell define 'femicide' as 'the murder of women by men motivated by hatred, contempt, pleasure, or a sense of ownership of women' (Caputi & Russell 1990: 1). Later they termed it simply 'sexist terrorism against women', citing Marc Lépine's December 1989 murder of 14 women in the engineering faculty at the University of Montreal during which he screamed 'You're all fucking feminists' (Caputi & Russell 1992). Lépine's three-page suicide note blamed his life failures on women (Pitt 1989: 9).

Opposition to men's domination over women and the subordination of females has existed on record since at least the twelfth century. It took particular flight in the fourteenth century in France. The term 'feminism' was devised during the nineteenth century and simultaneously paralleled (and in some cases was deeply enmeshed in) the global development of movements for working-class equality growing out of the industrial revolution, most notably Marxism. Feminism was also linked to political liberalism. It is, at its core, an ideology that has withstood the test of time, asserting the need for equality of the sexes. Despite its very broad diversity, the feminist movement has had, at its heart, the common goal of achieving equality of the sexes across the political, economic, legal, and social spheres. Duerst-Lahti asserts:

> Unlike patriarchy – which can be used to mean a system of rule, a way to organise households, an ideology, and more – feminism has always been recognised as a political ideology. It is marked by the suffix 'ism', and indisputably has sought more political power for women, two dimensions of ideologies. It also was recognised as ideological because it challenged the ideology of masculinism that was both unnamed and made largely invisible due to its hegemonic position.
>
> *(Duerst-Lahti 2008: 165)*

This central idea has shaped different forms of political action, from those seeking to reform the political system to those calling for the abolition of capitalism and class society. Such politically driven activity, which challenges dominant power structures, has not only produced verbal and structural repercussions, it has often resulted in physical violence against its advocates. Some scholars have framed a competing ideology grounded in antifeminism that seeks to return women to the domestic sphere and a subordinated status. Arthur Brittan asserts that masculinism is this competing ideological frame:

> [Masculinism] [i]s the ideology that justifies and naturalises male domination. As such, it is the ideology of patriarchy. Masculinism takes it for granted that [1] there is a fundamental difference between men and women, [2] it assumes heterosexuality is normal, [3] it accepts without question the sexual division of labour, and [4] it sanctions the political and dominant role of men in the public and private spheres.
>
> *(Brittan 1989: 4)*

Blais and Dupuis-Déri explore the concept of antifeminism, which they assert is generally 'posited on the existence of a higher order, be it the will of God, human nature, national destiny, or social stability' (Blais & Dupuis-Déri 2012: 22).

Developing the concept of 'masculinism' to reflect contemporary developments in antifeminism, they argue: 'Masculinism asserts that since men are in crisis and suffering because of women in general and feminists in particular, the solution to their problems involves curbing the influence of feminism and revalorising masculinity' (Blais & Dupuis-Déri 2012: 22).

To the extent that masculinism captures a small group of politically motivated actors (men and women) who assert that women's rights have gone too far and that men have been victimised and thus need to reclaim their manhood, the concept works reasonably well. The argument that it is grounded in a belief in the 'existence of a higher order' makes the important link between fundamentalist religion and the manosphere. Yet a key challenge is how to identify people who subscribe to these beliefs (or elements of these beliefs) unless an individual self-labels (rather than being labelled). Like feminism, it may be argued, masculinism works on a spectrum, with contested versions of what constitutes the ideal man and the root causes of their 'crisis'. Furthermore, masculinist activity, as abhorrent as it may seem, is not illegal. Nor does the concept capture new developments that demonstrate a vociferous and holistic hatred of women made evident through the targeting of women for terrorist violence. The same may be said for the concept of 'toxic masculinity', which has evolved from psychology. It is used to describe socially constructed aspects of masculinity, including sexism and violence, that can be harmful to both men and women. The concept has become particularly prevalent in contemporary discourse, yet it does little to shape public policy.

Ideological masculinity: A new paradigm

Whilst the concepts of femicide and masculinism draw attention to the possibility of 'sexist terrorism' and masculinism as 'the ideology of patriarchy', neither is framed or developed appropriately to have the necessary impact on public policy. In particular, they are not addressed by the field of countering violent extremism, which is pertinent to the allocation of resources for challenging this new threat.

The emergence of the 'manosphere' and the apparent increase in angry men congregating online and hiding behind a veil of anonymity to vent (at best), threaten, and degrade women are historically unprecedented. In 2018, the Southern Poverty Law Center (SPLC) designated two organisations run by individuals examined in this chapter as hate groups: 'A Voice for Men' run by Paul Elam and the 'Return of Kings' run by Daryush Valizadeh. The organisation commented: 'The vilification of women by these groups makes them no different than other groups that demean entire populations, such as the LGBTIQ community, Muslims, or Jews, based on their inherent characteristics' (Southern Poverty Law Center 2019).

In defining male supremacist groups, the SPLC, which has decades of experience in identifying and working to challenge extremist groups in the United States, stated:

> Male supremacy misrepresents all women as genetically inferior, manipulative, and stupid and reduces them to their reproductive or sexual function – with sex being something that they owe men and that can or even should be coerced out of them. Driven by a biological analysis of women as fundamentally inferior to men, male supremacists malign women specifically for their gender. A thinly veiled desire for the domination of women and a conviction that the current system oppresses men in favor of women are the unifying tenets of the male supremacist worldview.
>
> *(Southern Poverty Law Center 2019)*

The SPLC's recognition of male supremacist groups as 'hate groups' is a key step toward shifting the terrain. The organisation outlines key elements of an ideology centred on the subjugation of women. However, it does not extend its logic to the individuals and small groups emerging from male supremacist circles who may seek to forcibly enact their subscribed ideology through threatening or actually killing women. We must, as Duerst-Lahti (2008: 192) argues, recognise gender ideology (in this case male supremacy) as an inherently *political* ideology centred on social change.

This form of *ideological masculinity* is radical. It seeks to promote a return to a perceived period of male supremacy 'lost' to women's rights and self-effacing men. Those who subscribe to this ideology believe that women's empowerment has left men victimised and discriminated against. They stand vigorously against the notion of gender outside the female-male binary and, more broadly, against LGBTIQ communities.

They play out their anger and resentment through violent acts and justify their actions as a reclaiming of what they believe is rightfully theirs. Demagogic actors draw on elements of ideological masculinity, including beliefs that powerful elites have conspired to suppress men, that women must be forcibly consigned to the domestic sphere, and that a return to a past era of perceived male supremacy is the only path forward.

Understanding male supremacy as a political and ideological orientation is key to shifting the public policy and legislative inertia. However, it will very likely result in an increase in violent extremism and terrorist action directed against women and girls on the basis of their gender.

Ideology and violent extremism

Ideology is a key element of how we understand violent extremism and terrorism. As a concept, violent extremism (and Countering Violent Extremism or 'CVE') has emerged at the fore of policymaking across Western governments, despite the difficulty in gaining consensus on a universal definition. Striegher distinguishes the term from terrorism by noting that extremism is an 'ideology or viewpoint' that does not necessarily reach the threshold of an act of terrorism (Striegher 2015: 76). An act of terrorism requires an act of intimidation, coercion, or physical violence.

As the below indicates, however, ideological motivation is a key element of definitions of both violent extremism and terrorism.

The United States Department of Homeland Security developed a Countering Violent Extremism Task Force with a particular emphasis upon enhancing engagement with communities, building expertise, and countering extremist narratives (Department of Homeland Security 2016). An August 2011 policy, *Empowering Local Partners to Prevent Violent Extremism in the United States*, defines violent extremists as 'individuals who support or commit ideologically-motivated violence to further political goals' (Department of Homeland Security 2011). The United States Code of Federal Regulations defines terrorism as the 'unlawful use of force and violence' to further social or political objectives (United States 2019). Key elements of the US government, including the Department of Defense (DoD) (United States Department of Defense 2019) and the United States National Counter Terrorism Center, refer to an ideological or philosophical motivation for the act of violent extremism (Joint Chiefs of Staff 2010).

The UK House of Commons has noted that it is important that the ideology behind violent extremism be clearly understood and challenged (United Kingdom House of Commons 2010), whilst the United Kingdom Terrorism Act (2000) defines terrorism as the use or threat of an action designed to influence the government or intimidate a section of the public *and* the use or threat is made for the purpose of advancing a political, religious, or ideological cause (United Kingdom Government 2020).

In the Australian context, the Federal Attorney-General's Department, the agency responsible for countering violent extremism, defines it as 'the beliefs and actions of people who support or use violence to achieve ideological, religious, or political goals' (Australian Government 2015). Similarly to the United Kingdom, the Australian definition under the Criminal Code Act 1995 (Cth) identifies a 'terrorist act' as an action done or threat made with the intention of advancing a political, religious, or ideological cause *and* it seeks to coerce or influence by intimidation a government or intimidate the public or a section of the public (Australian Government 2020).

Incels, pick-up artists, and others in the so-called 'manosphere' regularly encourage extremes of physical and sexual violence against the women they believe have deprived them of their 'rights' to reproduction and sexual pleasure. Many others attack feminists on the basis of their argument for gender equality. Violent extremism has already escalated to terrorism. If these acts were carried out by the same men under the guise of a religious or specifically far-right agenda, they may well have been labelled as terrorists.

The violent language and actions of ideological masculinity fit neatly into the definition of violent extremism, which involves 'the beliefs and actions of people who support or use violence to achieve ideological, religious or political goals'. It includes terrorism and other forms of politically motivated and communal violence. It also includes the language and symbolic behaviours that threaten or support such violence.

To this extent, processes of radicalisation leading to male supremacist terrorism might be considered to have much in common with other violent extremist groups, including alienation, anxiety, and misinterpellation (Roose 2016). In the aftermath of a May 2020 terror attack in Toronto, the Toronto Police stated: 'Terrorism comes in many forms, and it's important to note that it is not restricted to any particular group, religion, or ideology' (Toronto Police 2020).

Assessing the prevalence of ideological masculinity and male supremacism

The final section of this chapter draws upon research conducted with Ipsos Public Affairs, a global social and market research firm. Developed as a collaboration between Ipsos, Professor Bryan Turner, and myself, the data is based on a global online survey of the Ipsos panel. The research was carried out in June and July 2019. The survey generated responses from over 19,000 respondents across 28 countries on topics including attitudes to democracy, the rule of law, women's rights, and trust in institutions.

Drawing on the dataset, I explore the prevalence of extreme anti-women attitudes across the countries studied, comparing the United States, United Kingdom, and Australia though responses to two key propositions:

1. Women deserve equal rights to men; and
2. Rights for women have gone too far.

The first proposition measures a baseline for notions of gender equality, or what might be considered 'hard-line misogyny' (hard prejudice), which encompasses the concept, already touched upon in the discussion of the manosphere, that women can be prejudicial to women. The second proposition captures what might be considered 'soft misogyny' (soft prejudice), the notion, common in the 'manosphere', that there is now an imbalance and women have more rights than men. The difference between the propositions allows us to capture the 'I'm not sexist but' proposition that defines contemporary misogyny.

Citizens from all three countries (amongst others) contribute to the 'manosphere'. Thus, grouping them together offers an insight into the multinational dimension of the online space and its potential influence. Female respondents were adjudged to be appropriate comparators to men for the purpose of determining the extent to which anti-women attitudes exist in the wider community, therefore, they are included in the data tables (Table 4.1 and Table 4.2).

Young men under 35 years of age were the demographic most likely to disagree with the statement that women deserve equal rights to men (Table 4.1). Their numbers were highest in the United States (5.53%) and lowest in the United Kingdom (2.93%). Importantly, disagreement with the statement fell significantly as men got older, a pattern also evident in women, suggesting that exposure to the struggles of second-wave feminism in the 1970s had a marked and continued

TABLE 4.1 Women deserve equal rights to men (percentage of respondents who disagree or strongly disagree), by gender, country, age (Great Britain, United States, and Australia)

	18–34	35–54	55+	Total
Great Britain (M)	3.98	2.93	2.43	3.13
United States (M)	4.97	5.53	0.60	3.57
Australia (M)	5.90	5.48	1.98	4.71
Great Britain (F)	1.82	1.07	1.23	1.35
United States (F)	1.83	0.96	1.20	1.32
Australia (F)	4.12	1.53	0.58	2.16

Source: Ipsos-Roose-Turner Global Masculinity Index, June 2019 (Ipsos et al. 2019)

Great Britain base n = 817; United States base n = 753; Australia base n = 976

TABLE 4.2 Rights for women have gone too far (percentage of respondents who agree or strongly agree), by country, gender, age (Great Britain, United States, and Australia)

	18–34	35–54	55+	Total
Great Britain (M)	27.28	25.91	29.01	27.30
United States (M)	36.29	25.22	18.46	26.52
Australia (M)	36.93	30.19	28.17	31.97
Great Britain (F)	14.52	11.42	18.23	14.06
United States (F)	21.83	26.03	25.39	13.28
Australia (F)	26.83	22.47	17.09	22.38

Source: Ipsos-Roose-Turner Global Masculinity Index, June 2019 (Ipsos et al. 2019)

Great Britain base n = 806; United States base n = 737; Australia base n = 951

impact on individuals, though it could also suggest that as men marry and have children, including daughters, their attitudes may change.

Australian women under the age of 35 (4.12%) were more than twice as likely to disagree with the statement that women deserve equal rights to men as their counterparts in Great Britain and the United States (2%). Australian women in the 35–54 and 55+ age groups were also more likely to disagree.

The table above is significant for two reasons. First, it demonstrates that embedded anti-women prejudice is particularly evident amongst younger men, it may decline with age, and it also exists amongst some young women. Second, it also reveals a potential constituency for violent extremist views grounded in masculinity. Whilst on the face of it the charts reveal that a small percentage of the community subscribes to anti-women views, across an entire population the notional number of approximately

1 in 26 men adds up to a significant number (in the millions) who do not agree that women deserve equal rights to men. It is likely that those potentially drawn to violent extremism against women would be located within this group. Further, as indicated by the size and scope of manosphere websites, such as *MGTOW: Men Going Their Own Way* with is more than 30,000 members, the online environment has allowed like-minded men to find one another and develop ideological strands and sub-strands centred on the subjugation of women.

In a similar manner to hard misogyny, young men under the age of 35 led the way on the measure of soft misogyny. They agreed or strongly agreed with the statement that women's rights have gone too far (Table 4.2). The numbers were highest amongst men in Australia (36.93%) and the United States (36.29%), and they were lowest in the United Kingdom (27.28%). Similarly, apart from in Great Britain, where there was a slight rise in the 55+ age range, agreement with the statement fell as men got older, which suggests that older men have historic context on women's political struggle for equality, and they may be less exposed to the hard edge of the labour force where protections for women, such as maternity leave, are legislated and embedded in organisational culture.

Importantly, women were likely to agree with the proposition that rights for women have gone too far in numbers much higher than anticipated. Agreement was highest amongst women aged 18–35 in Australia (26.83%) and the United States (21.83%), while it was lowest in the United Kingdom (14.52%).

The percentage of the population agreeing with the statement that rights for women have gone too far is significant – more than one in three men in Australia and the United States, and more than one in four in Great Britain. Many of these men agreed with the statement that women deserve equal rights to men. They likely perceive themselves as somehow challenged or disadvantaged by the extension of women's rights, despite a continued gender pay gap, under representation of women in government and corporate leadership, women's greater burden when it comes to household labour, and a higher prevalence of poverty amongst women across the life course. This may demonstrate that 'manosphere' rhetoric has successfully infiltrated mainstream political discourse and that there are increasing levels of anxiety and anger about job security and declining status amongst men in both the blue-collar and professional workforce.

The fact that women subscribe to the perspective that rights have gone too far may speak simultaneously to the symbolic violence of contemporary misogyny, whereby women adopt the very ideas that subordinate them, and it may indicate that women are members of socially conservative groups or religious denominations that have traditionally exhibited hostility toward both rights and women's empowerment.

Conclusion

Anti-women attitudes and violence against women are not new developments. They have been deeply entrenched in religion and key social institutions throughout history. Even the Marshallian conception of citizenship has been accused of focusing primarily on working men and relying on the domestic subordination of women. The rise of neoliberal economics has opened pathways for women into the workforce whilst simultaneously entrenching a gender pay gap. Yet, despite persistent inequality in the workforce, the combination of women achieving success in non-traditional areas of the work and the feminisation of the service economy, particularly at a time when blue-collar, manual-labour jobs are becoming increasingly insecure and precarity is increasing in white collar professional work, has led to anxiety, alienation, anomie, and, most tellingly, anger and resentment.

On the spectrum of anti-women prejudice, it is possible to start at the 'soft' end with anti-women institutions, such as the Catholic Church. Throughout its history the Catholic Church has denied women the possibility of spiritual leadership. Evangelical men's movements exhibit a modern, distorted form of hyper-masculine muscular Christianity. Similar developments are evident in Islam, Judaism, and the majority of faiths. These groups provide a logical base receptive to the new populist demagogues' regurgitation of notions of 'traditional family values' and their engagement with select religious leaders who share similar values. However, the combination of the collapse of key social institutions driven by neoliberal economic policies and the emergence of social media as a key organising tool for activist groups has led to the birth of vociferously anti-establishment and anti-women political agendas. They are embodied in loose clusters and groups, such as the 'alt-right' and MGTOW, which seek to portray a hegemonic hyper-masculinity that belies their status as subordinated men operating on the fringes of society. For the new populist demagogues, such individuals and groups offer a ready-made constituency and a fast-track to political power.

As alarming as these developments might appear, they are minor compared to the ideologically driven movements that explicitly seek to cause psychological and physical harm to women. Influential individuals incite physical and sexual violence through couched language and 'satire'. Online activists threaten to rape and murder feminists. Incel terrorists are motivated to kill women on the basis of their gender. The development of ideological masculinity, whereby gender becomes a political identity and a base of violent action, must be viewed, not as being isolated from, but as being closely linked to the rise of the new demagogues, who display the same anti-women behaviours and deploy the same religiously and politically inflected rhetoric professing to restore a long-lost period of male supremacy.

References

AIHW (Australian Institute of Health and Welfare). (2019). *Family, Domestic, and Sexual Violence in Australia: Continuing the National Story*. Canberra: Australian Government.

Anderlini, S.N. (2018). Challenging Conventional Wisdom, Transforming Current Practices: A Gendered Lens on PVE. In B. Austin and H. J. Giessmann. (Eds.), *Transformative Approaches to Violent Extremism* (pp. 21–36). Berlin: Berghof Foundation.

Australian Government. (2015). *Living Safe Together: Preventing Violent Extremism and Radicalisation in Australia*. Canberra: Attorney-General's Department, Australian Government.
Australian Government. (2020). Criminal Code Act 1995 (Cth), Part 100.1: Definitions. *Federal Register of Legislation*.
Barbalet, J.M. (1993). Citizenship, Class Inequality, and Resentment. In B.S. Turner (Ed.), *Citizenship and Social Theory* (pp. 36–57). London: Sage.
Beauchamp, Z. (2018). Incel, the Misogynist Ideology that Inspired the Deadly Toronto Attack, Explained. *Vox*, 25 April.
Beierle, S. (2018). All videos by Tallahassee Yoga Shooter Scott Beierle/'Scott Carnifex'. *Youtube*. Retrieved 20 August 2019 from https://www.youtube.com/watch?v=8Ca00hcOND8.
Besley, T., Folke, O., Persson, T., & Rickne, J. (2017a). Gender Quotas and the Crisis of the Mediocre Man. *LSE Business Review Blog*. Retrieved on 20 June 2018 from https://blogs.lse.ac.uk/businessreview/2017/03/13/gender-quotas-and-the-crisis-of-the-mediocre-man.
Besley, T., Folke, O., Persson, T., & Rickne, J. (2017b). Gender Quotas and the Crisis of the Mediocre Man: Theory and Evidence from Sweden. *American Economic Review*, 107 (8), 2204–2242.
Blais, M. & Dupuis-Déri, F. (2012). Masculinism and the Antifeminist Countermovement. *Social Movement Studies*, 11 (1), 21–39.
Briggs, R. & Silverman, T. (2014). *Western Foreign Fighters: Innovations in Responding to the Threat*. London: Institute for Strategic Dialogue.
Brittan, A. (1989). *Masculinity and Power*. Oxford: Basil Blackwell.
Burton, T. (2019a). A Notorious Pickup Artist Found God: Lots of Angry White Radicals Do. *Washington Post*, 31 May.
Burton, T. (2019b). The Religious Hunger of the Radical Right. *The New York Times*, 13 August.
Campbell, B. & Manning, J. (2014). Microaggression and Moral Cultures. *Comparative Sociology*, 13 (6), 692–726.
Caputi J. & Russell, D.E.H. (1990). Femicide: Speaking the Unspeakable. *Ms.*, 1 (2), 34–37.
Caputi J. & Russell, D.E.H. (1992). Femicide: Sexist Terrorism Against Women. In J. Radford & D.E.H. Russell (Eds.), *Femicide: The Politics of Woman Killing* (pp. 13–21) New York: Twayne Publishers.
Connell, R. (2005). *Masculinities*. 2nd ed. Cambridge: Polity Press.
Connell, R. & Messerschmidt, J.W. (2005). Hegemonic Masculinity: Rethinking the Concept. *Gender and Society*, 19, 829–859.
CNN. (2016). Exit polls. *CNN*, 23 November. Retrieved from https://edition.cnn.com/election/2016/results/exit-polls.
Daily News Editorial Board. (2018). Profile in Rage: Too Late, New York Republicans Distance Themselves from Gavin McInnes. *NY Daily News*, 16 October. Retrieved from https://www.nydailynews.com/opinion/ny-edit-mcinnis-20181015-story.html.
Department of Homeland Security. (2011). *Empowering Local Partners to Prevent Violent Extremism in the United States*. Washington, DC: United States Government.
Department of Homeland Security. (2016). *Department of Homeland Security Strategy for Countering Violent Extremism*. 28 October. Washington, DC: United States Government.
Du Mez, K. (2017). Donald Trump and Militant Evangelical Masculinity. *Religion and Politics*, 17 January. Retrieved from https://religionandpolitics.org/2017/01/17/donald-trump-and-militant-evangelical-masculinity.

Duerst-Lahti, G. (2008). Gender Ideology: Masculinism and Feminism. In G. Goertz & A. Mazur (Eds.), *Politics, Gender, and Concepts: Theory and Methodology* (pp. 159–192). Cambridge: Cambridge University Press.

Elam, P. (2010). If You See Jezebel in the Road Run the Bitch Down. *A Voice for Men*, 22 October. Retrieved from https://avoiceformen.com/feminist-violence/if-you-see-jezebel-in-the-road-run-the-bitch-down.

Elam, P. (2018). Men's Movement: Personal and Political (ICMI'18 Speech). *A Voice For Men*. Retrieved on 20 January 2020 from https://avoiceformen.com/featured/mens-movement-personal-and-political-icmi18-speech.

Galston, W.A. (2018). *Anti-Pluralism: The Populist Threat to Liberal Democracy*. New Haven, CT: Yale University Press.

Green, J. & Shorrocks, R. (2019). The Gender Backlash in the Vote for Brexit. *SSRN*. Retrieved from https://ssrn.com/abstract=3429689.

Hage, G. (2011). Multiculturalism and the Ungovernable Muslim. In R. Gaita (Ed.), *Essays on Muslims and Multiculturalism* (pp. 165–186). Melbourne: Text Publishing.

Huffington Post. (2013). Gavin McInnes Launches Expletive-laden Tirade About Women in the Workplace. *HuffPost*, 6 December.

Ipsos, Roose, J.M., & Turner, B.S. (2019). Global Masculinity Index Survey Developed and Conducted by Ipsos Public Affairs, Joshua Roose, and Bryan S. Turner. June.

Joint Chiefs of Staff. (2010). *Joint Pub 3–07.2: Antiterrorism*. Washington, DC: United States Government.

Kassam, A. (2018). Woman Behind 'Incel' Says Angry Men Hijacked Her Word 'As a Weapon of War'. *The Guardian*, 26 April.

Kelly, A. (2017). The Alt-right: Reactionary Rehabilitation for White Masculinity. *Soundings: A Journal of Politics and Culture*, (66), 68–78.

Kimmel, M. (2018). *Healing from Hate: How Young Men Get Into – and Out of – Violent Extremism*. Oakland, CA: University of California Press.

Kimmel, M. & Bridges, T. (2011). Masculinity. *Oxford Bibliographies*. Oxford: Oxford University Press Online. doi:10.1093/OBO/9780199756384-0033.

Lewis, J., Lewis, B., Cameron, R., Pond, P., Ghumkhor, S., & Mohamud, H. (2017). *Mediating Extremist Violence: A Report on the Role of Media, Far-Right Politics, and Gender in Extremist Violence and Social Cohesion in Victoria*. Melbourne: RMIT.

Lichter, D.T., Price, J.P., & Swigert, J.M. (2019). Mismatches in the Marriage Market. *Journal of Marriage and Family*, 82 (2), 796–809.

Littler, J. (2017). *Against Meritocracy: Culture, Power, and Myths of Mobility*. London: Routledge.

Martinez, D. (2016). Nigel Farage on Trump's Sexist Comments: 'This is Alpha Male Boasting'. *The Independent*, 9 October.

May, C. (2013). 'Godfather of Hipsterdom' Gavin McInnes: Feminism Makes Women Miserable. *Daily Caller*, 23 October.

Mazza, E. (2015). Gavin McInnes, Fox News Guest, Says Women Are 'Less Ambitious' and 'Happier at Home'. *HuffPost*, 15 May.

McDowell, L. (2003). *Redundant Masculinities: Employment, Change, and White Working Class Youth*. Oxford: Blackwell Publishing.

McInnes, G. (2016). The Gavin McInnes Show 165. *Compound Media*, 16 June.

McInnes, G. (2017). The Gavin McInnes Show 171. *Compound Media*, 28 June.

McSmith, A. (2014). UKIP's Women Problem. *The Independent*, 8 October.

Mead, L. (1997). Citizenship and Social Policy: T.H. Marshall and Poverty. *Social Philosophy and Poverty*, 14 (2), 197–230.

MGTOW. (2020). *MGTOW: Men Going Their Own Way*. Retrieved from https://www.mgtow.com.
Mudde, C. (2018). Why is the Far Right Dominated by Men? *The Guardian*, 17 August.
New York Times. (2016). Transcript: Donald Trump's Taped Comments about Women. *The New York Times*, 8 October.
Oxford Dictionary. (2015). Femicide. In A. Stevenson (Ed.), *Oxford Dictionary of English* (3rd ed.). Oxford: Oxford University Press.
Peucker, M. & Smith, D. (2019). Not a Monolithic Movement: The Diverse and Shifting Messaging of Australia's Far-right. In M. Peucker & D. Smith (Eds.), *The Far-Right in Contemporary Australia*. New York: Palgrave.
Pitt, D.E. (1989). Montreal Gunman Had Suicide Note. *The New York Times*, 8 December.
Robinson, S. (2000). *Marked Men: White Masculinity in Crisis*. New York: Columbia University Press.
Ross, J. (2016). Who Really Supports Donald Trump, Ted Cruz, Ben Carson, Marco Rubio, and Jeb Bush – in 5 Charts. *The Washington Post*, 15 December.
Rodger, E. (2014). My Twisted World: The Story of Elliot Rodger. Retrieved from https://assets.documentcloud.org/documents/1173619/rodger-manifesto.pdf.
Roose, J.M. (2016). *Political Islam and Masculinity: Muslim Men in the West*. New York: Palgrave.
Sassen, S. (2014). *Expulsions*. Cambridge, MA: Harvard University Press.
Shanahan, R. (2019). Typology of Terror – The Backgrounds of Australian Jihadis. *Lowy Institute*. 21 November.
Shklar, J.N. (1989). *American Citizenship: The Quest for Inclusion*(The Tanner Lectures on Human Values). Delivered at the University of Utah, 1–2 May.
Shklar, J.N. (1990). *American Citizenship: The Quest for Inclusion*. Cambridge, MA: Harvard University Press.
Southern Poverty Law Center. (2019). Male Supremacy. *SPLC*.
Standing, G. (2011). *The Precariat: The New Dangerous Class*. London: Bloomsbury.
Statista. (2016). Share of Votes in the Brexit Referendum of 2016 in the United Kingdom, by Gender. *Statista*. Retrieved from https://www.statista.com/statistics/567922/brexit-votes-by-gender.
Striegher, J. (2015). *Violent Extremism: An Examination of a Definitional Dilemma*. The Proceedings of [the] 8th Australian Security and Intelligence Conference, Edith Cowan University Joondalup Campus, Perth, Western Australia, 30 November – 2 December (pp. 75–86).
Toronto Police. (2020). Media Release: Terrorist Activity and Attempted Murder – Terrorist Activity, Homicide #12/2020. *Royal Canadian Mounted Police/Gendarmerie royale du Canada*. Retrieved from https://www.rcmp-grc.gc.ca/en/news/2020/dufferin-and-wilson-avenue.
Tyson, A. & Maniam, S. (2016). Behind Trump's Victory: Divisions by Race, Gender, Education. *Pew Research Centre*, 9 November.
United Kingdom Government. (2020). Terrorism Act (2000), c. 11, Part 1, Section 1, Terrorism: Interpretation. *legislation.gov.uk*. Retrieved from https://www.legislation.gov.uk/ukpga/2000/11/section/1.
United Kingdom House of Commons. (2010). *Preventing Violent Extremism: Sixth Report of Session 2009–10*. London: House of Commons.
United Nations. (2019). Why We Must Eliminate Violence Against Women. *United Nations International Day for the Elimination of Violence Against Women: 25 November*. Retrieved on 30 November 2019 from https://www.un.org/en/events/endviolenceday.
United States. (2019). 28 CFR Section 0.85 – General Functions. *Code of Federal Regulations*.

United States Department of Defense (DoD). (2019). DoD Dictionary of Military and Associated Terms. *DoD*. Retrieved from https://www.jcs.mil/Portals/36/Documents/Doctrine/pubs/dictionary.pdf.

Valizadeh, D. (2015a). What is Neomasculinity. *Roosh V*, 6 May. Retrieved from https://www.rooshv.com/what-is-neomasculinity.

Valizadeh, D. (2015b). How to Stop Rape. *Roosh V*, 16 February. Retrieved from https://www.rooshv.com/how-to-stop-rape.

Vieten, U.M. & Poynting. S. (2016). Contemporary Far-Right Racist Populism in Europe. *Journal of Intercultural Studies*, 37 (6), 533–540.

Wetherell, M. & Edley, N. (1998). Gender Practices: Steps in the Analysis of Men and Masculinities. In K. Henwood, C. Griffin, & A. Phoenix (Eds.), *Gender and Psychology. Standpoints and Differences: Essays in the Practice of Feminist Psychology* (p. 156–173). London: Sage Publications Ltd.

World Bank. (2019). Gender-based Violence (Violence Against Women and Girls). *World Bank*, 25 September. Retrieved on 20 October 2019 from https://www.worldbank.org/en/topic/socialdevelopment/brief/violence-against-women-and-girls.

World Health Organization. (2017). Violence against women. *WHO*, 29 November. Retrieved on 20 November 2019 from https://www.who.int/news-room/fact-sheets/detail/violence-against-women.

Yuval-Davis, N. (2019). Autochthonic Populism, Everyday Bordering, Construction of 'the Migrant'. In G. Fitzi, J. Mackert, & B.S. Turner (Eds.), *Populism and the Crisis of Democracy: Volume 3: Migration, Gender and Religion* (pp. 69–77). London: Routledge. 69–77.

5

BREXIT AND THE WHITE WORKING-CLASS

Introduction

For better or worse, 23 June 2016 was a date that will shape the future of the United Kingdom for centuries to come. The United Kingdom European Union membership referendum (known variously as the 'EU' or 'Brexit' referendum) asked voters a simple question:

> Should the United Kingdom remain a member of the European Union or leave the European Union?

The vote, which was an attempt by Prime Minister David Cameron to placate factions within the British Conservative Party, was never expected to succeed. Yet succeed it did. Despite the widespread perception that citizens of the United Kingdom would vote to remain part of the EU, over 17.4 million, a majority, voted to leave (51.89%), whilst just over 16.1 million (48.11%) voted to remain. The referendum attracted 72.21 per cent voter participation. If the vote had been a general election, it would have represented the largest voter turnout since 1992 (United Kingdom Electoral Commission 2020). The campaign was defined by highly polarised and hostile rhetoric and the assassination of Jo Cox, the pro-remain MP for Batley and Spen (and mother of two young children), by a far-right British nationalist.

Whilst David Cameron resigned in the aftermath of the vote, Parliament had no such luxury. The vote provided a chance of a lifetime for pragmatist anti-EU politician (and future Prime Minister) Boris Johnson and populist UKIP founder Nigel Farage to mobilise those feeling threatened by rapid social change, economic insecurity, and immigration. The disaffected voters were largely outside of the main capital cities, where everyday multiculturalism, relatively abundant jobs, and economic opportunity were concentrated. Writing just before the vote, *Guardian* columnist Paul Mason made a tellingly accurate prediction:

> In many working-class communities, people are getting ready to vote leave not just as a way of telling the neo-liberal elite to get stuffed. They also want to discomfort the metropolitan, liberal, university-educated salariat for good measure. For many people involved, it feels like their first ever effective political choice.
>
> *(Mason 2016)*

A significant age gap emerged in the voting. A survey conducted in March 2016 (prior to the vote) by YouGov found that young people ages 18–24 (75%) and 25–49 (54%) were more likely to vote in favour of remaining within the EU compared to 50–64 year olds (44%) and those 65+ (33%) (YouGov 2016). A further breakdown reveals significant social differences. Voters with high educational qualifications and incomes were much more likely to vote to remain irrespective of age (Speed 2016). Urban population centres, Northern Ireland, and Scotland were also much more likely to vote to remain.

The city of Birmingham, England's 'second city', stood as an exception to the other large British cities. It stunned the nation by voting to leave the EU by a small, but decisive, 50.4 per cent (leave) to 49.6 per cent (remain), a margin of just 3,000 votes. More compelling was that key wards in the outer ring of the city voted to leave the EU at numbers that were amongst the highest in the United Kingdom, including Shard End (Hodge Hill constituency), where 75.64 per cent of citizens voted to leave, and Kingstanding (Erdington constituency), where 71.13 per cent of citizens voted to leave.

The vote to leave the European Union lifted the proverbial lid on long-building social ferment, a potent mix of anger, diminished trust, alienation, and anxiety amongst primarily invisible citizens in the de-industrialised, working-class towns of the United Kingdom.

A brief history of Birmingham

The Domesday Book of 1086 records Birmingham as a small village. It only started to grow significantly in 1166 after a charter allowed the town to develop and hold a marketplace. It became an important regional town by the fourteenth century. Birmingham was a leading nucleus of the industrial revolution in the eighteenth century. It served as an innovation hub for printing, engineering, and manufacturing, becoming known as the 'city of a thousand trades'.

During the Midlands Enlightenment of the eighteenth century, leading scientific, technological, mechanical, and philosophical minds clustered in collectives, such as the Lunar Society of Birmingham (1765–1813). Members of the Lunar Society – abolitionists, manufacturers, poets, philosophers, entrepreneurs, and scientists – congregated on the full moon to investigate and explore a wide variety of challenges, including, but not limited to, electricity, mechanics, and geology. The group, restricted to 14 men at any one time, fused 'useful knowledge' with 'technical knowledge' and became a key intellectual impetus behind the Industrial Revolution that shapes the world to this day (Jones 2008).

Importantly, during the same era Birmingham was a centre of religious nonconformism. The Church of England and established aristocracy were weaker in Birmingham and, arguably, remain so to this day. One key figure in the movement, Joseph Priestley, was a philosopher, scientist, and theologian. Priestley was close to several members of the Lunar Society, and his interactions with them shaped his work on oxygen and gasses during his time in Birmingham (1780–1791). Priestley was driven from Birmingham by violent riots, during which his home and churches were burned to the ground. He moved to Middlesex before emigrating to Pennsylvania. Like Birmingham, Pennsylvania was a bastion of religious freedom and an industrial centre key to scientific and intellectual development. Priestley also wrote key theological texts and developed Unitarian doctrine (the rejection of the Trinity central to the majority of Christian denominations), which influenced Thomas Jefferson, the US founding father, author of the Virginia Statute for Religious Freedom (see Chapter 3), and the third US president.

During the twentieth century, Birmingham proved a pivotal industrial centre during war time. At the conclusion of World War I, Prime Minister David Lloyd George declared that 'the country, the empire, and the world owe to the skill, ingenuity, and resource of Birmingham a deep gratitude' (Ward 2005: 185). During the interwar years, Birmingham made a concerted effort to develop housing, relocate residents from inner-city slums, and develop civic spaces and amenities, including building over 50,000 houses. In 1924, during the same period of development, future Prime Minister Neville Chamberlain defeated Labour candidate Oswald Mosely, who went on to found the British Union of Fascists in 1932, by just 77 votes.

Birmingham rode out the Great Depression with a peak unemployment rate of 17.7 per cent compared to 20.7 per cent for the rest of England (Cherry 1994: 126). William Temple, just prior to becoming the Archbishop of Canterbury, gave social welfare a religious legitimacy by claiming 'the State is a servant and instrument of God for the preservation of justice and for the promotion of human welfare' (Prochaska 2006: 94). In World War II, Birmingham resumed its central war-production role, including building the Spitfire bomber. Between 9 August 1940 and 23 April 1943, the city was subjected to the 'Birmingham Blitz' by the German Luftwaffe, which killed 2,241 and seriously injured 3,010 local residents, while another 3,682 were harmed. (BBC 2005). The Blitz led to greater state intervention in the day-to-day provision of medical and housing resources. Historian A.J.P. Taylor argued that '[e]vacuation was itself a disguised welfare scheme, and the most dangerous period of the war became paradoxically the most fruitful for social policy … The *Luftwaffe* was a powerful missionary for the welfare state' (Taylor 1965: 455).

The impact of the war on church life was devastating. As a result of a number of compounding factors, including a lack of clergymen and church resources, in Birmingham the number of curates fell from 178 in 1939 to just 38 in 1948 (Prochaska 2006: 93).

The immigration debate: From Griffiths to Powell

The increasing visibility of migration, first from the Caribbean and then from South Asia, caused ponderable consternation in some parts of Birmingham. The town of Smethwick, which is located four miles west of Birmingham city centre and was held by Oswald Mosely for Labour between 1926–1931, before he founded the British Union of Fascists, was bombed by the Luftwaffe on many occasions and up to 80 local residents were killed. In the post-war era, it became home to a significant number of Indian Sikh and Afro-Caribbean migrants. In 1964 Conservative candidate Peter Griffiths was elected. He was widely associated with an anti-black campaign slogan that made national headlines, and defended its use as a 'manifestation of popular feeling' and 'exasperation, not fascism' (Jeffries 2014). The constituency was arguably the 'most racist town in Britain' (Jeffries 2014). To prevent blacks from obtaining housing in the area, the local council sought to enact a policy for the compulsory acquisition of empty houses, which would only be let to whites. At the time there was a housing shortage, and whites claimed that migrants were being given priority, which, as we will see, continues to be a common theme more than fifty years later, irrespective of its validity. The council scheme prompted a visit from US civil rights activist Malcolm X just nine days before his assassination in New York. It was only prevented by the Labour housing Minister blocking funding to the council.

In 1968 the Labour Government sought to introduce the Race Relations Act (1968), which was to supersede the Race Relations Act (1965). The 1968 Act made discrimination on the grounds of colour, race, ethnic, or national origin illegal, and it applied to the provision of housing, employment, and the provision of public services. It was in the context of the Act being introduced that Enoch Powell, the Conservative MP for the constituency of Wolverhampton South West, delivered his 'Rivers of Blood' speech to the West Midlands Area Conservative Political Centre in Birmingham on 20 April 1968:

> But while, to the immigrant, entry to this country was admission to privileges and opportunities eagerly sought, the impact upon the existing population was very different. For reasons which they could not comprehend, and in pursuance of a decision by default, on which they were never consulted, they found themselves made strangers in their own country.
>
> They found their wives unable to obtain hospital beds in childbirth, their children unable to obtain school places, their homes and neighbourhoods changed beyond recognition, their plans and prospects for the future defeated; at work they found that employers hesitated to apply to the immigrant worker

the standards of discipline and competence required of the native-born worker; they began to hear, as time went by, more and more voices which told them that they were now the unwanted.

(Powell 2007)

The speech cited conversations with white members of Powell's constituency of Wolverhampton, who felt they were being forced from their neighbourhoods, which aroused feelings of irreversible detrimental social change and impending violence:

For these dangerous and divisive elements the legislation proposed in the Race Relations Bill is the very pabulum they need to flourish. Here is the means of showing that the immigrant communities can organise to consolidate their members, to agitate and campaign against their fellow citizens, and to overawe and dominate the rest with the legal weapons which the ignorant and the ill-informed have provided. As I look ahead, I am filled with foreboding; like the Roman, I seem to see 'the River Tiber foaming with much blood'.

(Powell 2007)

As my contemporary research (discussed below) demonstrates, Powell's sentiments continue to resonate to this day amongst the white working-class in Birmingham.

The collapse of manufacturing

Whilst debates about immigration never dissipated, they were ultimately sidelined by what might be considered the calamitous collapse of manufacturing in Birmingham in 1976. Preceding the drop in manufacturing, there was a strike by 30,000 Birmingham engineers in solidarity with the National Union of Mineworkers, which was the first general miners' strike since 1926. It led to a 21 per cent pay rise for miners and cost the Conservative Prime Minister Edward Heath his job (Griffin 2013). The strike in Birmingham contributed significantly to the formation of the Thatcher government's militant approach to union-busting.

Birmingham lost over 200,000 jobs in the manufacturing sector in the decade from 1971 to 1981. A GDP per capita that was amongst the highest in the United Kingdom in 1976 fell to the lowest by 1983 (McCabe 2014). Amidst a climate of economic hardship, the city saw significant social unrest, including the Handsworth riots in July 1981, which were part of a broader series of riots between black youths and the police. The same district again experienced riots in 1985, which were blamed on tensions between the police and minority communities as well as unemployment.

The election of Margaret Thatcher as leader of the Conservative Party in 1975 and her subsequent election as Prime Minister (May 1979–November 1990) ushered in the institutionalisation of neoliberal economic policies across the country, including deregulation, attacks on trade unions and collective bargaining, privatisation of state assets, and increasing casualisation. The effects seen and felt in

Birmingham were experienced across the country. Speaking to the Birmingham Chamber of Industry and Commerce on 21 April 1980, Thatcher posited Birmingham as a bellwether for the nation.

> A City whose leaders have had a powerful influence on British national life for generations. Birmingham has been the pacemaker of British industry. And all this long before Government created a Ministry of Industry.
> When it has prospered, so has Britain.
> When it has faltered, so has the national economy.
> In short, what goes for Birmingham usually goes for Britain.
> *(Thatcher 1980)*

The speech, which was delivered at the beginning of Thatcher's prime ministership and in the immediate aftermath of the so-called 'Winter of Discontent' characterised by significant trade union strikes, proved even more instructive in its outlining of a neoliberal economic agenda based on three perceived factors for economic decline: 'too much government', 'the attitudes of many employees', and 'patchy' management 'saved by subsidies' (Thatcher 1980).

At the Birmingham meeting Thatcher outlined a nine-point agenda that included cuts in spending; decreased government borrowing; a shift toward printing less money (monetarism); latitude for businesses to 'decide what to pay your employees, what to charge for your goods, what dividend to pay on capital and what to invest overseas'; the introduction of a Competition Act; privatisation; lower income taxes, 'especially for higher management'; incentivisation of small businesses; and the narrowing of legal immunities for picketing and 'blacking' boycotts, including 'legislating to reduce Social Security benefits for strikers families' (Thatcher 1980). Subsequent governments to the right and left of the political spectrum enacted these policies.

Contemporary demography of Birmingham

Birmingham has grown into a multicultural, highly diverse hub characterised by a service-based economy in the city centre. As of 2017, it was the 'youngest' city in Europe, with residents under 25 years of age accounting for almost 40 per cent of the population (Harris 2019). Importantly, in 2016, at the time of the European referendum, unemployment in Birmingham was at 9 per cent (the highest of the major cities in England), compared to 4.9 per cent nationally. In October 2016, the welfare claimant rates in Perry Barr (7.8%) and Erdington (7.8%), which are neighbourhoods near the key area of focus for this chapter, were the sixth and seventh highest in the United Kingdom (Mirza-Davies et al. 2016). In June 2019, the claimant rate stood at 8.6 per cent for the city, compared to 3.4 per cent nationally (Birmingham City Council 2019). At that time just 69.7 per cent of Birmingham residents aged 16–64 were economically active in some form of employment or small business (Birmingham City Council 2019).

Multiculturalism

Birmingham has experienced exponential multicultural growth and demographic change in the twenty-first century. In 2001, White British residents (not including Irish, Gypsy, Irish Traveller, or other) constituted 65.54 per cent (641,345) of the population, whilst by 2011 their numbers had declined to 53.14 per cent of the population (570,217) (Birmingham City Council 2019).

In the same period of time, Asian or Asian British (Pakistani) residents rose from 10.7 per cent of the population to 13.5 percent of the population (Office for National Statistics 2001; Birmingham City Council 2018). Other Asian British residents (including Indian, Bangladeshi, Chinese, and other) rose from 9.4 per cent to 13.1 per cent of the population. The total percentage of Asian British in Birmingham stood in 2011 at 26.6 per cent of the population. Abbas (2006) observed that ethnic minorities in Birmingham are concentrated in inner city areas, forming a 'middle ring' around the central business district. He also noted that the majority of Pakistanis in the city originate primarily from the Mirpur district of Azad Kashmir and surrounding areas (Abbas 2006).

Individuals of mixed heritage and those of Black Caribbean descent both constituted 4.4 per cent of the population compared to 2.3 per cent mixed heritage and 1.1 per cent Black Caribbean for England as a whole. Those born in European Union countries outside the United Kingdom represented just 2.7 per cent of the city's population, challenging the narrative that the Brexit vote in Birmingham was about immigration from European Union countries.

Extremism and terrorism

Birmingham suffered its first terror attack on 21 November 1974. Two Irish Republican Army bombs exploded, killing 21 people and injuring 182. Like many other major cities, it suffered subsequent acts of terrorism, including an anti-Muslim attack in 2013 by a Ukrainian-born far-right activist terrorist (BBC 2013). Most significant for the purposes of this chapter, however, was the 2014 'Trojan Horse' affair involving an anonymous letter that was delivered to Birmingham City Council in November 2013 alleging that Salafist Muslims were seeking to, in effect, take over the governance bodies of a number of Birmingham schools in order to change their curriculum, values, and ethos. It alleged that Muslims would segregate classrooms, put pressure on female students to cover their hair, ban sex education, and disallow teaching any faith other than Islam in religious education class. Reported in March 2014, the affair received national coverage and headlines, arousing tensions in Birmingham that simmered up until the EU referendum and beyond.

Whilst it is notable that there have been no Islamist terror attacks in Birmingham, the city and its Muslim population, nonetheless, have been thrust into the centre of the national stage amidst a wave of Islamic State attacks across the United Kingdom (particularly in London) and a number of individuals leaving the city to join the Islamic State movement in Iraq and Syria. A controversial 2017 report by the Henry Jackson Society, a Libertarian think tank, found that outside of London, the West Midlands (18%) and Birmingham (14%) were the second most common places of residence for Islamist terrorists (Stuart 2017: 8).

White nationalism

Beyond the speeches of Mosley, Powell, and others, white nationalists, like Islamists, have an historical presence in Birmingham. In 2006 the British National Party (BNP) targeted the Kingstanding Ward, won the vote, and gained its first councillor before a countback declared the BNP member's election void. Far-right groups have used Birmingham as symbolic terrain to make a national point through marches and rallies. The English Defence League (EDL) held its first two marches in Birmingham in August and September 2009, which led to violence and arrests. The EDL marched again in October 2011 and July 2013.

Whilst there is significant division within Birmingham, it is also clear that Birmingham has become symbolic to both left progressive and right-wing activists as an example of British multiculturalism. Some view it as a young city defined by street culture, a growing economy, and opportunity. Others see it as a highly divided, ghettoised, economically stagnant city that has left behind indigenous white working-class individuals – the extension of Enoch Powell's dystopian vision.

Farage as a new (same old) demagogue

It is into this context that Nigel Farage, the long-established figurehead of the anti-European 'leave' campaign, emerged. He was described by one *New York Times* op-ed as 'the British Crisis in human form … one of the most effective and dangerous demagogues Britain has ever seen' (Seymour 2019a). Farage possessed the requisite cultural capital to connect with those who were laying the blame for their challenges at the feet of the European Union.

Farage was a member of the Conservative Party from his youth. He was inspired by figures, including Enoch Powell, whom he met whilst at Dulwich College. Farage later drove Powell to speak at a UKIP Rally and asked Powell (unsuccessfully) to stand as a UKIP representative in the 1994 elections. Shortly before his death, Powell wrote: 'I think that the UKIP will provide some of those who are opposed to British membership of the European Union with an opportunity for recording their opposition at the election' (Hope 2014).

Farage carved out a career as a stockbroker (like his father before him) before he founded UKIP in 1993, become its leader in 1996, and was elected to the European Parliament as a staunch leave advocate in 1999. Farage won subsequent five-year terms in 2004, 2009, and 2014.

A polished campaigner known for his signature pink shirts and 'man of the people' tan coat, Farage embodied the eccentricities of those employing populist tactics, past and present. Farage's capacity to shape his persona according to context extends to his speech. In an address to the European union in 2016 shortly after the referendum vote, Farage positioned himself as being on the side of the 'little people' – working men and women who felt alienated from the opportunities presented to their urban and educated counterparts by EU membership:

> Thursday was a remarkable result, it was indeed a seismic result, not just for British politics, for European politics, but perhaps even for global politics too. Because what the little people did, all the ordinary people did, what the people who have been oppressed over the last few years and seen their living standards go down, they rejected the multinationals. They rejected the merchant banks, they rejected big politics, and they said, 'Actually, we want our country back. We want our fishing waters back, we want our borders back. We want to be an independent, self-governing, normal nation'.
>
> *(Farage 2016)*

In an earlier debate with Nick Clegg in April 2014, Farage said that immigration rates, tied to the European Union, had 'left the white working-class effectively as an "underclass", which would be a disaster for our society' (BBC 2014). In April 2015, at the height of the general election campaign, Farage sought to supplant the British Labour Party as the traditional representative of working people, stating: 'We represent the interests of working people who need a fair deal and the five million small entrepreneurs in this country … We are speaking for them. They have got nobody else to speak for them' (Hall 2015). Subsequent electoral efforts by Farage were unsuccessful, and he returned to the role of outsider contrarian, where he is arguably most dangerous.

Despite his privileged roots and youth, Farage deliberately adopts a disposition more likely to endear him to working-class voters and, in particular, British working-class masculinity. One editorial claimed that prior to the referendum Farage had made UKIP, not Labour, Britain's most working-class party (Blackhurst 2014). Farage is known for holding numerous press conferences in pubs, and he is often pictured with a beer or cigarette in his hand. He openly admits to having been to lap-dancing clubs and derides as politically correct those who would decry such behaviour (Hattenstone 2009). Starck argues that Farage displays two forms of masculinity dependant on context: 'city masculinity', which constructs a 'charismatic strongman persona', and 'gentleman masculinity', which appeals to English nationalist voters (2020: 43). Seymour argues that, beyond targeting working-class voters, Farage is 'keenly attuned to the prejudices of middle England, its anguished resentment, and its yearning for adventure … the adventure of violent chaos' (Seymour 2019b).

Whereas members of the alt-right obfuscate and code their language in memes and satire, the hard-line far-right demagogues closer to real political power have historically had few qualms about threatening or enacting violence. Nigel Farage repeatedly threatened violence if the United Kingdom fails to leave the European Union as a result of the referendum vote. Speaking in 2016, Farage commented:

I think it's legitimate to say that if people feel they have lost control completely, and we have lost control of our borders completely as members of the EU, and if people feel that voting doesn't change anything then violence is the next step ... I find it difficult to contemplate it happening here, but nothing's impossible.

(Simons 2016)

Speaking in 2017, Farage stated that a failure to deliver Brexit would result in civil war: 'I'm enjoying my life. But if they don't deliver this Brexit that I spent 25 years of my life working for, then I will be forced to don khaki, pick up a rifle, and head for the front lines' (Peck 2017).

Demonstrating the emergence of a cohort of global populist demagogues, Farage was the first British politician to meet with Donald Trump after his 2016 election and raised issues with the new president, including the possibility of reinstating the Oval Office bust of Winston Churchill, which had been removed by President Barack Obama (Swinford 2016). Farage's attempt to form the mass-based political Brexit Party during the 2019 election arguably demonstrates greater aspirations for significant political power than he might otherwise admit. The Brexit Party listed a number of policy interventions, such as a reduction in annual immigration; tax cuts, including the abolition of inheritance tax; and reform of the Supreme Court, in effect politicising the judiciary (BBC 2019). In this context, the European Union referendum campaign might be understood as a means to an end: real political power.

It is worth considering the framing of Nigel Farage's pre-Brexit public writing and speeches. To provide insights into the psychometric properties of Farage's speech, I undertook a Linguistic Inquiry and Word Count (LIWC) analysis of a sample of over 33,000 words from between 1 Jan 2013 and the 2016 referendum, which were taken from sources such as speeches at UKIP conferences, internal communications, newsletters, and his 'Farage on Fridays' column in the *Daily Express* newspaper.

Despite the common cultural framing of Britain as the 'Motherland', Farage was almost eight times (7.88) more likely to use male gender references (1.43) than female gender references (0.17) (Table 5.1). Even accounting for English language bias toward male references (Pennebaker et al. 2015), the data arguably demonstrates that Farage has a very specific demographic in mind in his public work: working-class British men.

TABLE 5.1 Frequency of gender references in Nigel Farage's pre-EU Referendum public statements

Corpus	Male	Female
Gender references in Nigel Farage's pre-EU Referendum statements	1.34	0.17

Source: Ipsos-Roose-Turner Global Masculinity Index, June 2019 (Ipsos et al. 2019)

Sample size: 33,066 words (2013–2016)

The emotional tone and content of Farage's speech is similarly revealing. The LIWC program developed by Pennebaker and colleagues features three generic emotional categories that are particularly valuable here: anger, anxiety, and sadness. Anger may be regarded as being focused on the present, and it leads to an increased likelihood of confrontation with the individual or group that one is angry at (Roose et al. 2020). Anxiety may be regarded as an anticipatory emotion. It is focused on potential future risks and harms, and it is a motivation to seek relief from the threat (Roose et al. 2020; Derryberry 2001). Sadness is past oriented and reactive to the loss of something valued (Roose et al. 2020).

Whilst pitched more positively (2.84) than negatively (1.78) overall, Farage was 1.37 times more likely to communicate anger in appealing to his audience (.55) than anxiety (.40) and 1.83 times more likely to use anger than sadness (Table 5.2).

Taken together, it is arguable that the public speeches, media commentary, and other public communications of Nigel Farage were aimed at males, and the primary emotion that they emphasised was anger regarding the current state of the United Kingdom

Boris Johnson: Pragmatic populism

Boris Johnson, at the time of writing, had managed to turn the debacle that followed the Brexit vote to his favour. He attained office without a popular vote after Theresa May resigned in July 2019 after winning a vote by Conservative party members. *The Economist* magazine described Johnson as their 2018 'man of the moment', a 'demagogue, not a statesman', and pejoratively as the 'most irresponsible politician the country has seen for many years' (Economist 2018).

Johnson's language since his election has adopted an increasingly provocative tone and parallels populist language in its framing, such as the 'Surrender Act'. However, Johnson has far more in common with the establishment in British politics (racism and bigotry included) than he does with the stated aims of Nigel Farage. Johnson may indeed be considered a demagogic actor. Yet he also previously ruled out cooperating with the Brexit Party and was highly critical of Trump, demonstrating a less nihilistic approach than his contemporaries. His adoption of populist framing is a matter of political survival and, to this extent, it is demonstrative of the power of far-right political rhetoric once it takes hold. Consequently, I am more concerned in this chapter with the political program of Nigel

TABLE 5.2 Frequency of emotional tone (anger, anxiety, sadness) in Nigel Farage's pre-EU Referendum public statements

Corpus	Anger	Anxiety	Sadness
Emotional tone in Nigel Farage's pre-EU Referendum statements	.55	.40	.30

Source: Ipsos-Roose-Turner Global Masculinity Index, June 2019 (Ipsos et al. 2019)

Sample size: 33,066 words (2013–2016)

Farage and the Brexit Party, who shift the debate, than I am with Johnson and the Conservatives. who follow it.

Religion, masculinity, and Brexit

To recall, the dominant thesis concerning the relationship between religion and populism is that populists have 'hijacked' religion for their own nefarious purposes. As Roy argues, when the populists refer to Christianity, they deploy it as an identity with the explicit goal of excluding Islam from Europe. For them Christianity is a cultural factor, not a value system (Roy 2018). Indeed, this characterisation captures an element of those proposing the notion of Europe as a Christian continent under attack from Muslim migrant hordes. However, in the context of the referendum to leave the European Union, it overlooks two key dimensions. First, it fails to recognise that the 'populists' said relatively little about religion in the lead up to the poll. Second, it neglects the perspectives of religious leaders themselves on the role of religion in the lives of those who voted, whether it was to leave or remain.

Speaking as UKIP leader in April 2015, Nigel Farage stated his support for giving 'some Christians refugee status, given that with Iraq and Syria there's almost nowhere for them to go', though he quickly qualified the statement by limiting the numbers to 'a few thousand' (Lodge 2015). A week later he stated that the United Kingdom is a 'fundamentally Christian nation' and that Christianity 'should be recognised by government at all levels' (Farage 2015). In the UKIP election campaign, he released a pamphlet titled 'Valuing our Christian Heritage', which called for a 'reasonable accommodation' allowing believers to refuse to serve same-sex couples (UKIP 2015). Farage's 'message', set on a background of hymn books, stated:

> Christianity plays a significant part in my vision for the future of Britain. I have been saying for a long time that we need a much more muscular defence of our Christian heritage and our Christian Constitution. This does not of course mean we should be disrespectful of other faiths, only that ours is fundamentally a Christian nation and so we believe Christianity should be recognised by Government at all levels.
>
> Sadly, I think UKIP is the only major political party left in Britain that still cherishes our Judaeo-Christian heritage. I believe other parties have deliberately marginalised our nation's faith, whereas we take Christian values and traditions into consideration when making policy.
>
> *(UKIP 2015)*

The statement does not, *prima facie*, constitute racism or exclusivism. It mimics many calls by politicians seeking a constituency amongst minority voters. In the coded nature of the language, however, a Christian exclusivism emerges. In calling for a 'muscular defence' of 'our Christian heritage and our Christian Constitution',

Farage alludes to the nineteenth-century concept of 'Muscular Christianity', a movement defined by patriotism, discipline, steadfastness, and self-sacrifice. Rosen notes that the movement, which was labelled 'Muscular Christianity' by detractors before the term was appropriated by adherents, paradoxically arose among notably liberal men, 'the Christian socialists who had fought for the Chartists for improvements in living conditions' (Rosen 1994: 17). The appropriation of the term, however, embraced the spirit of chauvinism and empire:

> While some may have seen in the movement a gentle, liberal but realistic and hardworking social activism, for many in Victorian England muscular Christianity meant macho: Tom Brown boxing bullies at rugby and bloodying townies at Oxford, Amyas Leigh heroically hacking wily Spaniards, and Guy Heavystone dismembering menacing Irish peasants.
>
> *(Rosen 1994: 17)*

When Farage, a man who stated that he prays 'sometimes', calls for a muscular defence, he is arguably tapping into the collective memory of Christians and their nostalgia for a time when Christianity was, indeed, the exclusive faith in the United Kingdom. He is utilising the base of a cultural disposition grounded in cultural rejection of other traditions, in particular amongst protestant Christians. To this extent, the 'populist' Farage may be seen to be, superficially at least, 'hijacking' religion for his own cause. Yet to gain a full picture, it is important to consider the dynamics of how the issue of the EU referendum played out in the Church of England and, as importantly, how people from the Church of England voted.

Christianity and the Brexit vote

To outsiders, and particularly foreigners, the Church of England occupies a privileged position in the British social and political context, with the Queen as its head, guaranteed state funding, and political representation. It also appears theologically consistent. The Archbishop of Canterbury is the key spiritual leader, the central pivot for official proclamations in his role as Chair of the General Synod, and the recognised *primus inter pares* (first among equals) of bishops worldwide. Yet its outward-pointing face masks significant diversity within the Church, including internal cleavages and international influences on both theology and practice.

In the lead up to the vote, the Archbishop of Canterbury directly attacked Farage, stating that Farage's remarks on the connection between European Union membership and sexual assaults were 'inexcusable pandering to peoples worrying and prejudices' (BBC 2016). The Archbishop, as a matter of tradition, stated a neutral official position that 'There is no official Christian or Church line on which way to vote' in the referendum, and voting was a matter of individual conscience. Paradoxically, he then cited the historical origins of the European Union as an attempt to prevent the reoccurrence of war and made a case for remaining within the EU grounded in Christian theology:

> The principles Jesus taught, and which have so shaped us also include love for the poor, the alien, and the stranger. The EU came together in a Europe broken beyond description by war and has shaped a continent which until recently has contributed to more human flourishing, and more social care, than at any time in European history. Jesus taught us to love our neighbour, and when questioned about what that meant gave the extraordinary story of the Good Samaritan. In that story the one who turns out to be a neighbour is the one who shows respect, mercy, and love to the stranger, even to an enemy ... We each have to make up our own minds. But for my part, based on what I have said and on what I have experienced I shall vote to remain.
>
> *(Welby 2016)*

Welby's statement would appear to support the 'hijacked' thesis. Yet two key developments undermine such a conclusion. First, there was within the Church of England opposition to Welby and to support for the Leave campaign. Second, members of the Church of England overwhelmingly voted to leave.

Self-proclaimed 'Rebel Priest' Reverend Jules Gomes, who previously served as Dwelly Raven Canon at the Liverpool Cathedral, framed Welby's intervention as elitist and out of touch:

> First, Welby appealed to universal virtues. 'Sacrifice, generosity, vision beyond self-interest, suffering for others, helping the helpless, these are some of the deeply Christian principles that have shaped us.' 'Duh? Who does he mean by "us"?' replied your poor, marginalised, Northerner – fazed by Welby-speak. 'Does he mean Jean-Claude Juncker and the European Commissioners and the 10,000 Eurocrats paid more than Dave Cameron? Or does Welby mean that we – the poor, working-class, elderly, pensioners, from the North of England should be making the sacrifice and suffer for the glitterati in Brussels?'
>
> *(Gomes 2016)*

Also writing shortly after the vote, Mark Rylands, the Bishop of Shrewsbury, a town to the northeast of Birmingham, cited immigration as a key factor shaping his support to leave the European Union and drew upon an argument commonly used in the build-up to the vote:

> The UK has a proud history of welcoming migrants and has benefited from the presence and contribution migrants make to society. Unrestricted EU immigration, however, means that we end up discriminating against non-EU nationals. This seems especially perverse when the UK has strong relationships with many other countries of the world through the Commonwealth, not just with the EU.
>
> *(Rylands 2016)*

Rylands makes a particularly interesting point. The Bishop appears to suggest that the Church may be reinvigorated by migration from nations with Church of England congregations, rather than the primarily Catholic EU migrants or Muslims who migrated en masse. Writing in November 2018, Giles Fraser, Rector of the South London Church of St Mary's, Newington, recalled a meeting to discuss the way forward for churches after Brexit: 'Within the Church of England, there exists a split between the bishops and their congregations – bishops being overwhelmingly pro-Remain and regular churchgoers being slightly pro-Leave with occasional ones being significantly pro-Leave' (Fraser 2018).

Despite their campaigning, those employing populist tactics did not 'hijack' religion. Euroscepticism and social conservatism were already deeply embedded amongst the Church leadership, leaving Christian voters, whether affiliated purely on the base of identity or at a more substantive level, to vote with their feet.

Research by Woodhead and Smith (2018) based on referendum exit polls found that identifying as Church of England (Anglican) was an important independent predictor of voting leave, even when other factors, such as age and region, were taken into account. Across all demographic characteristics, Woodhead and Smith found that whilst 54 per cent voted to leave across their sample, 66 per cent of those who identified as Church of England voted to leave. For those not identifying with any religion just 47 per cent voted to leave. Importantly, compared to Roman Catholics and people of no faith across England, Church of England members were more likely to view the EU as overly bureaucratic (76%), a factor in less safe borders (65%), an influence on the availability of local work (66%), and a negative impact on British sovereignty (62%) (Woodhead & Smith 2018).

The gulf between cultural affiliation and those actively engaged in the Church, who are likely to be influenced by Church leadership, is a significant issue facing the Church of England above all other Christian denominations.

It is important to consider the dimensions of contemporary religion in Birmingham in order to consider the extent to which it may have played a role in the vote to leave (or remain) in the European Union.

Religiosity

According to the UK Census (Office for National Statistics 2001; Office for National Statistics 2011), Christianity in Birmingham declined significantly from 59.13 per cent of the population in 2001 to 46.07 per cent in 2011. The numbers are likely to decrease in the next census. Whilst there were small rises in the Buddhist (0.30% to 0.45%), Hindu (1.98% to 2.08%), and Sikh communities (2.93% to 3.02%), the largest gains in 2001–2011 period were in 'No Religion', which increased from 12.44 per cent of the population in 2001 to 19.27 per cent in 2011, and Islam, which grew from 14.33 per cent of the population to 21.85 per cent.

In 2019 the Vicar of St. Mark's Church in the Kingstanding parish, an area with approximately 8,500 parishioners, reported that approximately 50 were regular church goers 'on a Sunday', something he ascribed to social class: 'In England church is still a very middle-class thing. Getting working-class people to engage is difficult. They want to know what God is going to do for them' (Roose 2019).

The Dean of the Birmingham Cathedral, the Very Reverend Matt Thompson, also revealed the considerable diversity of religious denominations in Birmingham, a diocese of approximately 1.3 million, with 20,000 regular church goers:

> The Church of England has sometimes struggled in urban areas. In the north you might point to some areas with Methodism and non-conformist denominations. Birmingham is by no means an Anglican city. There is strong Catholic representation and from other denominations too.
>
> *(Roose 2019)*

The Reverend John Latham from the Catholic Diocese of Birmingham noted that the Catholic Dioceses were 'holding firm' (Roose 2019). Whilst services were attended primarily by older women, he noted that young families were also active.

The picture on Pentecostals and Brexit is not as clear as it may seem. Dr. Joe Aldred, a Bishop in the Church of God of Prophecy, which has over half a dozen churches across the city, stated that whilst he voted to remain for pragmatic reasons (remaining made travel across Europe easier for his family), he noted that the European Union had frozen out Commonwealth countries, including his birthplace of Jamaica. He noted further that at least some Pentecostals had a deep-seated distrust of the EU and voted to leave:

> Some Pentecostals see Europe as the antichrist. The UK needs to leave to weaken it. I suspect that Pentecostals would have been split. The public narrative of Pentecostals would have been to leave. I hear it more articulated among the white-led Charismatics.
>
> *(Roose 2019)*

Bishop Aldred noted further that mainstream churches were appropriating Pentecostal practices in a bid to win younger audiences: 'Baptists and Anglicans are increasingly behaving like Pentecostals. They would say it is a move of God' (Roose 2019).

On this point the Very Reverend Matt Thompson said:

> The other thing I think fuelled the Brexit vote. There was a whole period of time when those who are indigenous felt that they are missing out. When it came to jobs, housing, opportunities, they were slipping behind. They or their children were starting to lose out. People were getting a lift up the educational level they never had.
>
> *(Roose 2019)*

In a similar vein to the leadership of the Church of England, the Catholic Church leadership was overwhelmingly on the side of the remain campaign.

With many noting the relationship between Catholic teaching and the European Union, it was no surprise that the Vatican issued a statement that leaving 'would not make a stronger Europe' (Telegraph 2016). In a similar vein, the result shows the disjuncture between church leadership, laity, and the culturally affiliated.

In contrast to religion as a discrete, yet important, contributing factor, there is little debate that white, working-class men played a significant role in shaping the vote's outcome. Macleavy argues that the foregrounding of a number of issues – gender and, in particular, masculinity as a key mechanism through which to understand the Brexit vote, economic stagnation and deindustrialisation, shifting gender boundaries, and constructions of 'acceptable' masculinity – left some men in crisis:

> Whilst some men have been able to adjust and harness new labour market opportunities, it does appear that there are others for whom the spatially uneven effects of economic restructuring have served to fuel personal and political anxieties … By foregrounding gender and its intersectional articulations – with, for example, conceptions of 'valued' forms of work – we can better unpack the emotions that the Brexit vote has galvanised and address the array of problems from which they emerge, rather than treating connections to a 'crisis of masculinity' as self-evident or straightforward.
>
> *(Macleavy 2018)*

The remainder of the chapter turns to a comparison of national-level findings on key indicia related to masculinity, interviews with experts actually living in Birmingham, and local ethnographic work focused primarily on older white, working-class men from Kingstanding, though with broader reference to Shard End.

Kingstanding, Birmingham

Given its ethnographic dimension, it is important to situate the research that was undertaken. Birmingham is, irrespective of celebratory proclamations, a city deeply divided – between north and south, inner and outer, and white working-class, migrant middle-class, and wealthy white communities at the fringes of the city. It is telling that the city had the second largest number of COVID-19 cases in the United Kingdom outside of London in March 2020 (Rodger 2020). One of the men I interviewed defined the division within Birmingham along the lines of football clubs:

> If you go north of the city, anything that side is ours. Anything that side is blues. It's a football line that is. It's like in London you get north and south of the river, West Ham and Millwall, well there's always divides.
>
> *(Roose 2019)*

Whilst work has been undertaken to break down geographic divisions caused by the construction of a ring road through the city in the 1960s, class and racial barriers still exit. One notable example is the Mailbox, a high-end mall that is home to the BBC and designer shops, that has an entrance at the top of a long, sparse flight of stairs, which are guarded by layers of security guards looking down onto the inner-city side of the mall.

The Kingstanding village, located in the Erdington ward, is a short drive from the city centre. The majority of the area's housing was constructed as council tenancies during the 1930s and 1940s. Village life centres on a six-pronged roundabout, with shops, medical facilities, restaurants, and utilities interspersed with gambling outlets and pawn brokers. Numerous churches of all denominations are scattered within a short walk of the village centre – many more than one would think would be needed given the size of the location. Church-run schools are also a consistent feature of the landscape. The name of the town suggests a distinctly Christian historic landscape, even if church attendance figures are a shadow of what they once were. Perhaps most tellingly, after decades of Labour party loyalty, in 2014 the Kingstanding ward voted in Conservative councillors.

The chapter turns now to an exploration of dimensions of the key factors of masculinity, which draws on the June–July 2019 Ipsos survey (Ipsos et al. 2019) and interviews I conducted in Birmingham in July 2019, three years after the vote and at a time of ongoing national political tension about its enactment (Roose 2019).

Work, meritocracy, and social trajectory

Precarity across Great Britain is felt across genders and age groups. A sense of secure employment and income was highest amongst young men aged 18–34 (52.03%), dropped slightly amongst men aged 35–54 (49.19%), and was lowest amongst men over the age of 55 (41.30%) (Table 5.3). Less than half of all men in Great Britain (47.92%) felt their employment and income were stable and secure. These are concerning figures, which are likely to be even lower in the post-COVID-19 environment.

TABLE 5.3 My employment and income are stable and secure (percentage of respondents who agree or strongly agree) by gender and age, Great Britain

	18–34	*35–54*	*55+*	*Total*
Male	52.03	49.19	41.30	47.92

Source: Ipsos-Roose-Turner Global Masculinity Index, June 2019 (Ipsos et al. 2019)

Base n = 792.

The men I engaged with in interviews demonstrated a nuanced understanding of the Labour market grounded in often brutal experiences at its coal face:

CHRIS: Getting less and less a job for life. Jobs for life ain't there anymore. Plus, people find other things that come along that pay a bit better. Full time employment is down. The figures are down. Salary pensions, they're all gone. Foreign labour.

MICKEY: All agency workers. From abroad. The shift towards agency workers is the problem. And they haven't got full-time jobs, but the figures say they have. But they've only got a job for today.

CHRIS: They can be got rid of the next day. No notice. One phone call. You've got no sick days. Mid-size companies don't want to employ people that might get pregnant.

MICKEY: Even the big companies like Jaguar Land Rover, which is one of the big employers round here. I have a mate who is a supervisor there and it's all agency … Birmingham City council the same.

LEE: There's no holiday pay, there's no sick pay, if they've got no work for you tomorrow, they can sack you. You've got no grievance.

MICKEY: Back to the agency and you lose a day. And if they need you again next week … That's how agencies work. And they're growing more and more. There's less workers' rights than there was 20 years ago. You've got nothing to protect you.

INTERVIEWER: So, is the pay going down?

LEE: No, the pay is going up. That pushes up inflation, so you pay more for your stuff.

(Roose 2019)

Asked about whether trade unions played any role in protecting their rights and conditions, there was a collective laugh:

CRAIG: They killed the trade unions.

MICKEY: Maggie did that.

LEE: Unless you're a Southern Rail worker, then you can bring the tubes to a standstill while the rest of the world is going on.

(Roose 2019)

Matt Thompson, Dean of the Birmingham Cathedral, noted that trade unions were a key mechanism through which workers could built upward social trajectories, and that they often did this in tandem with the churches:

MATT THOMPSON: They were one of the ways that people improved themselves, developed themselves. They had a great role in working-class education. Some for the church did too, with language education, some of those were housed in church halls and so on. The church and trade unions in some districts had a good relationship. But membership from the 1970s to now has fallen off a cliff. Some of that was hard to defend, closed shops and so on. But convening power was central to working-class identity. The decline of the trade union goes with a decline in the potential for social mobility.

(Roose 2019)

Despite this precarity, there was a general belief that hard work had to some extent pay off.

Belief in the meritocracy

As Littler outlined (Chapter 4), the concept of meritocracy is a key platform of neoliberalism. Yet hard work and reward are also key elements of the dignity of work throughout history. Hard work amongst the working-classes might typically be associated with working overtime or extra shifts if and when available, not 'slacking off' on the job, and showing fiscal discipline by saving. Importantly, despite years of neoliberal economic policy, the extent of belief in the meritocratic compact remains remarkably high. The proposition that 'hard work will ensure I can build a better future' is highest amongst young men aged 18–34 (75.37%), followed by men aged 35–54 (68.74%) and men aged 55+ (68.07%). Only 3 in 10 men in total do not subscribe to the notion that hard work will be rewarded.

Amongst the working-class men that I got to know, there was a general recognition that the standard of living had risen:

BRADLEY: We call ourselves working-class, but our standard of living is better than our parents.
PAUL: Born lucky, our generation.
BRADLEY: We don't like to be called middle-class. Middle-class make you think you're a bit of a numpty, so we like to be called working-class, but living has improved.

(Roose 2019)

There was a clear pattern of belief across both white working-class men and non-whites in Birmingham, however, about who actually deserved work. When I asked Charlie, a small business owner of Indian heritage, why people had voted to leave the European Union in Birmingham, he immediately told me 'Indians voted to

TABLE 5.4 Hard work will ensure I can build a better future (percentage of respondents who agree or strongly agree), by gender and age, Great Britain

	18–34	*35–54*	*55+*	*Total*
Male	75.37	68.74	68.07	70.81

Source: Ipsos-Roose-Turner Global Masculinity Index, June 2019 (Ipsos et al. 2019)

Base n = 810

stay because of our kids' future'. Pressed on whether immigration was an issue in the vote, Charlie waved his arms toward the street:

CHARLIE: Around here they don't work. They are old people, they don't work, they are on the dole. My kid was telling me don't vote for out, we are staying in – now they all work – 26 and 24. English people don't work – the Asian people work. I've been here the last 34 years – I don't work for 6 months because I break my legs, otherwise I work. Factory, bakery, own business, deliveries ... They [white people] run away from work.

(Roose 2019)

Another man of Pakistani heritage told me:

IMRAN: We have to work hard. A lot of us have a house in Pakistan and a house here to pay off.

(Roose 2019)

By contrast, men I spoke to in Kingstanding directed the exact same language and attitude toward Asian and Muslim communities:

CHRIS: You've got people coming here with seven kids. They aren't coming to do any type of work, get a house and sit there on their arse. And we're working.
MICKEY: When the Pakis come, they know exactly what they're doing.
CHRIS: It's about eating the benefits system.
MICKEY: And that's the problem.

(Roose 2019)

Ultimately, despite their precarity and being, as one noted, an injury away from unemployment, there was a strong emphasis upon respect and solidarity between members of the working-class:

CRAIG: Between the working-class there has always been respect. We have always respected each other. It doesn't matter where you go in the country. If you go into a pub after work, in work clothes, you can go into any fucking pub in the world, well in this country. And the accent doesn't mean anything. You're a working man There is respect I believe between the working-class.

(Roose 2019)

The dignity of work and the sense of self-respect it imparts is an overlooked dimension in discussions about merit. The belief that one can develop an upward trajectory through hard work and, simultaneously, find solidarity with other workers and develop a source of meaning in work is an aspect of why working men, in particular, feel alienated when they deprived of them. It may explain why working-class men are drawn to narratives propounded by those employing populist tactics.

Hope for a better future

If the idea that hard work will be treated on its merits and lead to upward mobility is the cornerstone of capitalism, then hope grounded in the belief that one can build a better life for one's family and loved ones is arguably the mortar that binds the entire structure together. This sense of hope is a key measure of whether an individual is likely to support the political status quo or seek change.

Nationally, in the UK population there is a significant deficit of hope that individuals can build a better lives for their families. Hope is typically highest in youth and lessens over a lifespan. With a similar level of optimism to those believing that hard work leads to upward social trajectories, 68.17 per cent of men aged 18–34 believed they could make a better life for their family, compared to just 55.40 per cent for men aged 35–54 and 48.18 per cent of men aged 55+ (Table 5.5). Overall, more than 4 in 10 men in Great Britain do not believe they can build a better life for their family.

For the men I engaged with in Kingstanding, the sense that they or their children could make a better life in England was tied directly to their belief that immigration was driving down the standard of living and safety:

MICKEY: Housing's gone to fuck. Everyone lived here since the fifties, and then the oldies died. And every house they had, it's all gone to (pause) … Our children, you couldn't get a council house around here, you have to buy your own house. Because the council allocate houses to every …
LEE: From abroad …
MICKEY: They literally give you … White people …
LEE: You don't get nothing … It's gone too far.
SHANE: Every street now has got burqas on.
LEE: They walk around in the day; in the night-time they flood the streets.
MICKEY: They walk around in the day because they don't work … When we was growing up, when we was teenagers, it wouldn't have happened around here. Nowadays you get mugged.
LEE: This country is just getting fuller and fuller and everyone will be fighting for scraps because there won't be enough to go around.

(Roose 2019)

TABLE 5.5 I feel that I can make a better life for my family in this country (percentage of respondents who agree or strongly agree), by gender and age, Great Britain

	18–34	*35–54*	*55+*	*Total*
Male	68.17	55.40	48.18	57.57

Source: Ipsos-Roose-Turner Turner Global Masculinity Index, June 2019 (Ipsos et al. 2019)

Base n = 798

Yet, despite the pessimism, the men interviewed did not consider the potential to improve beyond the means of possibility:

CHRIS: This place needs a good politician who can grab it by the balls.
INTERVIEWER: Does it need to be a bloke?
CHRIS: No. The last great leader of this country wasn't.

(Roose 2019)

The Very Reverend Matt Thompson was able to point to less visible social factors shaping hope and belief in a better future for residents of Birmingham, including austerity economics, an element of neoliberalism designed to tame government spending:

> Some of the traditional roots to a good life are no longer available. The social fabric of the city, in common with other places in the country, is becoming stretched due to austerity. Some of the safety nets no longer work. Can we get on the housing ladder? Seemingly not, when it was the case for their parents. Now, at the moment, it feels like it has gone miles away. People's journey through life is now feeling uncertain.

(Roose 2019)

In the context of economic uncertainty and the declining status of blue-collar working-class men through largely invisible structural means, the parallel increase in rates of migration, particularly from the European Union and South Asia, ultimately leads to one, if not the most significant, factor shaping the vote to leave the EU: immigration.

Immigration

Immigration was arguably the key defining feature of political discourse in the lead up to the European Union referendum. It is important to consider that the referendum occurred at the height of the European migration crisis, defined by the largest influx of migrants and refugees to Europe since the Second World War. Those employing populist tactics, including Farage, actively exploited xenophobia, particularly amongst the older generation. Among men (and women) over the age of 55, 42 per cent believed minorities threaten national unity (Table 5.6).

Research in Birmingham revealed that it was proximity and personal impact, rather than more abstract concerns about an influx of refugees into Europe or overseas terrorism, that shaped the attitudes of older white working-class men:

CHRIS: In the northeast you have all these places of new estates that have been built for foreigners.
MICKEY: For foreigners, for foreigners, and it's fucking wrong. It's wrong. You know what I mean?

TABLE 5.6 Minorities undermine or threaten national unity (percentage of respondents who agree or strongly agree), by gender and age, Great Britain

	18–34	35–54	55+	Total
Male	30.06	29.66	42.44	33.56

Source: Ipsos-Roose-Turner Global Masculinity Index, June 2019 (Ipsos et al. 2019)

Base n = 780

CHRIS: My brother's there and can't get a council house.

MICKEY: Nice houses … nice houses.

CHRIS: My mate has to go and rent off a foreigner who's only been in the country ten years. He can't get a council house, and he's got four kids. He'll be on a five-year waiting list.

RESEARCHER: Why would the council deny them housing?

SHANE: Because they're Asian themselves. Looking after their own. They say that we still need lots of migrants, but people around here are concerned about where they come from. Like I said, we're anti-Islamic, I think I can speak for all of us on that one.

CHRIS/MICKEY: Yeah, yeah.

RESEARCHER: So you're not afraid of Islam?

SHANE: No, no, not at all.

MICKEY: You'll find that people around here are anti-Islam, not racist. Islamophobia is not a word that we agree with because a phobia is a fear, and no one's scared of it. You know what I mean?

(Roose 2019)

As one conversation at a pub in Kingstanding turned to immigration, those walking past stopped to listen and join in. When I asked about the potential damage a withdrawal from the EU could cause the British economy, a middle-aged woman interjected:

UNIDENTIFIED WOMAN: Why should we be told what to do by Germany, France, and Italy? We won the war. You're saying our men won two world wars and … It's them that need us. I'll tell you what we need. Enoch fucking Powell. But he's dead.

JOHN: You must have heard of Enoch?

UNIDENTIFIED WOMAN: They called him a racist, but he wasn't a racist. The speech wasn't about that. He said there will be rivers of blood. He was on about what might happen in the future.

JOHN: There is rivers of blood. A knife murder every 24 hours.

FREDDIE: It's basically is rivers of blood, and it's all … who's doing it. I ain't being racist. You look at the stats. Who's stabbing who?

(Roose 2019)

The intersection of religion, anti-immigration attitudes, and the vote to leave the EU came to a head in the following part of a conversation, which is quoted at length:

RESEARCHER: This was the first time you voted Shane, what motivated you?
SHANE: Islam. It's nothing to do with Europeans, is it.
CHARLIE: People weren't bothered about northern European workers. All European workers tend to be Christian. We're a Christian continent. Certain things, unless they're willing to adapt, ain't gonna fit, and we've got to change our life. Which it seems we've got to.
SHANE: We've got to.
CHARLIE: We've had to bend over backwards
RESEARCHER: You have all said you're not religious, you're not practicing, but you draw the line at Islam. You're all saying you're Christian and that this place is Christian?
COLLECTIVE: Yep.
CHRIS: It's not a Christian decision on my part. It's a self-survival thing. What's happening to my country.
MICKEY: Leicester is 50 per cent Asia. London is long gone. Birmingham is 50 per cent. There is places in this country, little northern towns, Dewsbury, Burnley, where they're raping all our kids. Everything that is wrong with the place is to do with Islam or the Prophet. So, what we do, we'll go back to our roots. And if it was another religion, we would say it's them, it's them, it's them.
CHRIS: What we perceive to be the problem.
MICKEY: It's not perception. It's them mate.
CHRIS: The suits in town. They live in the countryside. In little gated villages. They don't have to come to Birmingham at seven o'clock at night.
MICKEY: It looks like Mogadishu. You going into Birmingham city centre at night? Don't take any expensive ...

(Roose 2019)

For the older white working-class men I engaged with, voting to leave the European Union was an act targeted at somehow contributing to stemming Muslim migration:

MICKEY: A Paki will marry a poor Portuguese girl because she is EU and she is allowed to be here. She's on about 5 grand a year. Abdul, he gives her 5 grand to marry 'er. You know what I mean? It gives him a passport.

(Roose 2019)

Later in the conversation, another at the table said:

CHRIS: I suppose because it's Commonwealth. We're paying the price of empire. But why do I have to pay it? Why does he have to pay it? My kids? I don't get any great benefit from the Victorian era. Do you know what I mean?

MICKEY: People voted [for Brexit], but it wasn't particularly against Europeans.
CHARLIE: None of them, none of them want to fit in. None of them. If they weren't here, they wouldn't have been a Brexit.
MICKEY: It was always against Islam.

(Roose 2019)

Where to for Birmingham?

Birmingham has a proud history. It played a significant role in English, European, and, indeed, world history. It was the birthplace of the industrial revolution and associated industrial enlightenment and a pivotal hub for innovation and manufacturing of armaments during two world wars. The city's residents, 'Brummies', have overcome significant challenges to develop a unique pride and dignity that belies Birmingham's working-class origins.

However, Birmingham also has a deep undercurrent of political and religious intolerance. From attacks on non-conformist religious figures of the eighteenth century to becoming the birthplace of British Fascism in the 1930s (albeit instigated by an aristocrat seeking to mobilise workers), the unique conditions of the city would bring out both the best and, at times, the worst of the industrial working-class. The city faced significant challenges after World War Two. Severe impediments to growth were imposed by central government, and there was an influx of migrants from across the Commonwealth, most noticeably from the Caribbean and Ireland. Whilst the Birmingham economy thrived, the period also marked the emergence of significant racial tensions and local politicians, most notably Enoch Powell, prepared to exploit them.

The recession that led to the collapse of manufacturing in the 1970s and early 1980s devastated the city. In some ways the city is still recovering from the recession's effects. Birmingham became a launching point for Prime Minister Margaret Thatcher's neoliberal 'nine-point plan', which involved attacks on trade unions, started the disintegration of working-class solidarities, and introduced economic and social policies that continue to negatively impact working people in the city to this day.

During the 1980s and 1990s, mass migration into the city from South Asian communities changed the face of key areas. Whilst Eastern Europeans migrants settled in the city, the arrival of the South Asian communities in clusters to the east of the city and their collective movement into the middle-class were most noticeable to local white working-class inhabitants. Whilst the white population and key facets of pre-1980s life, including local churches, declined in numbers, the new communities built religious centres – and lives – across the city. These communities, including Pentecostals and Muslims, are typically associated with high religious commitment, and they benefit from increased intra-community bonds of solidarity – social capital. However, a distinct lack of bridging social capital between cloistered and geographically distinct communities saw the fostering of a deep-seated resentment amongst some sections of the white working-class at a time when their historical connections with the city, sense of solidarity, and dignity in work were being steadily eroded.

Austerity measures across the city impacted not only unemployment, but the provision of resources and services to those areas that required them most. At the time of the referendum in 2016, unemployment in Birmingham was almost double the national average, and the welfare rate was almost three times the national average.

In the twenty-first century, the sustained decrease in the number of white residents in the city and the number of white residents attending churches has been paralleled by exponential growth in Asian communities, particularly amongst Pakistani and Bangladeshi Muslims, who have kinship networks and financial responsibilities in their countries of heritage. Nigel Farage (demagogic populist) and Boris Johnson (pragmatist) both stepped into and exploited this context. Farage, in particular, sought to target the anger and anxiety prevalent amongst the white male working-class.

It is important to understand, however, that when Farage refers to Christianity's centrality to the United Kingdom or when working-class men refer to England as a Christian nation, the religion is not being hijacked. Indeed, a strong counter-cultural claim is being made – liberal, city-dwelling church leaders have hijacked Christianity and forgotten the significance of the relationship between church and nation. Kingstanding in Birmingham is quite literally the epitome of the notion of England as a Christian nation. It has numerous churches, church schools, and associated childcare centres. While the church was once a feature of social life alongside the solidarities gained from trade union membership and the dignity derived from meaningful work, all have suffered a catastrophic failure. Even those who are not actively involved in church life but identify with it on a personal basis feel a relative and disproportionate sense of loss in the context where 'high faith, high visibility' religious traditions grounded in the intersection of race, minority status, and faith (including Islam and Pentecostalism) emphasise solidarity and community. However, while Pentecostals have been a feature of the Birmingham landscape since the 1940s and 1950s, when it was brought in by Afro-Caribbean migrants and elements were appropriated under the practice of ecumenism, Islam remains well and truly outside that space to all but the staunchest liberal members of Christian churches.

The sense of loss and resultant anger, anxiety, and alienation manifest in ugly and very often hyper-masculine ways. The language of hatred and contempt, rather than fear, has become a key component of political and social discourse in the city. In the 1950s and 1960s, politicians drew on fear by targeting black migrants. In the contemporary era there is a well of hatred and contempt to draw upon. What might once have been framed as fear of Islam is, for many, less about fear than hatred, and this animosity played a significant role in the referendum vote among members of the white working-class. A key element of the equation appears to be the visibility and vicinity of the 'other' and their association with privileges not afforded to locals.

If the issue is to be addressed amongst the white working-class and, in particular, men of Birmingham, discussions around citizenship, social bridging capital, and improving intercultural understanding will not, in the first instance, cut it, for such engagements rely on a shared sense of power amongst participants. It is vital to address the sense of disempowerment felt by the remaining members of the white working-class in Birmingham. This is no longer a talk about the relative 'loss of white privilege'. It is about dignity in work and solidarities that are pivotal to forming a meaningful sense of manhood, building a sense of solidarity, and moving beyond precarity to social stability. This is the base upon which the real work to address social division in Birmingham – and arguably the United Kingdom – must take place.

References

Abbas, T. (2006). Muslims in Birmingham, UK: Background Paper for COMPAS, University of Oxford. *COMPAS: Centre on Migration Policy & Society*. Retrieved from https://www.compas.ox.ac.uk/wp-content/uploads/RR-2008-Muslims_Cohesion_Birmingham.pdf.

BBC. (2005). Local Events: Birmingham's Blitz Victims Remembered. *BBC Birmingham*, 7 October. Retrieved from http://www.bbc.co.uk/birmingham/content/articles/2005/10/04/memorial_feature.shtml.

BBC. (2013). Mosque Bomber Pavlo Lapshyn Given Life for Murder. *BBC News*, 25 October. Retrieved from https://www.bbc.com/news/uk-england-birmingham-24675040.

BBC. (2014). Nick Clegg and Nigel Farage in Heated BBC Debate over EU. *BBC News*, 3 April.

BBC. (2016). EU Referendum: Farage and Welby in 'Racism' Row. *BBC News*, 7 June.

BBC. (2019). Brexit Party: 12 Key Policies Explained. *BBC News*, 22 November. Retrieved from https://www.bbc.com/news/election-2019-50515516.

Birmingham City Council. (2018). Population and Census: Ethnic Groups. *Birmingham City Council*. Retrieved from https://www.birmingham.gov.uk/downloads/file/9741/2018_ks201_ethnic_group.

Birmingham City Council. (2019). Birmingham Labour Market Update. *Birmingham City Council*, July.

Blackhurst, C. (2014). Farage has Made UKIP, not Labour, Britain's Most Working-class Party. *The Independent*, 4 April.

Cherry, G.E. (1994). *Birmingham: A Study in Geography, History, and Planning*. Chichester, UK: Wiley.

Derryberry, D. (2001). Emotion and Conscious Experience: Perceptual and Attentional Influence of Anxiety. In P. Grossenbacher (Ed.), *Finding Consciousness in the Brain: A Neurocognitive Approach (Advances in Consciousness Research)* (pp. 221–224). Amsterdam: John Benjamins.

Economist. (2018). Our End-of-Year Awards Celebrate the Worst of Politics. *The Economist*, 6 December.

Farage, N. (2015). A Message from UKIP Leader Nigel Farage MEP. *Valuing Our Christian Heritage: UKIP Policies for Christians*. Retrieved from http://www.support4thefamily.org/UKIPChristian_Manifesto-1.pdf.

Farage, N. (2016). Address to European Parliament. Speech delivered to EU Parliament, Brussels, 28 June. *BBC News*. Retrieved from www.bbc.com/news/worldeurope-36650014.

Fraser, G. (2018). How the Church Lost its Flock over Brexit. *Unherd*, 23 November. Retrieved from https://unherd.com/2018/11/church-lost-flock-brexit.

Gomes, J. (2016). Bishops Choke on Brexit Humble Pie. *The Conservative Woman*, 30 June. Retrieved from https://conservativewoman.co.uk/rev-jules-gomes-bishops-choke-on-brexit-humble-pie.

Griffin, J. (2013). How Margaret Thatcher Changed the UK Mining Industry Forever. *BusinessLive*, 9 April. Retrieved from https://www.business-live.co.uk/economic-development/how-margaret-thatcher-changed-uk-3906525.

Hall, M. (2015). Ed Miliband's Love of Big Business Betrays Working Classes, Blasts Nigel Farage. *Daily Express*, 20 April. Retrieved from https://www.express.co.uk/news/politics/571546/Nigel-Farage-Ed-Miliband-working-class.

Harris, C. (2019). The Birmingham Economic Review 2018: People – Population and Employment. *University of Birmingham City REDI Blog*. Retrieved from https://blog.bham.ac.uk/cityredi/the-birmingham-economic-review-2018-people-population-and-employment.

Hattenstone, S. (2009). Nigel Farage, UKIP: Other Party Leaders Live in a PC World. *The Guardian*, 6 June.

Hope, C. (2014). Nigel Farage and Enoch Powell: The Full Story of UKIP's Links with the 'Rivers of Blood' Politician. *The Telegraph*, 12 December.

Ipsos, Roose, J.M., & Turner, B.S. (2019). Global Masculinity Index Survey Developed and Conducted by Ipsos Public Affairs, Joshua Roose, and Bryan S. Turner. June.

Jeffries, S. (2014). Britain's Most Racist Election: The Story of Smethwick, 50 Years On. *The Guardian*, 16 October.

Jones, P.M. (2008). *Industrial Enlightenment: Science, Technology, and Culture in Birmingham and the West Midlands 1760–1820*. Manchester, UK: Manchester University Press.

Lodge, C. (2015). Nigel Farage: UK Should Take in Christian Refugees but Send Others 'Back Where They Came From'. *Christian Today*, 22 April.

Macleavy, J. (2018). Leave-voting Men, Brexit and the Crisis of Masculinity. *LSE Brexit Blog*, 24 October. Retrieved from https://blogs.lse.ac.uk/brexit/2018/10/24/leave-voting-men-brexit-and-the-crisis-of-masculinity.

Mason, P. (2016) Brexit is a Fake Revolt – Working Class Culture is Being Hijacked to Help the Elite. *The Guardian*, 20 June.

McCabe, S. (2014). Benefits Street – and a Warning from History. *Birmingham Live*, 6 February.

Mirza-Davies, J., McGuinness, F., & O'Neill, M. (2016). *Briefing Paper No. 7738: Unemployment by Constituency*, October 2016. London: House of Commons.

Office for National Statistics. (2001). 2001 Census Data. *Office for National Statistics*. Retrieved from https://www.ons.gov.uk/census/2011census/2011censusdata/2001censusdata.

Office for National Statistics. (2011). 2011 Census. *Office for National Statistics*. Retrieved from https://www.ons.gov.uk/census/2011census.

Peck, T. (2017). Nigel Farage Would 'Pick Up a Rifle' if Brexit is not Delivered. *The Independent*, 17 May.

Pennebaker, J., Boyd, R., Jordan, K., & Blackburn, K. (2015). *The Development and Psychometric Properties of LIWC2015*. Austin, TX: University of Texas at Austin. doi:10.15781/T29G6Z.

Powell, E. (2007). Enoch Powell's 'Rivers of Blood' Speech. *The Telegraph*, 6 November.

Prochaska, F. (2006). *Christianity and Social Service in Modern Britain: The Disinherited Spirit*. Oxford: Oxford University Press.

Rodger, J. (2020). UK Coronavirus Map Shows How COVID-19 has Spread Across Birmingham and Midlands. *Birmingham Live*, 31 March. Retrieved from https://www.birminghammail.co.uk/news/midlands-news/uk-coronavirus-map-shows-how-18015713.

Roose, J.M. (2019). Research Interviews Conducted by the Author in Birmingham, July.
Roose, J., Flood, M., & Alfano, M. (2020). *Challenging the Use of Masculinity as a Recruitment Mechanism: Report to Department of Justice and Community Safety*. Australia: Victorian Government.
Rosen, D. (1994). The Volcano and the Cathedral: Muscular Christianity and the Origins of Primal Manliness. In D.E. Hall (Ed.), *Muscular Christianity: Embodying the Victorian Age* (pp. 17–44). Cambridge: Cambridge University Press.
Roy, O. (2018). 'A Kitsch Christianity': Populists Gather Support while Traditional Religiosity Declines. *LSE Populism and Religion Series*, 28 October. Retrieved from https://blogs.lse.ac.uk/religionglobalsociety/2018/10/a-kitsch-christianity-populists-gather-support-while-traditional-religiosity-declines.
Rylands, M. (2016). Why I Voted for Brexit. *Church Times*, 1 July. Retrieved from https://www.churchtimes.co.uk/articles/2016/1-july/comment/opinion/why-i-voted-for-brexit.
Seymour, R. (2019a). Nigel Farage is the Most Dangerous Man in Britain. *The New York Times*, 28 May.
Seymour, R. (2019b). A Dark Appetite for Adventure is Driving Britain's Hardline Brexit Folly. *The Guardian*, 2 September.
Simons, N. (2016). Nigel Farage Predicts 'Violence the Next Step' If Immigration is not Controlled. *Huffington Post*, 17 May.
Speed, B. (2016). How Did Different Demographic Groups Vote During the EU Referendum? *The New Statesman*, 24 June.
Starck, K. (2020). I am a Bull Trader by Nature: Performing Nigel Farage. *NORMA*, 15 (1), 43–58.
Stuart, H. (2017). *Islamist Terrorism: Key Findings and Analysis*. London: The Henry Jackson Society.
Swinford, S. (2016). Beaming Nigel Farage Becomes First British Politician to Meet Donald Trump Since Election. *The Telegraph*, 13 November.
Taylor, A.J.P. (1965). *English History 1914–1945*. Oxford: Oxford University Press.
Telegraph, The. (2016). Vatican Wants UK to Remain in the European Union. *The Telegraph*, 20 January.
Thatcher, M. (1980). Speech to Birmingham Chamber of Industry and Commerce, Metropole Birmingham, 21 April. *Margaret Thatcher Foundation*. Retrieved from: https://www.margaretthatcher.org/document/104349.
UKIP. (2015). Valuing our Christian Heritage. *Support 4 the Family*. Retrieved from http://www.support4thefamily.org/UKIPChristian_Manifesto-1.pdf.
United Kingdom Electoral Commission. (2020). Results and Turnout at the EU Referendum. *The Electoral Commission*. Retrieved from: https://www.electoralcommission.org.uk/who-we-are-and-what-we-do/elections-and-referendums/past-elections-and-referendums/eu-referendum/results-and-turnout-eu-referendum.
Ward, R. (2005). *City-State and Nation: Birmingham's Political History, 1830–1940*. West Sussex: Phillimore & Co.
Welby, J. (2016). Archbishop of Canterbury Justin Welby Makes a Deeply Personal, Principled, and Powerful Intervention Against Brexit. *Mail on Sunday*, 12 June.
Woodhead, L. & Smith, G. (2018). Religion and Brexit: Populism and the Church of England. *Religion, State and Society*, 46 (3), 206–223.
YouGov. (2016). YouGov Survey Results. 2–3 March. Retrieved from http://d25d2506sfb94s.cloudfront.net/cumulus_uploads/document/rzgxjhbyun/InternalResults_160303_EU.pdf.

6

TRUMP AND BLUE-COLLAR WORKERS

Introduction

On a chilly November evening, the night before the 2016 US presidential election, Democratic nominee Hilary Rodham Clinton stood on a stage in front of Independence Hall and addressed a crowd of over 33,000 Philadelphians. She was the favourite to win the presidency. She was joined onstage by two-term president Barack Obama (2008–2016) and her husband, Bill Clinton, himself a two-term president (1993–2001). Clinton was supported by performances from the perennial voice of the American working-class, Bruce Springsteen, and rock musician Bon Jovi, amongst others. Springsteen exhorted those watching to vote for Clinton based on her 'intelligence', experience, preparation, and 'actual vision' to encourage diverse Americans to 'come together to address problems in a reasonable and thoughtful way' (PennLive.com 2016). Clinton herself commented, 'I regret deeply, how angry the tone of the campaign became', and she urged Americans to vote to build 'bridges not walls' and to demonstrate that 'love trumps hate' (Clinton 2016).

On the same day, 125 miles (200 km) to the north in the town of Scranton, Pennsylvania (the birthplace of Clinton's father), Republican nominee Donald Trump stood alone on stage in a city Clinton had not visited for over three months. Trump almost immediately proclaimed, '[T]o all the people of Pennsylvania I say we are going to put the miners and the factory workers and the steelworkers back to work, we're bringing our companies back' (Trump 2016e). He added that Clinton was the last stand of 'special interests' and 'Wall Street', the 'face of failure', and the 'most corrupt person ever to seek the Office of the Presidency of the United States', which were themes that resonated throughout his campaign (Ibid).

The contrast in tone and form could not be more pronounced. The focus on the city of Philadelphia and the state of Pennsylvania, indeed, justified their respective efforts. Hilary Clinton swept Philadelphia. In some micro geo-voting blocs, such as the Carroll Park precinct (bounded by N53th and N54rd St), Clinton won by figures upwards of 99 per cent (4,422 votes) compared to 0.2 per cent (1 vote) (New York Times 2018). Her lead in the votes was particularly pronounced in the University City district of West Philadelphia and in the north of the city, where figures upward of 95 per cent were the norm. The same pattern was repeated in cities across the state.

However, as mapping demonstrates, the majority of Pennsylvania was a sea of red, with small, barely visible blue Democratic-party islands. Donald Trump's choice of Scranton, in Luzerne County, PA, for his election-eve speech was strategic. He sought to connect with local blue-collar workers in particular. Journalist Ben Bradlee Jr. wrote a book about the 2016 election vote in Luzerne County, seeking to understand the appeal of Donald Trump to residents:

> Trump connected strongly to his aggrieved constituency, especially when he called them 'the forgotten people'. That struck a chord, and the floodgates seemed to open to him. Trump was able to activate, own, and even weaponize the resentments that Luzerne residents had over issues that were long-standing and hard to solve, if not intractable.
>
> *(Bradlee 2018: 7)*

Bradlee Jr. further noted, 'It was the perfect moment for a nonideological and malleable populist to emerge, a candidate nominally a Republican but who didn't seem wedded to either party: Donald J. Trump' (Bradlee 2018: 39).

Formerly a Democratic Party stronghold that voted for Barack Obama at the 2012 election (52% to 47%), Luzerne County dramatically flipped, electing Trump with 58 per cent of the vote compared to Clinton's 39 per cent, a difference of 26,237 votes that delivered almost 60 per cent of Trump's margin in Pennsylvania. It constituted a stunning rejection of the Democratic Party and, in particular, Hilary Clinton in a blue-collar area that had been a traditionally solid base of political support. Voters not only rejected a leader they perceived to be intricately tied up both with the neoliberal policies that wrought devastation on their communities and the 'Washington elite', they actively embraced a Republican nominee who promised to bring the area back to its past glory, which existed before the lives of most voters. Writing on the reasons why workers turned against the Democrats in the 'Rust Belt', Michael McQuarrie commented:

> unions have been destroyed, with the Democratic Party complicit, and stunning economic decline has made it easy for narratives of zero-sum competition between different social groups to take hold. Democrats have offered precious little to prevent people in the Rust Belt from feeling embattled and forgotten. More to the point, the Clintons are avatars of free trade, financialization, and

identity politics, a triumvirate of characteristics that associates them pretty directly with what many people associate with the causes of Rust Belt decline and crisis.

(McQuarrie 2016)

Resentment and animosity worked hand in hand with nostalgia to shape their votes. Religion and masculinity played key, yet little understood, roles in the process. As in the case of the British vote to leave the European Union, the vote for Donald J. Trump as president had clear detrimental consequences for political civility, increased polarisation, and gave significant political momentum to far-right political actors within the United States.

A brief history of Pennsylvania

The mass of land now occupied by the state of Pennsylvania was – and still is – indigenous land, both prior to and since European colonisation. Without overlooking the devastating effects of colonisation on indigenous peoples that persist to this day, here I look to the period since white settlement.

The Commonwealth of Pennsylvania is central not only to the formation of the United States as one of its thirteen original states, but also the Industrial Revolution that drove its economic growth throughout the nineteenth and twentieth centuries. The origins of Pennsylvania (originally called New Wales before being renamed by King Charles II in honour of Admiral Penn) reflect the character of Admiral Penn's son, William. A committed Quaker and advocate for religious freedom in England, Penn was expelled from Christ Church Oxford (where he is thought to have been influenced by John Locke) for his refusal to conform to religious tenets. Following his expulsion, he studied in France, where he was influenced by Moses Amyraut at the Saumur Academy (Morris 2012: 190). Penn was imprisoned in the Tower of London for eight months in 1668. In *No Cross No Crown*, written whilst he was imprisoned, Penn simultaneously proclaimed Quaker moral values whilst he criticised the materialism of the established clergy (Penn 1669).

Penn sought to implement his vision of the ideal Christian Commonwealth (Adams and Emmerich 1990) where Quakers and other persecuted religious minorities could practice their faith without impost. To this end, the major city of Pennsylvania was called Philadelphia, derived from the ancient Greek: *philos* (beloved) and *adelphos* (brother). Its motto is 'let brotherly love endure'. While Pennsylvania was born out of a desire to build a heartland where Christians could practice unencumbered, the state played a key role in the political life of the nation. It was central throughout the process of gaining independence from the British, including the American War of Independence (1775–1783), the Declaration of Independence (signed in Philadelphia on 4 July 1776), and the Constitution of the United States (signed at Philadelphia's Independence Hall on 17 September 1787).

Philadelphia played a similarly important role in shaping the American Industrial Revolution (c.1760–1820). It was a key city in the American manufacturing belt, particularly in the areas of textile weaving, ship building, and railway production (De Geer 1927). The Pennsylvania countryside was particularly rich in oil and coal. It became a base for steel production, powering and providing raw resources for the state and the national economy. The industrial era and the decades on either side of it proved valuable for driving both economic and, as in Birmingham in the United Kingdom, intellectual progress. Early in the eighteenth century, Benjamin Franklin, aged just 21, formed The Junto (also known as the Leather Apron Club), a collective of philosophers, artisans, and businessmen who met to discuss and plan the betterment of society. The group produced numerous local developments, including Philadelphia's first library and its firefighting service. In 1743, Franklin and others founded the American Philosophical Society (APS), an expansion of sorts upon The Junto, which brought together leading scholars, scientists, and innovators. Early members included George Washington, John Adams, Thomas Jefferson, and James Madison (the first four US presidents) as well as leading judicial, scientific, and philosophical figures who defined the nation's intellectual, social, and moral compass. Very clear links emerged between the Birmingham-based Lunar Society and the APS. Franklin travelled to Birmingham in 1758 and again in 1760 in order to conduct electricity experiments with Matthew Boulton. At its peak, Philadelphia and Pennsylvania were the political, economic, and intellectual centres of American progress, particularly as it emerged out of the War of Independence. With this history in mind, it is possible to consider post-industrial developments in north-eastern Pennsylvania and, in particular, Luzerne County and Hazleton in greater detail.

Hazleton, Luzerne County, PA

Formed as an administrative district in 1786, Luzerne County is in north-eastern Pennsylvania. Located in the Wyoming Valley, the area was disputed by settlers from Connecticut and Pennsylvania as part of the Pennamite–Yankee Wars (1769–1784) and also during the American War of Independence (1775–1783). It was not until 1791 and the discovery of anthracite coal, however, that the economic significance of the area became apparent. Wilkes-Barre was incorporated as a Borough in 1806, and its population increased significantly with the discovery of an efficient mechanism to ignite and burn anthracite in 1808. Coal mining companies were formed throughout the area in subsequent decades, including the Hazleton Coal Company in 1836. St Gabriel's Catholic Church was founded by Bishop John Neumann in 1855 and aimed primarily at Irish immigrants who had moved to the area. Neumann, himself a Bohemian immigrant and the only American citizen to become a canonised saint, was at the time the Bishop of Philadelphia. Hazleton was incorporated as a Borough in 1856.

The city of Hazleton was incorporated on 4 December 1891, the same year it installed an electricity grid across the city. It was just the third electric system in the entire United States, indicating the city's status as an economic powerhouse. Whilst coal mining was the primary industry, other business areas also grew. The Duplan Silk Corporation, which was formed in New York in 1897, relocated to Hazleton in order to exploit the non-unionised labour of coal miners' wives and children (National Museum of American History 2019). It was, at the time, the world's largest silk mill. Migrants soon unionised, however, resulting in the 'Lattimer Massacre'. In September 1897, a local sheriff and 150 deputies fired on 400 unarmed, primarily Eastern European miners, killing 19 and wounding up to 50. It proved to be a defining moment in the history of the United Mineworkers and contributed to the union's rapid growth and militancy (Shackel 2018: 2). The population of Hazleton grew from less than 1,000 just after its incorporation as a Borough, to almost 7,000 by 1880 and 32,000 by 1920.

Post-World War One, the United States transitioned to natural gas and electricity as its primary energy sources, leading to reduced reliance on coal. In subsequent decades the transition started to have a serious economic impact on the Hazleton area and led to significant unemployment of up to 23 per cent in the mid-1950s. The economic challenges were compounded by two significant natural disasters in quick succession: Hurricane Hazel (1954) and Hurricane Diane (1955). The remaining coal mines were flooded beyond repair, damaging the town's economy. Dublin and Licht, who studied economic decline in Hazleton between 1920 and 1970, noted that at the time 'men also possessed ultimate authority in the household' (Dublin & Licht 2000: 86).

The unemployment and under-employment that resulted from economic stagnation, at best, and significant decline, at worst, drove men to seek employment in other towns, often hundreds of kilometres away. Those who obtained distant employment relied on carpooling and co-bunking with other men from the district, and they returned only on weekends, leaving local women to raise children alone (Dublin & Licht 2000: 89). As the economic crisis worsened, gender roles in Hazleton and the wider region often reversed. Men were confined to household duties, whilst women worked in local industries, such as garment manufacturing. Females became the primary breadwinners.

The Hazleton Community Area New Development Organisation, known as 'CAN-DO', was formed in 1956 to seek to arrest the economic decline in the area. It started with a community subscription to initially purchase land for industrial use and subsequently build 'speculative industrial shell buildings' (Greater Hazleton CAN-DO 2019). General Foam Corporation, the first business to move in, created 100 jobs in 1957. The initiative created economic momentum in the area, which was solidified by the construction of two key highways: Interstate 81 running from Canada to the Deep South in 1959 and Interstate 80 from New York to San Francisco in 1956. Both highways are within ten kilometres of the city centre. The area became known as the 'Crossroads of the East'.

Work in the CAN-DO area factories was often hazardous and had life-threatening implications for workers. A 1972 article in the *New York Times*, for example, detailed how nine workers in one of the original companies to move to the area in

1956, Kawecki Berylco Industries, were found to be suffering from chronic berylliosis, which causes irreversible deterioration of the lungs (New York Times 1972). A subsequent article detailed a strike by members of the Oil, Chemical, and Atomic Workers International Union at the plant (New York Times 1973). Despite the health issues and union activity, the CAN-DO model remained successful well into the late 1970s. As Longazel and Fleury-Steiner (2011: 53–55) note, the neoliberal approach adopted by the Reagan administration resulted in privatisation, devolution, and funding cuts for community development bodies such as CAN-DO. The organisation's approach became 'far more market-oriented' and focused on generating employment opportunities and providing significant tax-breaks to low-paying, anti-union companies. To this extent, Longazel and Steiner frame CAN-DO as a 'neo-liberal conduit' that significantly contributed to the city's changing demographics by attracting migrants who were prepared to work in conditions that were unattractive to locals (Longazel & Fleury-Steiner 2011: 54–56). In the context of the loss of more substantive employment opportunities, education and migration out of the city came to be viewed as being key to social mobility for the children of Hazleton inhabitants, which resulted in a shrinking town and an older demographic profile (Dublin & Licht 2000: 96).

The shrinking population and economic base meant that social institutions consequently also left the town, further eroding social capital. Whilst trade unions retained a presence in coal mining, they had significantly less scope to recruit within warehousing and factories, as indicated by the 6.63 per cent who reported union membership at the 2010 census (United States Census Bureau 2019). At the same time the Catholic Church, the leading church in the area by number of adherents due to the European population, was plagued simultaneously by significantly declining numbers and a child abuse scandal across the Scranton Diocese and Pennsylvania. The Church was forced to consolidate or shut down churches entirely. Between 1971 and 2018, the Catholic Church in Pennsylvania lost 36 per cent of its churches, dropping from 1,490 to 958. In the Diocese of Scranton, to which Hazleton belonged, the number of churches decreased by 50 per cent, from 240 to 120 (Sullivan 2019). It resulted in a significant number of empty, unattended church buildings scattered across the town, a situation discussed in my local interviews. The problem was not experienced by Catholics alone. The 2010 US Census indicated that only 6–11 per cent of households in the region were actively religious (United States Census Bureau 2019).

Lou Barletta: 'Trump before Trump'

The combination of a steep economic decline, the loss of social infrastructure, and an increase in street crime converged in the mid 2000s when the murder of a white Hazleton resident by two undocumented Latino immigrants acted as a catalyst for the introduction of *Ordinance 2006–18* (Hazleton, PA 2006), known as the Illegal Immigration Relief Act (IIRA) Ordinance, by the city's then Mayor, Lou Barletta (Longazel 2017: 9; McElwee 2018). Barletta became a strong local ally of

Donald Trump. The Act, which was passed in July 2006, enabled local authorities to fine landlords $1,000 a day if they rented to unauthorised migrants, allowed authorities to revoke the licenses of businesses that hired undocumented labourers, and declared English as the city's official language, preventing the publication of documents in other languages (Steil and Ridgley 2012: 1029). These actions brought Hazleton to the fore of the national debate about immigration and led to over one hundred other municipalities and states introducing similar legislation. The American Civil Liberties Union (ACLU) and its Pennsylvania chapter joined with a law firm and Latino Justice, a public interest group, to fight the law and its enforcement.

Steil and Ridgley noted that attempts to introduce ordinances such as the IIRA were central to defining boundaries between the local white population and outsiders:

> As much as the ordinance served to exclude undocumented immigrants, it simultaneously served to unify native-born white residents by repositioning Hazleton as 'small-town USA', no longer marginal but, instead, central to the defence of American 'quality of life'. Control over housing became a key form of spatial and territorial control through the creation of a location in which outsiders could be defined as not belonging and local citizenship could be imbued with new meaning.
>
> *(Steil and Ridgley 2012)*

The population of Hazleton in April 2010 stood at 25,340, while the estimated July 2019 population was 24,794, a drop of –2.5 per cent in size (United States Census Bureau 2019). Census methodologies make it difficult to determine the breakdown by race, though the census estimated Hispanic or Latino individuals constituted 56.9 per cent of the population, while white alone (not Hispanic or Latino) were 38.2 per cent. Those born overseas constituted 31.4 per cent of the population. Just 63.7 per cent of men over the age of 16 in the 2013–2017 period were in the labour force. Importantly, the median household income in the area in the same period was just 67.25 per cent of the United States median income, or $40,548 compared to $60,293. Approximately 22.5 per cent of the population lived in poverty, almost double the national average of 11.8 per cent. In 2017, the Mayor of Hazleton, Jeffrey Cusat, applied for and received from the Commonwealth of Pennsylvania designation as a financially distressed city (McElwee 2018).

As stark as these figures are, they do not represent the exponential growth of the Hispanic and Latino population in the region. In 1990 Hazleton was home to 249 individuals of Hispanic background, constituting approximately one per cent of the population. In 2000 the number had grown to 4.84 per cent (1,132); in 2010 it was 37.31 per cent (9454); and in 2018 it was estimated to be 54.2 per cent (United States Census Bureau 2019). The majority of Hispanics in Hazleton are of Dominican heritage. They settled in the area as a result of chain migration from New York, where large Dominican communities reside, or arrived directly from the Dominican Republic. The age profile of Dominican residents is significantly younger than the age profile of white residents, exacerbating the sense of change in the region.

Donald J. Trump and the blue-collar worker

It was into this changing and challenging environment that Republican presidential nominee Donald J. Trump would tread. He shocked not only the United States, but the world when he won the 2016 Republican nomination over far more established figures within the party's ranks. He brought with him much of the conservative, small-government Tea Party movement, which held considerable sway within the Republican Party. Trump was labelled a populist and demagogue well before he attained the presidency, most notably on the cover of the March 2016 issue of *Time* magazine. Drawing on the concept of 'demagoguery', Johnson argues that Trump's rhetorical style 'functions through a toxic, yet paradoxically abject masculine style whose incoherence is opaque to his critics but meaningful to his adherents', as it positions them as victims in contrast to a feminised political establishment (Johnson 2017: 23). Writing a day before the election, Robert E. Kelly summed up Trump as 'a demagogue straight out of Thucydides or Plato's fears about democracy: unstable, vindictive, lazy, short-tempered, self-aggrandising, and narcissistic' (Kelly 2016). Writing in the *New York Times* three years into the Trump presidency, Bob Bauer, White House Counsel under President Obama, argued:

> President Trump has made full use of the demagogic playbook. He has refused all cooperation with the House. He lies repeatedly about the facts, holds public rallies to spread these falsehoods, and attacks the credibility, motives, and even patriotism of witnesses. His mode of 'argument' is purely assaultive.
> *(Bauer 2019)*

Despite such labels, Trump foregrounded three key themes that continued to resonate throughout his Republican primary and presidential campaigns, particularly in Luzerne County: he promoted economic growth in blue-collar industries (driven by the reclamation of business from hostile foreign powers, such as China); called for restrictions on immigration, particularly from south of the American border; and criticised the American political 'elite'. His approach echoed with those of historical candidates who ran on similar platforms to appeal to white working-class supporters, particularly in the Rust Belt, including George Wallace in the 1968 election (Devinatz 2017). Trump appealed not only to fear, but to blue-collar nostalgia for an era defined by prosperity. He rallied support around a desire to 'Make America Great Again'. He offered an alternative to neoliberal economics in the form of a return to protectionist policies (despite later tax cuts to his business) and attacks on global institutions that embraced neoliberal economics.

At the launch of his candidacy, Trump equated the strength of the economy with employment, specifically 'jobs'. In doing so he spoke to those facing challenges in finding employment, laying the blame squarely on an external 'other':

> … our real unemployment is anywhere from 18 to 20 percent. Don't believe the 5.6. Don't believe it. That's right. A lot of people up there can't get jobs. They can't get jobs, because there are no jobs, because China has our jobs and Mexico has our jobs. They all have our jobs.
>
> *(Trump 2015)*

In a campaign speech in Wilkes-Barre, PA, on 25 April 2016, Trump restated this in a more specific context:

> I guess I'm a product of Pennsylvania. I love Pennsylvania. But you know, I'll tell you what – but I had to do this. So I went to the statisticians and they talked about your area. I said, give me some stuff in the area.
>
> So it's been hit hardest – among the communities in America, it's been really hit hard. Then they talk about the Scranton region, lost half of its manufacturing jobs since 1990. Our region here lost 6,000 manufacturing jobs since the recession in 2007. That's a lot of jobs. And you know where they're going. They're going to China, they're going to Mexico, they're going to Japan, they're going to Vietnam. The state of Pennsylvania has lost more than 35 percent of its manufacturing jobs since 2001.
>
> *(Trump 2016b)*

These same countries, particularly Mexico, are positioned as not only economic competitors from abroad, but a fifth column of illegal migrants within, undermining the American social fabric. In his candidacy announcement Trump stated:

> When Mexico sends its people, they're not sending their best. They're not sending you [points at crowd]. They're not sending you [points at crowd]. They're sending people that have lots of problems, and they're bringing those problems with us. They're bringing drugs. They're bringing crime. They're rapists.
>
> *(Trump 2015)*

Trump sought to tap into concerns about Hispanic migration to the area in his Wilkes-Barre, PA, speech:

> Now here's something I don't like. Foreign born population in Pennsylvania has surged to one million, reducing wages and reducing jobs. Not good folks, not good, right? All right, we're going to change it. We're going to change it.
>
> *(Trump 2016b)*

In a 7 November 2016 speech in Scranton, PA, on Election Eve, Trump took specific aim at neoliberal economic policies and perceived political corruption:

> In one day, we are going to win the great state of Pennsylvania and we are going to take back the White House. This election will decide whether we're ruled by a corrupt political class or whether we are ruled by yourselves, the people. It is time to reject a failed political elite that has bled this country dry. To all the people of Pennsylvania, I say, we are going to put the miners and the factory workers and the steel workers back to work. We're bringing our companies back.
>
> *(Trump 2016e)*

Trump's vulgarity, both prior to his election and throughout his campaign and presidency, is a hallmark of populists. When used strategically, it is designed to appeal to the common working man. Indeed, Trump's rallies were often marked by hyper-masculine displays by Trump, who yelled, targeted media, and bashed dissenters in the audience (Roose 2017). Yet for all the criticism of Trump's apparent incoherence, particularly in speech-making, he has resonated with blue-collar workers (amongst others) for reasons outlined by Liberman, whose analysis of a July 2015 speech noted:

> The false starts and parentheticals may actually make the speech better, at least for people who are open to liking Trump and endorsing his ideas, by giving an impression of enthusiasm and genuineness. It would be a mistake to underestimate his considerable effectiveness as a public speaker, even if he doesn't speak in conventionally coherent textual paragraphs.
>
> *(Liberman 2015)*

A Linguistic Inquiry and Word Count Analysis enables a deeper engagement with Trump's strategic engagement with voters. It draws on a sample of over 51,600 words from speeches made by Trump during the 2016 election campaign, including his Pennsylvania speeches and a number across the 'Rust Belt'. According to the analysis Trump's male references were three times as prevalent (0.56) as female references (0.19) (Table 6.1). Despite controversies in relation to Trump's treatment of women and sexual impropriety, the gender division is not as pronounced as it might have been and may arguably reflect structural inequality in English language use. In Trump's Election Eve speech in Scranton, for example, he addressed men and women on more equal terms: 'And we will massively cut taxes for the middle-class, the forgotten people – the forgotten men and women of this country, who built our country. We will massively lower taxes. It's in our plan' (Trump 2016e).

This stands in contrast to the contemporary preoccupation with Trump as outspoken misogynist, despite its apparent validity.

TABLE 6.1 Frequency of gender references in Trump 2016 campaign material

Corpus	Male	Female
Gender references in Trump 2016 campaign material	0.56	0.19

Source: Ipsos-Roose-Turner Global Masculinity Index, June 2019 (Ipsos et al. 2019)

Sample size: 51,662 words (2014–2016).

In another Scranton speech earlier in the campaign, Trump urged women to avoid voting for his opponent, inverting claims of his sexism, by suggesting that Clinton would undermine women in future leadership roles:

> I don't want to hear that. I do want to hear it eventually because I want to see a woman become president. She's a disaster. She'll set you back a long way, women, if that happens. It'll be a long way before it happens again. You better be careful what you wish for.
>
> *(Trump 2016d)*

The point here is not what the researcher or even the reader makes of Trump's statements. Rather, we must position ourselves, reflexively, in the shoes of an active listener in Wilkes-Barre, Hazleton, or anywhere else in Luzerne County, who may take at face value statements made by a national celebrity who has brought the spotlight of national and, indeed, international attention to the listener's struggling hometown.

When emotional anchors are considered, it is clear that Trump drew on anger (0.58), focused on the present, as a mobilising devise. Present-focused anger represented over 55 per cent of emotional references, which was significantly higher than past-focused sadness (.33) or future-focused anxiety (.14) (Table 6.2).

Trump skilfully utilised anger, for example, in a campaign speech in Vandalia, OH:

> People are fed up with what's going on. And by the way, they're fed up, they're fed up with the stupidity in Washington. They're fed up with the stupidity of trade deals and labor deals. They're fed up with the fact that they haven't had an increase in the last 12 years if you can believe it. The middle-class, the workers aren't being taken care of in this country. We're

TABLE 6.2 Frequency of emotional tone (anger, anxiety, sadness) in Trump 2016 campaign material

Corpus	Anger	Anxiety	Sadness
Emotional references in Trump 2016 campaign material	.58	.14	.33

Source: Ipsos-Roose-Turner Global Masculinity Index, June 2019 (Ipsos et al. 2019)

Sample size: 51,662 words (2014–2016).

losing our jobs. We're losing our factories. They're going to China. They're going to Mexico. [Audience Boos].

(Trump 2016a)

In his Pennsylvania speeches, in particular, Trump stuck to the issues of jobs, immigration, and political elites. The difference between his campaign and his opponent's was pronounced. No more so than on Election Eve, when Trump spoke alone on a stage in Scranton, PA, whilst Clinton was surrounded by celebrities and political elites, including two presidents, during her speech.

Religion, masculinity, and Trump

The election of Donald J. Trump constitutes the most substantive challenge to the perspective that populists have 'hijacked religion'. The relationship between Trump and evangelical Christianity, in particular, has been well documented. Despite his background of sexual and what might be considered 'moral' indiscretions, his vulgarity, and his continued abuse of the truth, Trump successfully courted the evangelical Christian vote. During the campaign, Trump often began his rallies with prayers. He received endorsements from high profile evangelical leaders, including Liberty University President Jerry Falwell Jr., who stated:

> In my opinion, Donald Trump lives a life of loving and helping others as Jesus taught in the great commandment ... He cannot be bought, he's not a puppet on a string like many other candidates ... who have wealthy donors as their puppet masters.
>
> *(Costa and Johnson 2016)*

FitzGerald argues that the Christian right has evolved from a mere movement into an organised faction within the Republican Party, suggesting the political power 'trumps' moral indiscretions (FitzGerald 2018). Berlinerblau (2019) asserts that, in this context, the intersection of Republican politics and white identity politics constitutes a clear political reason for Trump's election. Although Berlinerblau also draws on the work of Martin Luther on the role of princes to argue a theological consideration:

> for Christians ... today's Evangelicals also view themselves as confronted by an unspeakable and demonic foe. That foe, however, is not Catholicism and the Roman Church, but modern 'secularism' ... Far from being God-ordained, as it was in the age of Luther, today's conservatives view secular authority as affiliated with all that is demonic.
>
> *(Berlinerblau 2019: 25–28)*

Berlinerblau observes that in a world where evangelical Christians perceive that their values and, indeed, their existence are under attack, Trump, a white Protestant like themselves, is seen as carrying out God's work: 'Why can conservative

Christians accept a man like Donald Trump? Because he knows precisely how to slay the secular beast, his personal shortcomings be damned' (Berlinerblau 2019: 29). A reading of Trump's speeches to religious supporters appears to support this thesis. On the campaign trail, Trump stated his complete support for the State of Israel, which holds a particularly important place in American evangelical identity:

> The importance of faith to United States aside is really the people who go to church, who work and work in religious charities, so important, and share their values. These are the foundations of our society. We must continue to forge our partnership with Israel and work to ensure Israel's security. Keeping people of faith safe from threats like radical Islam, whether protecting them here or standing by Israel, all of us need to confront together the threat of radical Islam.
>
> *(Trump 2016c)*

Trump's relationship with the American Christian Right is symbiotic and irrefutable proof that religious actors are prepared to work closely with populist politicians where and when it suits their own political agenda.

Religion and voting behaviour

In comparison to the United Kingdom and, indeed, many Western nations, religious identity and practice amongst those who identify as such in the United States is particularly thick. It is important to consider the central role of religion in the development of the United States polity and, indeed, nation. A haven of religious freedom for those who migrated, the United States has the largest Christian population in the world. Christianity is, to a great extent, inscribed in key elements of mainstream culture. It is clear that any politician who speaks the language of faith and of Christian identity has a strong potential base of support. Analysis of the 2016 election by the Pew Research Center found that Trump bested Clinton amongst Protestants (58% to 39%); white Catholics (52% to 45%); Mormons (61% to 25%); and, most compellingly, white, born again, evangelical Christians (81% to 16%), with minor parties making up the difference (Martinez & Smith 2016). The only faith groups to vote in favour of Clinton (and against Trump) were Hispanic Catholics (67% to 26%) and Jewish voters (71% to 24%) (Martinez & Smith 2016).

The remainder of the chapter is grounded in two sources of primary evidence: the Ipsos-Roose-Turner global masculinity survey conducted in June–July 2019 (Ipsos et al. 2019) and ethnographic research conducted in Hazleton (Roose 2019). A total of 26 interviews were carried out in Hazleton bars, cafes, and restaurants in late November and early December 2019 just as the first snowstorm of the season rolled in. Drawing on extensive mapping of the 2016 presidential election by the *New York Times* in combination with a broader body of writing about the city, it was possible to pinpoint key areas of focus for the research. Luzerne County, PA, was, in effect, a sea of Republican red, with two small islands of Democratic blue: Wilkes-Barre and small segments to the north-east of Hazleton.

Voting for the Democrats in Hazleton peaked in areas of Hispanic settlement in the downtown and inner-city regions of higher population density. The sector defined by the intersections of Church Street, Wyoming Street, and Broad Street hit a high of 60 per cent Democrat votes to 38 per cent Republican. More suburban parts of the city, such as Old Sugar Loaf to the north-east of the town centre, were more likely to vote Republican, with a margin of 54 per cent to 44 per cent. Rural regions surrounding the town, such as Stacie Manor just a couple of kilometres south-east from the city centre, saw 70 per cent of the local vote go to the Republicans, compared to 28 per cent to the Democrats. Initial ethnographic research efforts were concentrated in the south-eastern part of the city, where a range of voting responses were recorded and contrasts were most significant.

Work, meritocracy, and social trajectory

Precarity and associated insecurity are felt by almost half the workforce in the United States (Ipsos et al. 2019), a figure that is likely to have increased with the impact of COVID-19. Overall, 55.43 per cent of men aged 18–34, 52.24 per cent aged 35–54, and 58.81 per cent of men aged 55+ feel that their employment and income are stable and secure (Table 6.3). In total, 55.71 per cent of men feel stable and secure in work, leaving a sizeable constituency who do not. Those experiencing precarity are subject to concomitant flow-on effects on health, safety, and well-being (Quinlan 2013). It would be expected that this would be reflected in the research context.

Hazleton's transformation from key economic and industrial pivot at the beginning of the twentieth century to a textbook case of neoliberal individuation reliant on minimum-wage jobs, factories, and warehousing has had a significant impact on locals' experiences of the labour market. The majority of individuals I spoke with identified themselves as working class:

ZACH: I'm definitely working class. I've never had anything given to me. Or even a six-figure job or something like that. I'm blue collar, yeah.

JIM: We worked hard for everyone. When you're here 18 hours a day, you know you are.

Keystone Opportunity Zones (KOZs) are one mechanism used to attract businesses to Pennsylvania and Hazleton. In effect, they are special economic zones that encourage businesses to move to an area and create jobs by providing exemptions

TABLE 6.3 My employment and income are stable and secure (percentage of respondents who agree or strongly agree) by gender and age, United States

	18–34	*35–54*	*55+*	*Total*
Male	55.43	52.24	58.81	55.71

Source: Ipsos-Roose-Turner Global Masculinity Index, June 2019 (Ipsos et al. 2019)

Base n = 738

from state and local taxes. The businesses do not contribute to the funding that is central to the development of viable local infrastructures. As one local noted, the zones are often exploited by businesses to the detriment of local workers:

RICH: Back in the 1990s/early 2000s they set up KOZ zones. If you were a business and set up, they would wave all your county and school taxes. And then they would pack up and leave after their ten years were up.

Hazleton CAN-DO and the Downtown Hazleton Alliance for Progress are two such organisations, which sought to bring businesses into the region:

JEFF: All the jobs that are around here are just low paying jobs, minimum wage jobs. Most of them are not union. Humboldt and Valmont. That's all CAN-DO's stuff. Bring a lot of these low paying jobs in … Go behind Giant Supermarket, there's homeless people. It just never panned out. I am a hater of Amazon. All they do is shut mom and pop businesses down and take them over. They start their own delivery services. I think Jeff Bezos is a corporate pig. He just wants everything.

The question emerged as to whether unions had any role in representing local workers, particularly in a context defined by neoliberal economic freedom for large corporate giants in the area, such as Amazon. Dan, a local man in his thirties who had moved out of Hazleton but returned to look after his aging parents, noted:

DAN: I worked at Amazon a good six years ago. Amazon is one of the largest companies in America. They have a warehouse here, and they had one staff meeting. And they said, 'You have the option of joining a union. Sign this piece of paper'. Even if you would have got 500 to 1,000 people out of the 3,000 people, whatever it was, you're fighting Amazon.com, so like, good luck with that … [Laughing].

So you can go to Jeff Bezos and say, 'I want $2 more an hour for working my 10 hours', and that's going to get lawyered down to death so … So, not to say they [unions] don't exist. There are more specialised ones, like with the paper, like I said, with maintenance people. But as far as the general worker, in my opinion, I think entering a union job is very, very slim …

Especially the major corporations we're talking about. There are still big unions, but it has to be controlled now. Amazon is so messed up to begin with, that a union wouldn't help them. Bezos controls everything.

Justin, in his late thirties, asserted:

JUSTIN: Unions around here have pretty much kind of died out. Well, unions are kind of a thing of the past around here. The electrical union even pulled its office out of here. They're up at Wilkes-Barre now. But, you know, unions around here were a big thing in the 60s, 70s, and 80s, and that's kind of died off as far as I can see. They've been muscled out. By companies offering competitive wages. Not that they're great wages, but they're competitive. So, they're not going to muscle a union in or try to make it better for themselves, because its competitive. But, I do agree that the union helps the working man out a lot. A lot.

By contrast, one local religious leader in his thirties working in a non-union position argued:

MARK: In the past 30 or 40 years they haven't done much for working-class people. Someone goes to negotiate a contract, and they may not have your best interests at heart.

It is clear that stable, secure, traditional blue-collar work with large employers in Hazleton is rare. Whilst goodwill toward unions and the work that they do exists amongst older workers, younger workers, who have grown up in an era defined by neoliberal economic policies and large non-unionised workforces, may see unions as an impediment to entry into a competitive workforce.

Belief in the meritocracy

Despite numerous academic critiques, the United States continues to self-identify as meritocratic nation, where upward social mobility is possible through hard work. In total, 73.69 per cent of men aged 18–34, 71.48 per cent of men aged 35–54, and 77.39 per cent of men aged 55+ (with a total of 74.35%) subscribed to the principle that hard work would ensure they could build a better future (Table 6.4).

As in Birmingham, UK, a masculinity grounded in hard work and an egalitarian ethos based on respect for other working people has persisted, despite the immense changes brought about by the enactment of neoliberal economic policies:

ADAM: I guess you could go back to the coal working days when everyone was working in the coal mines ... That even goes back to respect. When you respect everyone who goes out and works every day, and we all get together and have a couple of beers at the bar and, you know, a couple of guys. That's respect. You take care of your family. Whether you're a doctor or coal miner, you get treated the same. It's changed.

TABLE 6.4 Hard work will ensure I can build a better future (percentage of respondents who agree or strongly agree), by gender and age, United States

	18–34	35–54	55+	Total
Male	73.69	71.48	77.39	74.35

Source: Ipsos-Roose-Turner Global Masculinity Index, June 2019 (Ipsos et al. 2019)

Base n = 748

Work is arguably the central defining component of Hazleton identity. Work grounded in physical labour has been central to how the city not only functions, but imagines itself – from its history as a coal mining town, where the tempo of city and home life was defined by the change of shift, through to the 10- to 12-hour, seven-days-a-week work days that define the contemporary rhythms of life. The work is changing, not only due to the individualisation of labour, which undermines working-class solidarities, but also due to efforts to attract new forms of intellectual capital to the city. KOZs offer tax breaks to certain segments of the economy: healthcare and life sciences, nanotechnology, advanced manufacturing and plastics, information technology, new media, back office finance, and Homeland Security (Downtown Hazleton Alliance for Progress 2016). The incentivised shift in businesses and jobs will see traditional masculinity grounded in physical work subordinated to masculinities equipped with the requisite cultural capital and bodily dispositions to achieve in a world where manual labour is less valued.

Even in the current economic climate in the city, one male in his early thirties noted that he had difficulty finding work without Spanish-language skills:

DAN: I got out of school in around 2008 when the whole housing bubble was happening. And a bachelor's degree didn't mean a whole lot, because you were competing against everybody that had previous experience and master's degrees and all that fun stuff. And, as far as this town is concerned, there's a lot of jobs now where you can go to any PNC Bank or any bank in this town, and you have to speak Spanish now. It's a requirement.

In the context of neoliberal conceptions of merit and American citizenship, a particularly potent venom is reserved for those who are seen as welfare recipients. As discussed in Chapter 2, Judith Shklar claims that, whilst short-term welfare may be socially acceptable, in a world where citizenship is defined by voting and the 'opportunity to earn', becoming dependent on welfare long-term is to be viewed as 'to lose one's independence and to be treated as less than a full member of society. In effect, people who belong to the underclass are not quite citizens' (Shklar 1990: 22). This negative view of welfare was particularly pronounced amongst the working blue-collar men I engaged with.

I quote two conversations here at some length. An initial question about the employment market quickly turned to conversations in which I was a mere bystander. These animated exchanges were focused on the topic of welfare recipients and, in particular, the perception that Latino residents of Hazleton were rorting the welfare system whilst *real* working citizens received nothing.

Mikey, a small business owner in his late fifties who, nonetheless, characterised himself as blue collar and working class, stated:

MIKEY: For people who want to work there is opportunity … I'm very frustrated. We tried basing it off an honest living, where you work for your money and you're not going to be out there peddling. And that's why they came here; and … for the free assistance on everything. Housing, cable, cars, everything. Because they don't speak English, they get their cable paid for. I'm not kidding, certain cable stations. Yes.

JEFF: They get access cards. They come here and get access cards. They get welfare here.

MIKEY: Well, yeah, because they'll put three different aliases from three different states. They collect from three different states. These people who come here are slick. And not by working wise either.

JEFF: They know the system.

MIKEY: Welfare fraud is a big thing. They have to get stricter. You know, conditions on being on it. Drug test them all. Make sure how many people are living in their occupancy. I've seen where four people [are] on their mail list, and 18 people are living in there.

JOHN: Food stamps, food stamps. They're buying shrimp, they're buying lobster. If you need it, you should only be able to buy [certain food with] food stamps. Not 20 pounds of shrimp, 15 pounds of steak. You sure as hell shouldn't be able to buy six lobster tails.

JEFF: We work every day. How many times a week do you eat lobster?

MIKEY: No way, hey.

JEFF: No. It's the ignorance. And that is why there is no respect. Not even for the system or anybody else. That's why hatred is there.

The sense that other groups in society and, in particular, Hispanic migrants to the city do not have to work, yet they receive generous government welfare support (irrespective of the validity or accuracy of the perception), undermines the idea that hard work (and, hence, merit) will be rewarded. It challenges the dignity of those who have remained in Hazleton as blue collar workers. New migrants are perceived to have greater access to societal benefits and luxury items, which ferments into resentment and, indeed, as Jeff suggested, 'hatred'. Yet, in a similar vein to migrants in Birmingham, UK, when local immigrants are confronted with such assertions, they respond with incredulity. One local Hispanic community member admitted that welfare fraud was 'a reality', however he also argued that local 'white people' refused to do the work that Hispanics were undertaking:

JOSE: Amazon pay $14–$16 a shift. Cargill pay $15–$16 a shift. White people, they don't do that job. They don't do. It's weird. White people say no.

There is a strong resonance between statements made by members of migrant communities in both the US and UK contexts.

Hope for a better future

Like the belief that hard work will be rewarded, hope plays an important role in the American dream. Hope for a better future remained reasonably consistent with the belief that hard work would be rewarded. In total, 71.94 per cent of men aged 18–34, 70.35 per cent aged 35–54, and 77.29 per cent aged 55+ (for a total of 73.36%) believed that they could make a better life for their family in the United States (Table 6.5).

TABLE 6.5 I feel that I can make a better life for my family in this country (percentage of respondents who agree or strongly agree), by gender and age, United States

	18–34	35–54	55+	Total
Male	71.94	70.35	77.29	73.36

Source: Ipsos-Roose-Turner Global Masculinity Index, June 2019 (Ipsos et al. 2019)
Base n = 738

A sense of hope that one can build a better future for their family is a key measure of whether an individual is likely to support the political status quo or seek change. For some, such as community leader 'Leon', Hazleton is seen as the epitome of the American dream for new migrants:

LEON: If you get that same job and transfer to a warehouse in Hazleton, and you and your wife work, you can make $64,000 a year if you both work at Amazon or Cargill or American Eagle or someone paying the modest sum of $15 an hour. And what you can do with that $64,000 is buy a home and live in a community that has far less crime. Far less crime.

One local contractor was similarly optimistic:

SAM: People earn more money in this city than they have since the manufacturing days. I've had one of the busiest years I've ever had this year. I'm going seven days a week right now. There seems to be more money. When Obama was in, it just seemed everyone had no money. It's not in the budget. You know what I mean? But I'm doing very good on the residential end, which means people have more money, fixing up their houses.

Others were less optimistic and thought opportunities were better during their youth.

DAN: I grew up in the Clinton era. There was an established middle-class, a surplus, economy booming. Now wars. People gave Republicans credit for the surplus, but happier times back then – the Clinton era.

Similarly to Birmingham, UK, the sense of optimism and hope in the area was diminished. Perceptions were largely rooted in references to migrants, who were considered to have changed the landscape of the area. However, as the research demonstrated, this has some nuance. Generation is an apparent indicator of attitudes toward new migrants, whilst shared religion had little influence in bringing people together across the racial divide.

Immigration

A question about whether minorities undermine or threaten national unity revealed that, nationally, 29.56 per cent of men aged 18–34, 23.72 per cent of men aged 35–54, and 25.50 percent of men aged 55+ (for a total of 29.56%) are likely

TABLE 6.6 Minorities undermine or threaten national unity (percentage of respondents who agree or strongly agree), by gender and age, United States

	18–34	35–54	55+	Total
Male	29.56	23.72	25.20	26.28

Source: Ipsos-Roose-Turner Global Masculinity Index, June 2019 (Ipsos et al. 2019)

Base n = 780

to be hostile toward immigration and particularly susceptible to political campaigning on the issue (Table 6.6).

Hazleton's recent history of political and legal challenges related to migration suggest that perspectives in the town may be more polarised than in more socially cohesive cities. Asked about whether he had observed any changes to the city over the length of time he had lived in it, Albert said:

ALBERT: Fights, street fights, and shit like that. Guns, drive by shootings, murders, drugs, a lot of drugs came to this town. They call this city, Hazleton city, 'the hub'. That's what they call it. Between here and New York and Philadelphia, they bring the drugs in and distribute. A lot of drug busts here. A lot of them. I don't let people [on drugs] come in here.

VINCE: On a daily basis, I wouldn't go out after dark if I was a teenager. I'm already 50-something years old. I don't care. I wouldn't let my kids out.

John cited the example of one elderly lady living in a predominantly Hispanic part of the city. He claimed that local gangs were trying to force her out so that Hispanics could buy her house:

JOHN: Trying to force them to leave is what they're trying to do to get a hold of the area.

MIKEY: They said they were really just going to hound everybody.

JOHN: Yeah. Because what they'll do, like, I know of one particular woman, she's 86 years old, and she's perfectly healthy enough to be living on her own, but now she is completely terrified.

MIKEY: Because they want to buy her house.

JOHN: They're egging her house, smashing her windows out, flatten the tyres on the car, and her neighbour, who is also elderly, they're doing the same thing to him. And her sons, she's 86, and they're also up there in age at this point. They're considering taking her out of there. One of them taking her in and selling her house. And that's what they want.

MIKEY: That's what they want. That's want they want. That's what they're trying to do.

BAR BYSTANDER: It's sad. It's really sad.

Irrespective of the validity and truth of the locals' claims, the narrative of an elderly woman being forced from her home by violent minorities resonates. This particular narrative bears strong parallels with a case cited by Enoch Powell in his *Rivers of Blood* speech, which was delivered in Birmingham, UK. Powell referred to an elderly war widow forced to choose between subletting to black migrants or facing eviction.

The action to restrict immigration by Hazleton Mayor Louie Barletta (the 'Illegal Immigration Restriction Act') was, irrespective of individuals' views toward him, viewed somewhat sympathetically by research subjects. However, my research engagements across Hazleton revealed generational differences between the attitudes of younger and older residents.

Referring to his workplace, Chris, in his twenties, talked about positive experiences with others, irrespective of their backgrounds:

CHRIS: On my line [that he supervises] there are three Caucasians, one African American, a couple Hispanic. A good group of guys. They are always there on time. They all want to work. It's not like there weren't bad apples before the influx. My group, we work really well together. We all get along, which is really nice.

Chris continued:

CHRIS: You do get a little bit defensive. We grew up here. This is your home. Our roots. A lot of the guys are now second generation, and it is their home too. I know guys who take vacation back to the DRC … The younger generation is getting more adapted. I think, for us, it is more of a live and let live. Don't bother us, we won't bother you. I think for the older generation, say 50+, they're an older generation, and they are more like, you know, stuck in those old stigmas. You know, hate's learned, and that's just what they grew up in.

Dan, also in his twenties, similarly stated:

DAN: Depending on who you talk to, there is a big generation gap. We're all immigrants to a certain extent. But what has happened in the past 15 years, as far as violence and drugs, if you talk to someone Bill's age, predominantly older white generation, they look at them as, you know, 'you brought violence and crime to our town' so.

Exposure to immigrants and second-generation Hispanic Hazletonians in schools and the workplace constitutes a form of everyday multiculturalism, which is not necessarily experienced by older residents.

Shared Christianity, yet little common bond

Both long-established locals of European heritage and recent arrivals of Latino heritage share a common Christian faith. Many Catholics, in particular, migrated to the region. Christianity should, in theory, serve as a form of bridging capital. However, it became clear that organised religion played very little role in bringing residents together on the basis of shared values. Linguistic and ethnic diversity were stronger factors. This has potential implications for understanding anti-Muslim prejudice. It also suggests that religion may be less of a factor than social distance.

The Christian geography of Hazleton, despite appearances, has been irreparably altered. Reflecting on the significant number of churches in Hazleton, Rich informed me that many were empty or had been sold off for private use, a result of cost-cutting:

RICH: There's only … I believe there's only like five or six Catholic churches left, and there used to be a ton of them. They brought a guy in from the Catholic Diocese of Scranton. He was only there for a brief period of time, but they brought him in as what they call the 'hitman'. And he was brought in to shut all of these places down and consolidate. You know what I mean? I always say Hazleton people lost their image when this happened … They shut a couple of bigger churches down. All that did was create empty buildings. It was just a bad thing. You know what I mean? They were saying 'not enough people were going to Church, so this is what we had to do'.

A local religious leader from a Baptist congregation with approximately 150 primarily white attendees commented on these developments:

RELIGIOUS LEADER: Their solution was, they were all Catholic, but they would have different ethnic Catholic churches. They all reported up the chain to the pope. They've consolidated all those churches into one. A lot of the people who were going to those churches weren't really pleased when they got closed down. I haven't seen competition between the churches. But I also haven't seen a lot of the churches reaching out in order to help either. Everybody kind of stays cloistered.

Mikey, who still regularly attended church with his sizeable family, switched churches when his congregation became primarily Hispanic:

MIKEY: I don't see no bond there. Because once they started speaking a different language, I ain't go there no more. It makes a big difference. You know? I want to understand what I'm hearing. It would be a big difference if we did it in Latin, the way it was meant to be done from the Bible, and all. None of us would understand it. There's always that potential for shared faith, that optimism.

A leader in the Latino community reflected on the more than 1,000 attendees at St Gabriel's Catholic Church and the simultaneous proliferation of over 80 local Pentecostal churches held in family homes and shopfronts:

They have turned into businesses. A pastor can say 'I hear the voice of Jesus', and those in their congregation pay 10 per cent of what they have made. Many are not high school grads. It is easy to sell a product.

(Roose 2019)

Such churches may technically be framed as Christian, yet they have little incentive to develop social bridging capital with other Pentecostal churches, lest they lose adherents to other churches or to other more established churches in more formal institutional settings, which are governed by elected committees.

Hazleton: Small town America meets neoliberalism and globalisation

Hazleton is emblematic of the intersection of causal factors shaping the appeal of the new demagogues. A once proud, heavily unionised, and religious blue-collar city, the decline of coal mining and subsequent population decline saw Hazleton face an existential crisis of sorts. Responses to the crisis evolved from a grassroots campaign to make the city more competitive in the 1950s, which led to the adoption of nothing short of full-scale neoliberal economic measures in the 1960s and 1970s. Economic development initiatives produced industrial estates offering primarily minimum wage, non-unionized employment. As unions packed up and left, so too did the Catholic Church, which employed its own form of austerity and fiscal conservatism, closed down churches, and sold Church properties. Traditional blue-collar masculinity, which was formed across a variety of European migrant experiences grounded in union solidarity and faith, took, it might be argued, a fatal blow.

The town's population changed in the late twentieth century in the wake of large-scale chain migration of largely Hispanic communities from New York, New Jersey, the Dominican Republic, Mexico, and Puerto Rico. Immigrants were drawn to the city at a time when local business leaders were desperate to boost the population size and, arguably, the pool of minimum wage labour necessary to continue to attract companies, such as Amazon, to the region. In the absence of any effective mechanism to integrate these primarily young, aspirational immigrants into the town, Hazleton gave rise to a 'Trump before Trump'. Louie Barletta, who to this day remains a trusted confidant of US President Donald Trump, was one of the most significant early populists to shape American responses to immigration. Hazleton's Ordinance 2006–18 (Illegal Immigration Relief Act) might have been defeated in the courts, at a significant cost to both social cohesion and the city, but its profound negative impact on the political landscape lives on. Other US cities adopted the platform, and it was a foundation of US President Donald Trump's approach.

Trade unions in Hazleton remain few and far between. Religion, however, is flourishing, particularly amongst the Pentecostal churches that thrive off individualisation in communities. While the empty shells of churches are highly visible across the Hazleton city landscape, the Pentecostal churches remain largely invisible, functioning behind shopfronts and in homes. Other churches adapted and evolved. The Irish St Gabriel's now has a primarily Hispanic congregation. Other churches, such as the Baptists, have primarily white and wealthier congregants. Despite ostensibly sharing the same Christian God, religion has failed to be a critical salve for the city's divisions.

Hazleton remains a city that is deeply divided, in particular between the largely Hispanic and Democratic-voting 'downtown' and the surrounding Republican-

and Trump-supporting areas. The downtown is currently the focus of efforts to develop a historical district (with as of yet unknown impacts on the predominantly Latino population living in the area) and to attract new forms of business investment beyond the factories, which are confined largely to industrial parks. Yet these efforts, because they seek to use tax-free economic zones, may well be of limited benefit to broader social cohesion and for funding local services. Hazleton is a city where solidaristic bonds have been replaced by neoliberal individualism. It is a city where the older generation of white blue-collar workers visibly display anger, anxiety, and alienation. They blame the most visible dimension of what, to them, constitutes the problem: Hispanic migrants. The younger generation of Hazletonians, who have grown up with everyday multiculturalism in their schools, workplaces, and streets, may well be less inclined to the racially charged scapegoating adopted by their elders. More broadly, efforts by groups, such as the Hazleton Integration project, have sought to break down such barriers, though the ultimate solution may well be time.

Even with time, the younger generation, entrenched as they are in the self-replicating logic of the neoliberal individualisation of workplaces and economic opportunity, may well be likely to remain attracted to messaging like that used by Trump in his 2016 campaign (and posturing for his 2020 re-election campaign). They may be drawn to the emphasis on rugged masculinity, faith, and economic prosperity, messages unlikely to be fathomed or recaptured by the identity-politics-driven Democrats in the foreseeable future. The mainstreaming of populist demagoguery appears here to stay.

More broadly, Pennsylvania has deep-seated traditions of tolerance, industrial innovation, scientific advancement, and entrepreneurialism grounded in the marriage of a fundamental concern with the human condition and notions of the common good. Hazleton, as a contemporary manifestation of neoliberal individualism and economic approaches, would do well to look to this heritage to map its way forward.

Post-script: Hazleton and the COVID-19 pandemic

In April 2020, Hazleton was suffering possibly the highest per capita coronavirus infection rate in the state of Pennsylvania. One possible contributing factor likely to be pointed to by those locals opposed to Latino migration to the town was the high mobility of Latino residents, who commuted between Hazleton and New York City or fled New York City, the worst hit metropolis in the world, although its significance was played down by local politicians (Thompson 2020). Other factors made transmission more likely, such as the warehouses and meat processing plants in the industrial area of the town or the businesses with precariously employed workers and limited or non-existent paid-leave entitlements, which made employees more likely to turn up to work unwell (Thompson 2020). In other cases, workplaces may have pressured employees to attend work irrespective of the risk (PennLive.com 2020). If Hazleton is indicative of the intersection of neoliberal economic policies, immigration, and the challenges facing male blue-collar workers in the United States, the city is also indicative of the intersection of neoliberal economic policies, immigration, and the COVID-19 pandemic. Hazleton's extremely high rates of infection are a clear sign that, despite best efforts to develop the city, what is required is a greater focus on working people rather than economic development.

References

Adams, A.M. & Emmerich, C.J. (1990). William Penn and the American Heritage of Religious Liberty. *Journal of Law and Religion*, 8 (1–2), 57–70.

Bauer, B. (2019). Trump is the Founders' Worst Nightmare: Once in the Oval Office, a Demagogue Can Easily Stay There. *The New York Times*, 2 December.

Berlinerblau, J. (2019). Donald J. Trump, the White Evangelicals, and Martin Luther: A Hypothesis. *Interpretation: A Journal of Bible and Theology*, 73 (1), 18–30.

Bradlee, B., Jr. (2018). *The Forgotten People: How the People of One Pennsylvania County Elected Donald Trump and Changed America*. New York: Little, Brown, and Company.

Clinton, H. (2016). Live from Philadelphia: Pre-Election Night Rally. *Hillary Clinton YouTube*, 7 November. Retrieved from https://www.youtube.com/watch?v=7JMlTpYFtkw.

Costa, R. & Johnson, J. (2016). Evangelical Leader Jerry Falwell Jr. Endorses Trump. *The Washington Post*, 26 January.

De Geer, S. (1927). The American Manufacturing Belt. *Geografiska Annaler*, 9 (4), 233–359.

Devinatz, V.G. (2017). Donald Trump, George Wallace, and the White Working Class. *Labor Studies Journal*, 42 (3), 233–238.

Downtown Hazleton Alliance for Progress. (2016). Keystone Main Street Developments. *Downtown Hazleton Alliance for Progress*. Retrieved from https://www.downtownhazleton.org/invest.html.

Dublin, T. & Licht, W. (2000). Gender and Economic Decline: The Pennsylvania Anthracite Region, 1920–1970. *The Oral History Review*, 27 (1), 81–97.

FitzGerald, F. (2018). *The Evangelicals: The Struggle to Shape America*. New York: Simon & Schuster.

Greater Hazleton CAN-DO. (2019). *Greater Hazleton CAN-DO Website*. Retrieved from https://www.google.com/search?client=safari&rls=en&q=Hazleton+can-do&ie=UTF-8&oe=UTF-8.

Hazleton, PA. (2006). *Ordinance 2006–18 (Illegal Immigration Relief Act (IIRA) Ordinance)*.

Ipsos, Roose, J.M., & Turner, B.S. (2019). Global Masculinity Index Survey Developed and Conducted by Ipsos Public Affairs, Joshua Roose, and Bryan S. Turner. June.

Johnson, P.E. (2017). The Art of Masculine Victimhood: Donald Trump's Demagoguery. *Women's Studies in Communication*, 40 (3), 229–250.

Kelly, R.E. (2016) Donald Trump: Straight from Plato's Nightmares. *The Interpreter*. Lowy Institute. Retrieved from https://www.lowyinstitute.org/the-interpreter/donald-trump-straight-platos-nightmares.

Liberman, M. (2015). Trump's Eloquence. *Language Log*, 5 August. Retrieved from https://languagelog.ldc.upenn.edu/nll/?p=20492.

Longazel, J. (2017). *Undocumented Fears: Immigration and the Politics of Divide and Conquer in Hazleton, Pennsylvania*. Philadelphia, PA: Temple University Press.

Longazel, J. & Fleury-Steiner, B. (2011). Exploiting Borders: The Political Economy of Local Backlash against Undocumented Immigrants. *Chicana/O-Latina Law Review*, 30, 43–64.

Martinez, J. & Smith, G.A. (2016). How the Faithful Voted: A Preliminary 2016 Analysis. *Pew Research Center*, 9 November.

McElwee, C.F. (2018). Chain Migration Comes to Hazleton. *City Journal*, Spring. Retrieved from https://www.city-journal.org/html/chain-migration-comes-hazleton-15832.html.

McQuarrie, M. (2016). Trump and the Revolt of the Rust Belt. *Blogs.lse.ac.uk*. Retrieved from https://blogs.lse.ac.uk/usappblog/2016/11/11/23174.

Morris, K.R. (2012). Theological Sources of William Penn's Concept of Religious Toleration. *Quaker Studies*, 16 (2), 190–212.

National Museum of American History. (2019). Duplan 'Martine' Silks. *Smithsonian*. Retrieved from https://americanhistory.si.edu/collections/object-groups/duplan-martine-silks.

New York Times. (1972). 9 Present or Former Employees of Kawecki Berylco Industries Inc, Found to be Suffering from Chronic Berylliosis. *The New York Times*, 29 October.

New York Times. (1973). Members of Oil, Chem, and Atomic Workers International Union are Striking Kawecki Berylco Plant near Hazleton. *The New York Times*, 18 March.

New York Times. (2018). An Extremely Detailed Map of the 2016 Election. *The New York Times*, 25 July. Retrieved on 20 September 2019.

Penn, W. (1669 [1872]). *No Cross No Crown: A Discourse Shewing the Nature and Discipline of The Holy Cross of Christ*. Philadelphia, PA.

PennLive.com. (2016). Bruce Springsteen is Voting for Hillary Clinton: Here's Why. *PennLive YouTube*, 7 November. Retrieved from https://www.youtube.com/watch?v=5kK2OwNf4l4.

PennLive.com. (2020). How Did Hazleton Become an Epicenter for the Coronavirus? *PennLive YouTube*, 19 April. Retrieved from https://www.youtube.com/watch?v=RtXxXrnuBDw.

Quinlan, M. (2013). Precarity and Workplace Well-Being: A General Review. In T. Nichols & D. Walters (Eds.), *Safety or Profit?: International Studies in Governance, Change, and the Work Environment* (pp. 17–32). New York: Baywood.

Roose, J.M. (2017). Citizenship, Masculinities, and Political Populism: Preliminary Considerations in the Context of Contemporary Social Challenges. In J. Mackert & B. Turner (Eds.), *The Transformation of Citizenship* (pp. 56–76). Abingdon, UK: Routledge.

Roose, J.M. (2019). Research Interviews Conducted by the Author, November–December.

Shackel, P.A. (2018). *Remembering Lattimer: Labor, Migration, and Race*. Chicago, IL: University of Illinois Press.

Shklar, J.N. (1990). *American Citizenship: The Quest for Inclusion*. Cambridge, MA: Harvard University Press.

Steil, J. & Ridgley, J. (2012). 'Small-town Defenders': The Production of Citizenship and Belonging in Hazleton, Pennsylvania. *Environment and Planning D: Society and Space*, 30 (6), 1028–1045.

Sullivan, R.D. (2019). Two U.S. Churches: One is Closing Down Parishes, the Other is Standing-room Only. *America: The Jesuit Review*, 19 April. Retrieved from https://www.americamagazine.org/faith/2019/04/19/two-us-churches-one-closing-down-parishes-other-standing-room-only.

Thompson, C. (2020). Some Blame Latinos for Hazleton's COVID-19 Outbreak, Echoing Divisions that Once Roiled City. *PennLive*. 20 April.

Trump, D. (2015). Announcement of Candidacy. *Factbase*. New York. 16 June. Retrieved from: https://factba.se/trump.

Trump, D. (2016a). Campaign Speech. Video recording. *Factbase*. Vandalia, OH. 12 March. Retrieved from: https://factba.se/trump.

Trump, D. (2016b). Campaign Speech. Video recording. *Factbase*. Wilkes-Barre, PA. 25 April. Retrieved from: https://factba.se/trump.

Trump, D. (2016c). Speech to Faith and Freedom Coalition. Video recording. *C-Span*. Washington, DC. 10 June. Retrieved from: https://factba.se/trump.

Trump, D. (2016d). Campaign Speech. Video recording. *Factbase*. Scranton, PA. 27 July. Retrieved from: https://factba.se/trump.

Trump, D. (2016e) Campaign Speech. Video recording. *Factbase*. Scranton, PA. 7 November. Retrieved from: https://factba.se/trump.

United States Census Bureau. (2019). Quick Facts: Hazleton City, Pennsylvania. *US Census*. Retrieved from https://www.census.gov/quickfacts/hazletoncitypennsylvania.

7

WESTERN ISLAMIC STATE FOREIGN FIGHTERS AND JIHADI MASCULINITY

Introduction

The rapid rise and fall of the Islamic State Movement was one of the most significant developments in global politics this century and, in the context of Islamic politics, in the past thousand years. The declaration of the *Khilafah* (Caliphate) on 29 June 2014 by Islamic State leader Abu Bakr al-Baghdadi (a former detainee at Abu Ghraib) served as a beacon to Salafi jihadists worldwide and signalled the emergence of the first such entity since the fall of the Ottoman Empire almost 90 years earlier. Al-Baghdadi stated that it was the intent of the Islamic State to conquer Rome and Spain (past historical ambitions for Islamic armies), and he subsequently urged Muslims to conduct *hijrah* (to immigrate) to the Islamic State, which was centred in the Syrian city of Raqqa. Despite depictions that associated the Islamic State with medieval barbarity, at its height it constituted a profoundly modern transnational global space. An estimated 30,000 men and women heeded the call from around the world, including up to 6,000 from Western Muslim communities in the United Kingdom, Europe, North America, and Australia.

Despite its occasional appeals to altruistic sentiment grounded in the oppression of Muslims, the Islamic State immediately became synonymous with extreme acts of savagery, destruction, atrocities, and the rape and forced marriage of women in conquered territories, most notably women of the Yazidi community, a monotheistic, Kurdish-speaking people native to northern Mesopotamia. The United Nations labelled violence against the Yazidi as genocide (United Nations Human Rights Council 2016). It very quickly became clear to intelligence agencies, scholars, and the world's media alike that Western Muslims and, in particular, Western Muslim men, including Australians who had migrated to join the Islamic State, were heavily involved in these activities (Edwards 2015).

The Australian Government estimated that, as of December 2018, more than 230 Australian Muslims had travelled to the war zone, up to 95 had been killed, and 110 remained in the region. Importantly, the passports of over 250 Australian Muslims were confiscated by authorities on suspicion they were making plans to join the Islamic State (Australian Government 2018). There have been a total of seven Islamic State-inspired attacks in Australia since 2015. A further eight plots were intercepted by authorities, including planned attacks on law enforcement and churches. Why has a small but committed group of primarily young Australian Muslim men travelled halfway around the world to join the Islamic State movement? Why have they sought to commit violent acts at home in the movement's name? Whilst some may have been genuinely motivated by altruism, it also may be that Islamic State recruitment narratives, which emphasise violence, have a particular resonance with at least some young men in local communities.

It must be noted from the outset that the Friday, 15 March 2019 terror attack on a mosque in Christchurch, New Zealand, that killed 51 Muslims and wounded another 49 was carried out by an Australian, Brenton Tarrant. It reveals some insights into the intense hostility evident amongst extremists on both sides of political discourse about the place of Muslims in the Australia and the West.

This chapter focuses on Australian-born Muslim men who joined or attempted to join the Islamic State movement between 2014 and 2017, the peak of the movement's existence on the international stage. Like other chapters, context is important. A brief historic overview of Australian multiculturalism and Islam is necessary, as is a consideration of literature on Muslim masculinities. The chapter then considers how and why the Islamic State movement may be considered to constitute a populist demagogic actor before analysing Islamic State recruitment narratives. Whilst interviews with Islamic State fighters were not possible, information sourced from Australian fighters, including targeted recruitment videos, blogs, social media posts, and a small number of interviews with family members provides a compelling insight into key factors shaping attraction to the Islamic State and, as importantly, provides a base for comparison with other men examined in this book.

A brief history of the white Australia era, 1901–1973

Before exploring the dimensions of contemporary Australia, it is vital to recognise the unbroken connection of Aboriginal and Torres Strait Islanders with the land for over 50,000 years and the history of theft and dispossession that followed white settlement in 1788. The nation we know as Australia is and always will be indigenous land. This section of the book, however, focuses on policies implemented after the Federation of Australia in 1901.

As a settler society geographically isolated from the British mainland and Anglosphere, notions of white superiority and a 'paranoid nationalism' (Hage 2003) have been dominant factors shaping the national culture throughout Australian history. Anne Aly and David Walker assert that:

Australia's history is marked by expressions of anxiety about invasion and the destruction of Australian culture. This culture is grounded in the tension between Australia's history as a European settler society and its geo-political position on the south-eastern fringe of Asia ... From the 1880s 'peril' has been a recurrent theme in Australia's history.

(Aly & Walker 2007: 204)

These anxieties led to the institutionalisation of xenophobia. The Immigration Restriction Act (1901), known colloquially as the 'White Australia Policy', effectively closed Australia to further immigration from Muslim and non-white nations. Geoffrey Stokes argues that 'White Australia' 'provided the official foundation of national identity and its exclusionary principles complemented other components of the Australian settlement, such as Wage Arbitration and Industry Protection' (Stokes 2004: 8).

Denied the right to become Australian citizens, many Muslims returned home, whilst others remained, often with their Aboriginal or Australian wives who had converted to Islam (Kabir 2005: 74). As the children of these marriages moved into adulthood in a social sphere characterised by racial intolerance and fear, many are believed to have shed their cultural 'baggage' and, hence, the number of identifiable Muslims in Australia started to decline from the beginning of the twentieth century, supplemented only by the arrival of acceptable white Muslim Albanians from Europe (Stevens 1989: 319; Jones 1993: 78).

The first Australian census of 1911 lists almost 4,000 Muslims. In addition to the already strong application of the White Australia Policy, a quota restricting non-British migrants was established in 1928 with the effect of limiting even the Albanian intake. Until the end of the Second World War, numbers fluctuated at between approximately 2,000–4,000 until the influx of refugees from Europe in 1947 (ABS 1911; ABS 1921; ABS 1922; ABS 1947; Omar & Allen 1996: 23). At this point, the number of Muslims in Australia was 2,704 or 0.04% of the national population. As a religion, Islam had virtually no representative influence with Australian governments at any level and, should policies have remained the same, any influence would likely have declined further over future generations.

In the First World War Turkey, a Muslim nation and the political centre of the Ottoman Empire (then the protector of Islam's holy places), was declared an enemy nation by Britain and Australia. In 1914 all Turkish citizens (as well as Germans and Austrians) in Australia were declared enemy subjects, subjected to surveillance, and required to report to police stations weekly (Kabir 2005: 96–97). Turkey's enemy status had wider implications for all Muslims in Australia, as the Sultan of Turkey, Abdul Hamid, was considered the temporal and spiritual leader of the Muslim world. Kabir argues that 'for some Muslims the news that Australia was at war with Turkey was shocking, and they considered Australia's involvement to be "horrendous"' (Kabir 2005: 100). Whilst it must be unequivocally understood that the vast majority of Muslims in Australia complied with the authorities (and many, in fact, pledged allegiance to the British Empire), one incident of note – a religiously motivated act of terrorism against civilians – did occur, which caused authorities to take significantly greater notice of the potential for enemy 'aliens' to attack Australia from within the nation's own borders. On New Year's Day morning 1915 in Broken Hill, NSW, two Muslim men, one Afghan and one Indian, ambushed a crowded picnic train carrying 1,200 passengers. They killed four civilians and wounded seven. Evidence revealed that one of the men, Gool Mahomed, had left Australia to fight with the Turkish Army, which at the time served the Ottoman Empire and Caliphate, on religious grounds. He had returned to Australia in 1912. The other man, Mullah Abdullah, was an imam to local Afghan cameleers and was noted for his fiery temperament (Stevens 2005). Suicide letters from both revealed that faith was the main inspiration for their actions.

During the Second World War, several Australian-born Muslims of Albanian and Javanese descent served in the Australian Army. As Kabir notes, 'though some Muslims in Australia may have been different in race and colour, their involvement in the war put them on an equal footing with ordinary Australians. Islam was never a criterion for discrimination during the Second World War' (Kabir 2006: 202). Service and, in some cases, death in service by Muslim Australians in the Second World War may be considered a little recognised, yet important, Muslim contribution to Australian society that signifies a commitment and loyalty to the nation and its people.

Between the end of the war in 1945 and the end of the White Australia Policy, the Australian Muslim population increased markedly as Turkish Cypriot Muslims and other 'white' Muslim refugees from Europe were accorded entry. The first Islamic societies were established locally and nationally in the 1950s. The Islamic Society of Victoria, an ethnically diverse society that had representation from the Arabic, Turkish, Yugoslav, and Indian Muslim communities, was established in 1957 (Cleeland 2001: 27). In 1958 the Migration Act was revised, allowing first Lebanese then skilled Turkish Muslims entry to Australia. By the time of the 1971 Census, the influx of refugees from Europe combined with Turkish and Lebanese migrants contributed to a significant increase in the Muslims population, which rose to 22,311.

It was not until December 1973 and the election of the Whitlam Labor government, after decades of Conservative rule, that the White Australia Policy was renounced and the official adoption of multiculturalism commenced. This would be the single greatest contributor to an increased and permanent Muslim presence in Australia.

Multicultural Australia, 1973–2001

The adoption of multiculturalism as official federal government policy signalled the biggest single shift in Australia's migration policy since European colonisation. It ushered in an influx of migrants from many non-English-speaking regions around the world. As official policy, multiculturalism accepted difference and promoted cultural and racial diversity. This period was one of immense growth in various

Muslim Australian communities. Representative bodies were consolidated at a national and state level as well as along ethnic lines. The Australian Federation of Islamic Councils (AFIC) was formed in 1976 with funding from Saudi Arabia. The AFIC increased its wealth through its authority to certify halal meat exports. Between 1972 and 1996, several major political issues impacted upon Muslim Australians and resulted in often severe discrimination by various segments of society. These included the Iranian Revolution of 1979; the American hostage crisis in Iran (1979–1981); terrorist attacks by Arab and Muslim groups in the Middle East related to the Arab-Israeli conflict; the bombing of a flight over Lockerbie, Scotland (1988); violent protests against Salmon Rushdie's *The Satanic Verses* (1988–1989); the First Gulf War (1990–1991); and consistent resistance to Muslim Australians building mosques within Australia throughout the whole period (Kabir 2005).

It is important to appreciate the significance of political and cultural developments in the period between 1973 and 2001, as they directly impacted the experiences of contemporary Australian Muslims. For a period of 23 years, multiculturalism was officially adopted and celebrated, particularly under the Labor governments of Robert Hawke (1983–1992) and Paul Keating (1992–1996). The policy faced its first significant challenge with the election of the Howard Liberal-National coalition government on 2 March 1996. This government arguably had the single greatest influence on Muslim consciousness in Australia because it strategically and deliberately drew attention to Muslim communities in order to gain symbolic and political capital.

Historian Robert Manne argues that it is impossible to grasp the Howard government and the positions it occupied without understanding the two 'peaceful revolutions' that profoundly reshaped the long-established Australian way of life (Manne 2004: 3–5). The first was a 'cultural revolution' brought about by the end of the White Australia Policy, the adoption of multiculturalism in 1973, and the increased acknowledgment of indigenous land rights through the recognition of native title in common law from 1992. The second revolution, according to Manne, was economic and involved the replacement of Keynesian and Deakinite (protectionist) economic principles with neoliberal free-market ideology. Extensive decentralisation and deregulation transformed Australia from one of the most protected economies to one of the least protected in the Western world (Manne 2004: 3–5). The economic shift echoed developments across the United Kingdom and United States. The combined impact of the two revolutions was powerful: 'Taken together, these revolutions threatened to wash away a great deal of what many Australians had unselfconsciously come to regard as an almost natural and even permanent way of life' (Manne 2004: 4–5).

From 1972 Australia went almost overnight from an insular, largely monocultural, and protected nation to one that was open to the world and the circumstances that prevailed within it. The 'field of power' dominated by White Australian cultural and political hegemony was in flux. The John Howard-led Liberal-National coalition sought to exploit the growing pains of Australian cultural politics and promised a cessation of many culturally-oriented policies that were portrayed as benefitting 'elites' at the expense of the (very broadly defined) 'Aussie battler' (Roose 2016). Andrew Markus argues:

> The conservative campaign sort acceptance for the return of an old ordering of national priorities, an old way of seeing and speaking. Its major themes were concerned with the folly of existing government policy, represented as a betrayal of the national interest and an appeasement of minorities.
>
> (Markus 2001: x)

This platform delivered the Liberal-National coalition a resounding victory in the 1996 federal election. The election of Independents Pauline Hanson and Graeme Richardson, both outspoken critics of multiculturalism, further underpinned the electoral mood of large parts of the Australian constituency at the time. Howard's tacit refusal to quickly condemn Hanson's now infamous maiden speech to Federal Parliament, which railed against Asian immigration and was considered by many to constitute open racism, loaned it an air of official credibility and signalled the approach that typified his government

To understand Howard's motivations, it is necessary to understand how neoconservatism intersected with the 'new racism'. Speaking in 2006, Howard expressed his admiration for and aspiration to live up to the examples of Ronald Reagan and Margaret Thatcher, the new right leaders of the 1980s (Howard 2006). As discussed in Chapter 2, Reagan and Thatcher were key to the introduction of neoliberalism as state policy across Western contexts.

A further series of events over the next several years enabled the Howard government to craft a campaign of divisiveness between 'us' and 'them'. The Howard government skilfully portrayed itself as the 'Aussie battler' against those perceived as having vested privilege. In 1999 the issue of asylum seekers (many of them Muslim) entering Australia came to the fore of the national agenda. Manne asserts that, in the history of the Howard government, 'no issue more sharply divided opinion in Australia – between those who were increasingly coming to be called the "elites" and the "mainstream" – than the government's treatment of asylum seekers' (Manne 2004: 35). It was during this era that the seeds of populist far-right Australian politicians, including Pauline Hanson, were sown, providing a platform for otherwise politically unacceptable views.

From 9/11 to the Islamic State movement

The '9/11' terrorist attacks on 11 September 2001 reverberated around the Western world. Australia was amongst the first nations to commit soldiers to the US invasion of the Muslim-majority nations of Afghanistan in October 2001 and Iraq in March 2003, which caused considerable consternation amongst many Australians, including Australian Muslims. Religion replaced nationality as a defining basis of whether an individual will become a potential threat. The two often were conflated. The emphasis upon Islam as a key contributor to terrorism reached its peak in the aftermath of the July 7/7 bombings in London, when British-born suicide bombers raised the issue of the loyalty of British and, more broadly, 'Western' Muslims. In an interview a week after the 7/7 attacks, Prime Minister Howard noted, 'We shouldn't complacently imagine that there aren't potentially suicide bombers in this country' (BBC 2005). The 2005 Anti-Terrorism Legislation Act was immediately rushed through Federal Parliament and was clearly aimed at addressing the Salafi Jihadist terrorist threat. Indeed, these laws would be utilised for the first time in police operations in Sydney and Melbourne in 2006 (and later 2009) that resulted in the arrest and conviction of Australian Muslims for planning terrorism.

Whilst physical internment of Muslim Australians was both unlikely and, as a result of the impact of multiculturalism, virtually impossible, arguably the Australian Government and conservative media commentators sought to intern Muslim Australians socially and politically through an intense campaign surrounding the manufactured concept of 'Australian values' and demands that Australian Muslims subscribe and show loyalty (Roose 2016).

The Cronulla Riots on 11 December 2005 in Sydney revealed the extent to which 'Middle Eastern' and 'Muslim' had become conflated in Australian discourse and highlighted the effects of sustained government and media attacks upon Australian Muslim populations. After a series of disputes in the weeks prior, over 5,000 primarily white Australian rioters attacked men of Middle Eastern appearance, resulting in a spiral of violence. Scott Poynting proposes that the Cronulla Riots and the violence used were directly linked to the policies pursued by the Howard government:

> Thus, if the state assaults, harasses, and vilifies Muslims as the enemy in the war on terror and thereby terrorises whole communities, then perhaps white-thinking citizens feel justified in personally attacking this enemy wherever they might encounter it ... The Arab 'other' has morphed into the Muslim 'other'.
> *(Poynting 2006: 88)*

The experiences of Cronulla indisputably had 'deep and lasting socio-political and emotional ramifications on the Australian national conscience' (Bliuc et al. 2011: 2). The images of mobs of white youths bashing brown-skinned young men served as a constant reminder of the threat Australian Muslims faced should they not 'know their place'.

In subsequent years Australian federal governments sought out 'moderate' Muslim voices for inclusion in various advisory councils and projects. The concept of 'moderate Islam' is heavily contested within Western Muslim communities. Islamists frame it as a corruption of a 'true' uncompromising Islam grounded in literal interpretation of text. 'Moderate' and more mainstream Muslim communities claim that wider Western and Islamic values are compatible, and Muslims can practice their faith uncorrupted as a minority. Many of these voices were from an older generation of Muslim leadership that was skilled at multicultural claim making. The door was largely shut to Australian-born Muslims, resulting in their further alienation from participation in formal political processes to achieve social change (Roose 2016).

These divisions, largely at the periphery of the 'silent majority' of Muslims and focussed primarily on building upward social and economic trajectories for Muslim families (Akbarzadeh & Roose 2011), continued into the new decade and became particularly pronounced in the aftermath of the violent 'Innocence of Muslims' protests in Sydney in September 2012.

The 2012 innocence of Muslims protests: A key turning point

Intra-community debates about the question of what it is to be an Australian Muslim are usually conducted behind a veneer of unity and kept either in-house or within online forums. Australian Muslims (outside of academia or activist organisations, such as Hizb ut-Tahrir) seek to make political distinctions between Muslims, argue about the place of Islam in the Australian public sphere, and publicly promote these perspectives. This changed with the release of a highly polarising film titled *Innocence of Muslims*. In September 2012, an Arabic-language trailer for the film was released through YouTube and almost immediately sparked international protests. The film was considered blasphemous and insulting by many Muslims. There was arguably little, if any, public indication that the protests would spread to Australia. However, on the evening of 15 September 2012, a protest demonstration by approximately 300 Muslims developed into violent clashes with the New South Wales police in the busy Pitt Street Mall and Hyde Park in Sydney.

Images of the unrest dominated national headlines across news and social media They depicted young, muscled, and bearded Muslim men wearing a mix of traditional garments and Western street-wear clashing violently with predominantly white, young, uniformed men from the New South Wales police force. Media coverage offered a visually spectacular example of the apparent threat posed by Australian Muslims (Roose 2013). Muslim women were also pictured. One notable example was of a woman who allowed a child to wave a placard calling for the beheading of those who insult the Prophet (Gardiner 2012). The protests were immediately condemned by senior representatives of Muslim communities in Sydney and throughout Australia as well as politicians from across the political spectrum. The Mufti of Australia, Dr. Ibrahim Abu Mohammad, condemned actions of 'violence and lawlessness' (Abu Mohammad 2012). At the same time, a group of 14 major Australian Islamic organisations, which joined together to condemn *Innocence of Muslims*, stated that such insults 'do not provide individuals with the right to react violently and retaliate' (Box & Gosper 2012). However, it became increasingly clear that a sharp division existed between hard-line Salafi elements in the communities and the established leadership.

Islamic State recruiters and key figures, including Khaled Sharrouf and Mohamed Elomar, were amongst those arrested for violence at the protest. Other groups included the 'Sixth Pillar' (i.e., jihad) linked to Sydney preacher Sheikh Feiz Mohammed. His DVD lectures, known as the *Death Series*, preach the centrality of violent jihad, martyrdom, and killing infidels. They featured in a 2007 BBC documentary, *Undercover Mosque*, which revealed that the videos were being sold in Birmingham mosques. Mohammed's lectures were also influential on Tamerlan Tsarnaev, one of the two 2013 Boston Marathon bombers.

The violent 2012 protest in Sydney, which featured a number of highly influential Islamic State Movement recruiters and foreign fighters before the movement grew into the powerful, albeit short-lived, force it became, is indicative of the environment created in Australia by a mix of highly polarised political rhetoric, securitisation, and Islamist organisation in the years leading up to 2014–2017.

Islamic State recruitment material

The methodology of this chapter, by necessity, differs from the previous two chapters. It was not possible to conduct ethnographic research with Islamic State foreign fighters or their supporters closer to home. As such, the chapter draws on a wide array of data to enable a broad comparison with the other two case studies focussed on religion, masculinity, and populism in the United Kingdom and United States. Pertinent information was sourced from Australian Bureau of Statistics (ABS) data from the national census, which is conducted every five years, most recently in 2016 (ABS 2016), and the Ipsos-Roose-Turner survey, with a specific emphasis on Muslim Australian responses in comparison to wider community responses (Ipsos et al. 2019). A Linguistic Inquiry and Word Count (LIWC) Analysis was conducted on Islamic State recruitment materials, including issues of *Dabiq* magazine (5 July 2014–31 July 2016) (ISIS 2014–2016) and *Rumiyah* magazine (5 September 2016–9 September 2017) (ISIS 2016–2017). In total, the analysis looked at 28 PDF editions of the two magazines, which totalled 720,314 words.

The magazines presented a particular data analysis challenge. LIWC software, targeted as it is at English-language texts, missed some important dimensions of the publications' Arabic vocabulary. Islamic State magazines and videos have a distinct discursive and linguistic repertoire that fuses colloquial Arabic; classical Islamic Arabic, which is often spelt differently (depending upon the author); and other idiosyncratic framing and structures, which are not found in standard English-language texts. Finally, the data was supplemented with recruitment videos featuring Australian fighters, their blogs, and some interviews with family members conducted in late 2019 to provide a holistic perspective (Roose 2019).

The small sample size of Muslim Australians in the Ipsos survey (Ipsos et al. 2019) made it difficult to draw wider conclusions about Australian Muslims, so it was excluded. The 2016 ABS Australian census data is referenced in its place (ABS 2016). While this makes it difficult to make direct comparisons to the other case studies, broader insights drawn from the analysis are comparable.

Demographic background

Much has been written, particularly in the media, about the socio-economic base of support for ISIS. While Muslims in France, Belgium, Germany, and the UK face significantly greater socio-economic challenges, very little detailed evidence exists, in part due to the lack of compulsory national censuses. Compared to its European counterparts, Australia has the advantage of a census conducted every five years that captures a wide variety of data, including religion statistics. Given Australia's very high per capita contributions to Islamic State foreign fighters, the census information is particularly useful.

Australia's highly diverse Muslim population grew exponentially in the twenty-first century. The population almost doubled between 2001 and 2011, rising from 281,576 to 476,292 (ABS 2001; ABS 2011). In 2016 it stood at 604,240 (ABS 2016). Despite significant diversity, Australian-born Muslims constitute the largest subgroup, representing 36.4 per cent of the Muslim population (ABS 2016).

Significantly, in 2016 at the peak of Islamic State recruitment, 70.3 per cent of all Australian-born Muslims were under the age of 20 (ABS 2016), compared to 31.35 per cent for the wider Australian community. This means that, at the time, seven out of ten young Australian Muslims had grown up in a hostile social climate defined by securitisation, media scrutiny, and broad social hostility. In comparison, just 12.12 per cent of overseas-born Muslims were under the age of 20 (ABS 2016). The data indicates that Australian-born Muslims were much more likely to be a target of Islamic State recruitment efforts. To understand this further, it is important to grasp the dimensions of masculinity, identity, and religiosity amongst Australian Muslims.

Muslim masculinities

In comparison to Muslim masculinities in Muslim-majority nations, research in Western contexts has been reasonably consistent in demonstrating that Muslim men occupy subordinated masculinities; and, through the practice of their faith, they either carve a space in wider society, or they directly challenge hegemonic (i.e., white) masculinities. It is an area of study that has grown exponentially.

Studies reveal that masculinity, particularly among the most disempowered young Muslim men, is viewed as performative, emphasising a 'hyper' masculinity through displays of 'physicality' and 'toughness' (Archer 2001; Tabar 2007; Hopkins 2007; Hopkins 2009). Based on research with young Lebanese men in Sydney, Australia, Greg Noble argues that these displays are the result of a lack of 'honourable recognition' and a lack of respect from wider society; the interplay of masculinity and emotion are embedded in social structures of disempowerment (Noble 2007: 341). This form of masculinity binds them together and defines them against those withholding respect and 'injuring' them.

Humphrey and Islam view incidents of injury as 'moments of crisis which challenge self-identity and cultural life' (Humphrey & Islam 2002: 206). The actual instant at which the injury is received may be considered a pivotal moment for identity construction, where 'cultural meaning is up for grabs' (Humphrey & Islam 2002: 206). Young Muslim men, due to the intensity of the focus upon their very existence, could be considered very likely to bear the emotional scars of a society that simultaneously demands their integration and conformity to dominant white hegemonic values, while it discriminates against them on many levels (Roose 2016).

Hage asserts that in multicultural Australia young Muslims are simultaneously promised opportunities and denied them by institutionalised racism, leading to their systematic exclusion. Hage labels this social process as 'misinterpellation' (Hage 2011: 172). The formation of citizens as willing subjects of the state through their active subscription to normative values and the process of ideological recognition (Althusser's 'interpellation') is corrupted by institutional racism and broader social hostility. This is particularly the case in a multicultural society that makes a compact with its citizens that, irrespective of ethnicity, culture, or religion, they can fulfil their personal aspirations and, simultaneously, belong. Recognition that this compact is a false promise designed to subdue, rather than fulfil, has considerable personal consequences:

> When the nation hails you 'hey you citizen', everything in you leads you to recognise that it is you that is being hailed, but when you do say 'yes it is me', you experience the shock of the rejection where the very ideological grid that is inviting you in the nation expels you through the petty and not so petty acts of exclusion that racists engage in in their everyday lives.
>
> *(Hage 2011: 173)*

Hage argues that it is precisely at this point that a 'shattering' occurs, and the individual needs space to 'pick up the pieces' (Hage 2011: 172). It is here that Islam, as the anti-racism ideology *par excellence*, plays a part in the lives of young Western Muslims that multiculturalism has not been able to play. It both provides a social space of belonging and 'stand[s] opposite multiculturalism as a competing governmentality rather than a culture that can be governed by it' (Hage 2011: 172).

Islam is clearly a more salient feature of identity for many young Western Muslims as a result of negative or hostile discourse and social pressure. In this context, it is possible to speak of the '9/11 generation' – young men who have grown up and formed their identities as Muslims and Australians in a context defined by engrained social prejudice and often intense social surveillance. Whilst some grew up and achieved success in education, business, and the professions, others did not. They became angry, disenfranchised, and alienated from both the wider Australian and Muslim communities. They grew up believing in the existence of a war on Islam and Muslims.

Concomitant flow-on effects have impacted how Muslim men engage with their faith (Hopkins 2007: 1128). Many made it a primary political identity as a means to develop solidarity and agency in the face of immense pressure (Cesari

2004: 42; Mandaville 2002: 221). For many of those drawn to Islam on this basis, the highly prescriptive form of Islam known as Salafism is a particularly attractive proposition. It provides order, rigidity, and structure to those who feel disempowered. Salafism is associated with Wahabbism, 'a strict, puritanical form of Islam that emphasises literal interpretation of the Quran and the absolute oneness of God' (Esposito 2010: 75). Salafism requires an unerring commitment to following the literal, textualist interpretation of the Quran and, as such, may be considered anathematic to more traditional approaches within Sunni Islam, which focus upon arriving at a position based upon both analysis of local cultural context (*urf*) and jurisprudential analysis derived from one of the four main *madhhabs* (schools) of Sunni Islamic thought (Roose 2016). Salafist scholars draw inspiration from textualist scholars, including, but not limited to, Ibn Taymiyyah (explored in Chapter 3) and the work of Muhammad ibn Abd al-Wahhab (1703–1792).

The Islamic State as a populist movement

The veracity of the Islamic State's claims to statehood and its power to constitute a caliphate were fiercely debated, as were the movement's claims to Islamic legitimacy. These are beyond the scope of the book. Suffice it to say that, for a limited period of time, the Islamic State controlled vast tracts of land and possessed the institutions necessary to make a claim to statehood, including the collection of taxes and the provision of healthcare, education, and law enforcement. The Islamic State was ultimately found wanting in international legitimacy, and its claims to statehood were met with hostility from powerful enemies.

In a similar vein, the claim to Islamic legitimacy and the establishment of a caliphate by the archetypal demagogic figure, Abu Bakr al-Baghdadi, in 2014 were not baseless. They had considerable historic precedent. Whilst not often viewed through a populist paradigm, al-Baghdadi and, in particular, the recruitment arm of the Islamic State employed populist tactics that are common across many contexts, as outlined in Chapter 2. They mobilised people against 'corrupt elites' (leaders of the Muslim world), attacked migrants (minority Christians and other groups, such as the Yazidi), attacked women's rights, and promised an imagined national community comprised of the 'majority' (the Caliphate). Islamic State messages and recruitment narratives targeted the sense of deep frustration, anger, anxiety, and alienation evident in Western Muslim populations, fusing Islamist and populist rhetoric in equal parts to attract new recruits. *Dabiq* and *Rumiyah*, the Islamic State magazines, were particularly effective at disseminating these narratives specifically to Muslims across Western contexts between 2014 and 2017.

Gender references in Islamic State material

Male references constituted 87.04 per cent (2.47) of gender references in *Dabiq* and *Rumiyah*, compared to 12.96 per cent (0.32) for female gender references.

TABLE 7.1 Frequency of gender references in Islamic State recruitment material

Corpus	Male	Female
Gender references in Islamic State recruitment material	2.47	0.32

Source: *Dabiq* and *Rumiyah* magazines (ISIS 2014–2016, ISIS 2016–2017)

Text word count: 720,314 words (5 July 2014–9 September 2017)

It is evident that the framing of recruitment material was targeted specifically at men. However, as outlined below, contesting Western gender norms was also a key theme evident in the recruitment material.

Representations of men and women in Islamic State propaganda

Throughout the magazines men are primarily depicted as warriors and the heads of families. The most potent celebration of Islamic State masculinity and manhood is reserved for Jihadist obituaries, which are published across both the *Dabiq* and *Rumiyah* magazines.

The first edition of *Rumiyah* featured the obituary of Melbourne man Ezzit Raad. Raad lost his brother to cancer at the age of 23, which was a key catalyst for his attraction to Jihadism (Roose 2016). He completed his high school studies and was a qualified electrician. However, he was also involved in rebirthing stolen cars. An observant Muslim, he became involved with the Benbrika Jama'ah. Australia's first convicted terrorists belonged to the organisation. Raad was imprisoned at the age of 24 for terrorism offences. Upon his release, having no discernible career trajectory, he departed Australia to fight and, as it turns out, die with the Islamic State movement. The *Rumiyah* obituary, however, represented him in very different terms:

> From a young age, the chivalrous muhajir [warrior] refused to be subjugated by the shackles of humiliation and this perishing world. He chose, instead, to surrender his soul in obedience of his Lord and to wield the weapons of faith and honor in defiance of the kafir masses.
>
> *(ISIS 2016–2017:* Rumiyah *Issue 1, 14)*

In contrast to the veneration of men as righteous warriors, in Islamic State magazines the ideal woman provides support and safety to her husband and is as pious as possible. In a regular *Dabiq* magazine column titled 'To Our Sisters', the author exhorts: 'My sisters, be bases of support and safety for your husbands, brothers, fathers, and sons. Be advisors to them. They should find comfort and peace with you. Do not make things difficult for them' (ISIS 2014–2016: *Dabiq* Issue 7, 51).

Women in the Islamic State are particularly valued as mothers of the next generation of Islamic State fighters: 'As for you, O mother of lion cubs … And what will make you know what the mother of lion cubs is? She is the teacher of generations and the producer of men' (ISIS 2014–2016: *Dabiq* Issue 11, 41). The framing of women as belonging in the domestic sphere resonates strongly with textualist Christian perspectives on the role of women.

Women as slaves and prostitutes

Despite the reverence of women's reproductive role in the Caliphate, there remains room in Islamic State literature for masculinity to be reinforced through sexual enslavement. The ready dehumanisation, misogyny, and brutality of the Islamic State apparatus becomes clear through its attempt to justify the enslavement of Yazidi women, who are framed as the equivalent of prostitutes in the West:

> Are slave-girls whom we took by Allah's command better, or prostitutes – an evil you do not denounce – who are grabbed by quasi men in the lands of kufr where you live? A prostitute in your lands comes and goes, openly committing sin. She lives by selling her honor, within the sight and hearing of the deviant scholars from whom we don't hear even a faint sound. As for the slave-girl that was taken by the swords of men following the cheerful warrior … then her enslavement is in opposition to human rights and copulation with her is rape?! What is wrong with you? How do you make such a judgment?
>
> *(ISIS 2014–2016:* Dabiq *Issue 9, 48)*

Islamic State theology and literature allows for polygamy, and men take multiple wives. It is represented not as a sexual benefit to men, but as support for women who may otherwise be left unmarried:

> Indeed, the legislation of polygamy contains many wisdoms. Amongst them is that women are greater in number than men, who face many dangers and hardships in their lives, such as war, hazardous work, and disasters. Likewise, young men tend to prefer virgins and abstain from marrying widows and divorcees, so who then would look after this group of women? … Furthermore, Allah might afflict a woman with infertility, but instead of divorcing her Islam has permitted the man to marry another woman while keeping his infertile wife honored and supported.
>
> *(ISIS 2014–2016:* Dabiq *Issue 12, 20)*

Western women, perhaps unavailable to those who left to fight with the Islamic State, are readily dehumanised and portrayed as representative of the wider moral decay in Western life: 'The Western woman is encouraged to compete with men in the workplace, to display of her body what no man ever displays, and to be more promiscuous than any prostitute has ever been' (ISIS 2014–2016: *Dabiq* Issue 15, 20).

Such messages resonate with manosphere depictions of women as shamelessly exploiting sexuality to derail men from the righteous path. The Islamic State offers young Western men a reconstituted sense of themselves as virile, courageous, and righteous warriors, in contrast to the sense of subordination and humiliation they may experience in Western contexts at the hands of hegemonic masculinity defined by arrogance, unbelief, institutional racism, and the infliction of pain. Women are, indeed, honoured as wives and mothers, so long as they are pious and submissive. Western women, by contrast, are prostitutes. Men are framed as protectors of women and children (overlooking the justification for the sexual enslavement of non-Muslim women and children). In contrast to the involuntary celibate (incel) movement, which emerged at approximately the same time half a world away and emphasised victimhood and beta masculinity (Ging 2017), the Islamic State very clearly adopted extreme patriarchy and hyper-masculinity.

Emotional references in Islamic State recruitment material

In a comparison of emotional references, words communicating anger (1.32) were significantly more evident across all 28 Islamic State magazine editions in contrast to words communicating anxiety (.28) or sadness (0.28) (Table 7.2). In other words, Islamic State magazines were almost five times more likely to mobilise anger in their framing of issues than they were to use anxiety or sadness.

Anger in Islamic State recruitment material

Throughout Islamic State recruitment materials significant anger is directed at the West on two fronts. First, it is against Western political leadership and democracy (broadly defined) for their perceived aggression, for the injustices they perpetrate against Muslims, and for propping up regimes across the Muslim world.

These are recurrent themes throughout both *Dabiq* and *Rumiyah*. An article in *Dabiq* provides context for this present-focused anger:

> For nearly two years, Muslims in the lands of the *Khilāfah* have watched their beloved brothers, sisters, and children being relentlessly bombed by crusader warplanes. The scenes of carnage, of blood and limbs scattered in the streets,

TABLE 7.2 Frequency of emotional tone (anger, anxiety, sadness) in Islamic State recruitment material

Corpus	Anger	Anxiety	Sadness
Emotional references in Islamic State recruitment material	1.32	.28	.28

Source: *Dabiq* and *Rumiyah* magazines (ISIS 2014–2016; ISIS 2016–2017)

Text word count: 720,314 words (5 July 2014–9 September 2017)

have become commonplace for the believers. The yearning for revenge has taken seed and has grown steadily in the hearts of the grieving widows, distressed orphans, and solemn soldiers; and the fruits are ready for harvest.

(ISIS 2014–2016: Dabiq Issue 14, 4)

Second, anger is directed against non-Muslim citizens in the West. They are viewed as being complicit because they participate in democratic elections and vote for anti-Muslim political leaders, as a piece in *Rumiyah* makes clear:

Crusader leaders who give the orders to brutally bomb the Muslims don't come from an abstract vacuum; rather, they come into power via the blessings of the constituency of their citizenry, those who partake in their democratic system or accept its results.

(ISIS 2014–16: Rumiyah Issue 2, 9)

Non-Muslim citizens are also viewed with disgust for being riddled with sin and vice. In a feature length video, Islamic State recruiter Neil Prakash references the violation of Muslim women as a key basis for attacks against Western targets. The highest level of anger of any source analysed, however, is displayed in a recruitment video featuring 17-year-old Abdullah Elmir, an apprentice butcher from Western Sydney who joined the Islamic State after telling his parents he was going fishing. Surrounded by several dozen fighters, Elmir looked directly into the camera. The embodiment of anger, he did not seek to justify violence, but to provoke it. Elmir directly challenged Western nations to fight:

You threaten us with this coalition of countries; bring every nation that you wish to us, whether its fifty nations or fifty thousand nations, it means nothing to us. Bring your planes, bring everything you want to us, because it will not harm us. Why? Because we have Allah. And this is something you do not have.

(The Guardian, 22 October 2014)

The overwhelming anger pervasive throughout Islamic State material is inescapably masculine. Women and children are resigned to the role of victims of Western aggression. The level of aggression, language, and imagery is deliberately confrontational and designed to provoke anger.

Beyond their perceived culpability as citizens of democratic states that elect leaders who attack Muslims, the Western public is viewed contemptuously as amoral and sexually deviant. *Dabiq* featured an article titled 'Clamping Down on Sexual Deviance'. Its title page included before and after photos of the execution of a homosexual man, who was thrown from the roof of a building in the Syrian town of ar-Raqqah. The article described the West:

Disease became rampant, the rate of children born outside of marriage skyrocketed, and the nuclear family was on its way to becoming a relic of the past. Rather than taking heed upon witnessing the destruction of their social fabric, and changing their 'way of life,' the kuffār [nonbelievers] defiantly persisted on their mission to eradicate their morals.

(ISIS 2014–2016: Dabiq *Issue 7, 42)*

Another key layer of anger in Islamic State magazines is directed toward other Muslims. Similarly, it is concentrated on two fronts: against leadership in the Muslim world and against Muslim leaders in the West, who are perceived to be directing Muslims away from true Islam and jihad. Expressing a profound sense of betrayal and frustration (key drivers of anger), an article in *Rumiyah* said of the Turkish government led by Islamist Recep Tayyip Erdoğan:

The Turkish government today, by entering into an open war with the Islamic State, is only cutting its own throat with its own knife, slicing its own veins with its own hand, hanging itself with its own ropes, and wrecking its own house – and indeed, the weakest house is that of a spider.

(ISIS 2016–2017: Rumiyah *Issue 3, 3)*

Similar disdain is reserved for Western imams and Islamic scholars who fail to support the Islamic State. An article in *Rumiyah*, which was accompanied by photos of dead and buried children, stated: 'Meanwhile, the "scholars" of the *tawaghit* and the "theorists" of the *Sahwat* denounced the flames of justice, doing so to draw closer to the thrones of the disbelieving tyrants and for the sake of *jahili* [ignorant] partisanship' (ISIS 2016–2017: *Rumiyah* Issue 5).

In the case of the Western Islamic State recruits, rejection from Western society may have triggered attachment to an alternate form of morality (in radical Islam), which arguably morphed into anger-fuelled violence and views of the West rooted in disgust and, consequently, hatred.

Anxiety in Islamic State recruitment material

Compared with anger, anxiety is relatively marginal in importance throughout Islamic State magazines. In relation to depictions of Muslims, anxiety and fear often have a theological base grounded in the *Sunnah*. In this context, fear is inverted from being afraid of one's immediate situation to being afraid of failing God. Thus, its connotations are not necessarily captured by a purely metric-driven reading of LIWC data. A speech by the official spokesman of the Islamic State in *Rumiyah* stated:

'O you who have believed, persevere and endure and remain stationed and fear Allah that you may be successful' (Al 'Imran 200). And reflect over the word of your Lord and consider it: 'And whoever fears Allah – He will make for him a way out and will provide for him from where he does not expect'.

(ISIS 2016–2017: Rumiyah Issue 9, 35)

Rather than existential anxiety based on social dislocation and misinterpellation, anxiety in the Islamic State stems from a fear of not serving God. It acts as motivation and empowerment. Thus, anxiety has positive masculine traits.

Sadness in Islamic State recruitment material

Whilst there is a significant difference between the deployment of anger and sadness in Islamic State magazines, it is important to consider how sadness is mobilised. Sadness and anger are often inextricably linked. Images of dead children in the magazines, for example, automatically stoke both emotions, despite the reader's lack of an intimate attachment to the victim. An article in *Rumiyah* by Abu Musab al-Zarqawi is one of the few sources that directly addresses sadness. It focuses on the significance of Muslims' low position in the worldwide status hierarchy:

> The suffering of this downcast *Ummah* does not cease to pain me. The ghosts of this defamed *Ummah* do not cease to haunt me. It is this *Ummah* of great glory and distinct honour, slapped with all kinds of debasement by the hands of treachery, so that the quilt of humiliation and insult were laid down.
>
> (ISIS 2016–2017: Rumiyah Issue 8, 20)

Sadness is expressed in a more nuanced manner in Islamic State recruitment videos. Young Muslim men speak directly to the camera and exhort other men to join. The format and technique require a level of personal engagement and vulnerability. The speaker seeks common ground with potential recruits. In *There is No Life Without Jihad*, Cardiff-raised recruiter Reyaad Khan makes a direct call to the viewer. He draws on feelings of depression and dishonour. He proposes jihad as an alternative that will lead to empowerment and happiness:

> I know how you feel. I used to live there. In the heart you feel depressed. The Messenger of Allah … said: The cure for depression is jihad in the cause of Allah. You feel like you have no honour, but the Messenger of Allah, Allah's peace and blessings be upon him, said: The honour of a believer is [sic] come with light, the honour of the *ummah* is jihad in the cause of Allah. All my brothers, come to Jihad and feel the honour that we are feeling. Feel the happiness that we are feeling.
>
> (al-Ḥayāt Media Center 2014)

In the same video, Australian Zakaryah Raad, who left Australia after serving time in prison for his role in enacting an illegal *Hadud* punishment (lashing) of another Muslim for drinking alcohol, spoke emotively about the impact of warfare on

Muslims worldwide: 'our sisters in Fallujah, day after day they give birth to deformed babies, look at the disgrace this Ummah is going through, look and see and wake up and understand why this is happening' (al-Ḥayāt Media Center 2014).

Collectively, the emotional layer of sadness in Islamic State videos revolves around the impact of war and negative treatment on Muslims. It relays an element of grief and signifies their perceived low position in Western hierarchies and international affairs. However, it also reveals the power of sharing vulnerability. The potent combination of anger and sadness is a recruitment mechanism. It builds rapport with other disaffected young men who may feel alienated and disengaged.

In the context of experiences of social hostility and entrenched disadvantage, which contribute to misinterpellation and anger, Australian Muslim men have moved from a subordinated hyper-masculinity in the local context to a Muslim hegemonic hyper-masculinity elsewhere. Carefully calibrated Islamic State messages show men as warriors and advertise a surplus of women not available in the homeland. The material offers a process of reinvention. Those with flatlining or diminishing social trajectories can become holy warriors and significant global actors merely by subscribing to Islamic State recruitment narratives.

Work, merit, and social trajectory

Unemployment and poverty are the most significant social issues facing Australian Muslim communities. Despite possessing higher-level qualifications than the wider community, particularly amongst overseas-born Muslims, Australian Muslims aged 15 or older who are in or available to the labour market were more than twice as likely to be unemployed (14.8%) compared to the total population (6.9%). Those who are employed are also more likely be in areas of the workforce typified by casual and precarious labour.

In an attempt to both capture and promote a sense of helplessness amongst Western Muslims, the Islamic State compared employment in countries such as Australia to slavery:

> The modern day slavery of employment, work hours, wages, etc., is one that leaves the Muslim in a constant feeling of subjugation to a *kāfir* master. He does not live the might and honor that every Muslim should live and experience … *Jihād* not only grants life on the larger scale of the *Ummah*, it also grants a fuller life on the scale of the individual. This life of *jihād* is not possible until you pack and move to the *Khilāfah*.
>
> (ISIS 2014–2016: Dabiq *Issue 3, 29*)

Jihad, in this sense, is framed as an alternative to the meaningless and precarious work that has come to characterise advanced neoliberal, capitalist economies.

In some cases, however, it is evident that socio-economic trajectory was not a recruitment factor. One Australian medical doctor, Tareq Kamleh, known colloquially in the Australian media as 'Dr. Jihad', left a well-paid position to join the Islamic State. In a letter to the Australian Health Practitioner Regulation Agency regarding his deregistration, Kamleh stated altruistic grounds as his motivation:

> I have come here as there are locals suffering from normal medical conditions despite being surrounded by war, with an overt lack of qualified medical care. Is it not my humanitarian duty to help these children also?! ... or only kids with white skin and blue passports?! ... I have no input or responsibility over the political or military actions of the state, if they are correct I wish them progression, if they are not, this is between them and God.
>
> (Davidson 2015)

His position was supported in my interviews with family members of Islamic State recruits in Melbourne. While they were typically reluctant to discuss actions overseas, they were more open to talking about why young men joined. One family member said, 'He had paid off most of a house in [a Melbourne suburb] and was on $100,000 a year as an electrical engineer. I asked him, "Why?" He said it was a higher calling. A higher calling' (Roose 2019).

Another family member distinguished between two groups who became Australian foreign fighters. One group demonstrated what would appear to be a form of misinterpellation, which resulted in their radicalisation. The other group were 'bad' from the outset:

> There are two types. The first were successful, intelligent, university educated. This one guy [name], he could have been Prime Minister if he was born another time. They all hit a roadblock, a hurdle that they couldn't overcome. The other group were looking for trouble.
>
> (Roose 2019)

This perspective differentiates between the men who come from what are considered 'good' family backgrounds and the men who were involved in criminal activity, drug use, or other nefarious behaviours before they rediscovered religion and became involved in Salafi Jihadist groups.

Belief in the meritocracy

Belief in the notion of meritocracy is undermined by experiences or accounts of discrimination. An important study by Booth, Leigh, and Varganova (2012) revealed that labour market discrimination is a key issue in Australia. Of the various ethnicities addressed in the study (Anglo-Saxon, Indigenous, Italian, Chinese, and Middle Eastern), among males the call-back rate was lowest for applicants with Middle Eastern names on their resumes – a pattern that was persistent across all job types. Given the conflation of Arabic names with Islam in the popular imagination, this comes as no surprise.

Jake Bilardi, an 18-year-old Anglo-Australian convert who would ultimately became a suicide bomber for the Islamic State, was a dedicated blogger. In one post, he critiqued the notion of Australia being a meritocracy and a successful multicultural society:

> Australia has long praised itself for its 'successful' multiculturalism programme, uniting more than 150 different ethnic and religious groups under the banner of Australian nationalism. They often point out the failures of similar programmes in Europe and proudly state that they are the only nation to have 'gotten it right', they deceive themselves though. While there are great numbers of Australian citizens from various lands, the extent of racism and marginalisation of minorities is often not acknowledged by the government. Coming from such an environment however allowed me to compare the world's self-proclaimed multiculturalism success story to the situation in the Islamic State and what I have found is the true abolition of racism and the destruction of all forms of racial and ethnic boundaries.
>
> *(Bilardi 2015)*

Representations of the Islamic State as a highly multicultural and tolerant society offered readers a sense of belonging and the possibility of developing the upward trajectory denied to them in Western contexts on account of their religion.

Hope for a better future

Muslims' disadvantaged position in the labour market translates into lower on average personal and household incomes. The Australian Council of Social Service (ACOSS) (2016) defined the 2016 poverty line (50% of median income) as $426.30 a week for an individual and $895.22 a week for a couple with two children. Vitally, well over half of Muslim households (58%) were living on less than $800 a week. Research by Riaz Hassan (2015) on the 2011 census revealed that 25.6 per cent of Muslim children lived in poverty (as defined by the benchmark) compared to 12.7 per cent for the wider population.

Islamic State recruiter Neil Prakash, from outer suburban Melbourne, had a history of drug use and was on a steep downward social and economic trajectory before he converted to Islam (Roose 2016). Prakash left Australia to join the Islamic State movement less than 18 months after his conversion. In 2016, when he was 24, he made a recruitment video targeted at Australian Muslims. In the video, Prakash portrayed the Caliphate as an ideal alternative to the Australia he left behind:

> Alhamdulillah. We came to establish a state. We came to give our blood, we came to pave the way toward establishing the Khilafah, Allah granted this to us and hamdulillah and now we have children walking the park, we have children going to school, we have hospitals, we have doctors, we have everything

here that we need. We left everything behind. Why? To be like the (Sahaba), where they left Mecca and went to Medina to establish a state. A land for the Muslims. A land of honour. So I invite the Muslims to come here. I tell you that this is the land of life.

(al-Ḥayāt Media Center 2015)

For those living in poverty and having difficulty developing an upward social trajectory, such vivid descriptions may well sound enticing because they offer a sense of belonging absent in daily life.

Immigration reversed: Belonging

Islamic State recruitment materials sought to demarcate a boundary around Muslims, differentiating between Islamic values and highly permissive 'liberal' and anti-Islamic values in wider society. *Dabiq* states:

> Your secular liberalism has led you to tolerate and even support 'gay rights', to allow alcohol, drugs, fornication, gambling, and usury to become widespread, and to encourage the people to mock those who denounce these filthy sins and vices. As such, we wage war against you to stop you from spreading your disbelief and debauchery – your secularism and nationalism, your perverted liberal values, your Christianity and atheism – and all the depravity and corruption they entail. You've made it your mission to 'liberate' Muslim societies; we've made it our mission to fight off your influence and protect mankind from your misguided concepts and your deviant way of life.
>
> (ISIS 2014–2016: Dabiq *Issue 15, 32*)

Anger, disgust, and anxiety merge seamlessly into a diatribe directed toward a faceless Western society. Often overlooked, however, is the emotion of shame. Many young Muslim men who departed to join the Islamic State as foreign fighters had histories of crime, drug use, and multiple sexual partners. They engaged in the practices denounced by Islamic State materials. However, their responsibility for deliberate, individual actions is absolved by joining the community of faith and casting blame, guilt, and shame on wider society. In this context, boundary marking is important. The once minority Australian Muslims find allegiance and belonging in the demarcated majority of shared Islamic values.

Conclusion

The demagogue-led Islamic State movement deployed the full repertoire of populist tactics to recruit Muslims from around the world, including over 6,000 individuals from Western contexts. It mobilised against perceived corruption and immorality, both in the West and Muslim-majority societies. It demarcated boundaries between true Muslims (us) and the non-Muslim 'other' (them). It attacked women's rights. It promoted the concept of an idealised community of the 'majority'.

Islamic State recruitment messages found a ready audience amongst a small, yet active minority of angry and alienated young men. Willing recruits had experienced misinterpellation and might not have felt themselves to be 'held in the arms of society'. Young Muslim men affected by subordinated masculinity, precarity, a lack of upward social mobility, tangible and institutionalised racism, and a sense of alienation were offered the opportunity to find belonging, acceptance, power, and authority in the Islamic State. Most importantly, recruitment materials offered the potential to gain respect and recognition and, thereby, overcome any sense of humiliation, shame, or wounded masculine pride. To this extent, Islamic State recruitment magazines were tailored to target the vacuum left by neoliberal economic policies and the absence of key institutions that facilitate citizenship. The emphasis on a textual, hard-line form of Islam as an alternate way forward mobilised anger particularly well. It fused local experiences with a bigger picture and communicated the need to build an alternate realty.

The young men who joined the Islamic State movement arguably share considerable commonalities with those who mobilised against the European Union in the United Kingdom or voted for Donald Trump in the United States. In all cases, religion and masculinity played an understated, yet nonetheless key, role in shaping political decision-making and actions.

References

ABS (Australian Bureau of Statistics). (1911). *Census of Housing and Population*. Canberra: Australian Bureau of Statistics.
ABS (Australian Bureau of Statistics). (1921). *Census of Housing and Population*. Canberra: Australian Bureau of Statistics.
ABS (Australian Bureau of Statistics). (1922). *Census of Housing and Population*. Canberra: Australian Bureau of Statistics.
ABS (Australian Bureau of Statistics). (1947). *Census of Housing and Population*. Canberra: Australian Bureau of Statistics.
ABS (Australian Bureau of Statistics). (2001). *Census of Housing and Population*. Canberra: Australian Bureau of Statistics.
ABS (Australian Bureau of Statistics). (2011). *Census of Housing and Population*. Canberra: Australian Bureau of Statistics.
ABS (Australian Bureau of Statistics). (2016). *Census of Housing and Population*. Canberra: Australian Bureau of Statistics.
Abu Mohammad, I. (2012). A Statement from the Grand Mufti of Australia Regarding the anti-Mohammad Film. *Islamicmedia.com*.
Akbarzadeh, S. & Roose, J.M. (2011). Muslims, Multiculturalism, and the Question of the Silent Majority. *Journal of Muslim Minority Affairs*, 31(3), 309–325.
al-Ḥayāt Media Center. (2014). There is No Life Without Jihad. *al-Ḥayāt Media Center*.
al-Ḥayāt Media Center. (2015). Abu Khaled Al-Cambodi. *al-Ḥayāt Media Center*, 21 April.
Aly, A. & Walker, D. (2007). Veiled Threats: Recurrent Cultural Anxieties in Australia. *Journal of Muslim Minority Affairs*, 27 (2), 203–214.

Archer, L. (2001). 'Muslim Brothers, Black Lads, Traditional Asians': British Muslim Young Men's Constructions of Race, Religion, and Masculinity. *Feminism and Psychology*, 11 (1), 79–105.

Australian Council of Social Service (ACOSS). (2016). *Report: Poverty in Australia: 2016*. Sydney: Social Policy Research Centre, University of New South Wales.

Australian Government. (2018). LinCT Conference. Melbourne. 10–12 December.

BBC. (2005). Australia PM Set for Terror Talks. *BBC News*, 15 July. Retrieved from http://news.bbc.co.uk/1/hi/world/asia-pacific/4684881.stm?.

Bilardi, J. (2015). Being White in the Islamic State: The Abolition of Racism. *Bilardi Blog Post* (archived), 15 January.

Bliuc, A., McGarty, C., Hartley, L., & Muntele Hendres, D. (2011). Manipulating National Identity: The Strategic Use of Rhetoric by Supporters and Opponents of the Cronulla Riots in Australia. *Ethnic and Racial Studies*, 34 (3), 1–21.

Booth, A.L., Leigh, A., & Varganova, E. (2012). Does Ethnic Discrimination Vary Across Minority Groups?: Evidence from a Field Experiment. *Oxford Bulletin of Economics and Statistics*, 74 (4), 547–573.

Box, D. & Gosper, S. (2012). Islamic Leaders Call for Halt to All Protests Over Film Deemed Offensive to Prophet. *The Australian*, 18 September.

Cesari, J. (2004). *When Islam and Democracy Meet: Muslims in Europe and the United States*. New York: Palgrave.

Cleeland, B. (2001). The History of Muslims in Australia. In A. Saeed & S. Akbarzadeh (Eds.), *Muslim Communities in Australia* (pp. 12–32). Sydney: UNSW Press.

Davidson, H. (2015). Isis Doctor Tareq Kamleh: I Don't Care About Losing Australian Citizenship. *The Guardian Australia*, 21 June.

Edwards, M. (2015). Australian Muslim Groups Condemn Islamic State's 'Barbaric' Use of Yazidi Slaves. *ABC News*. 22 January.

Esposito, J. (2010). *The Future of Islam*. Oxford: Oxford University Press.

Gardiner, S. (2012). 'Behead' Sign Child Deemed Safe as Mother Talks to Police. *The Sydney Morning Herald*, 18 September.

Ging, D. (2019). Alphas, Betas, and Incels: Theorizing the Masculinities of the Manosphere. *Men and Masculinities*, 22 (4), 638–657.

The Guardian. (2014). Islamic State: Australian Teen Abdullah Elmir Warns Tony Abbott in Isis Message. *The Guardian*, 22 October. Retrieved from https://www.theguardian.com/world/video/2014/oct/22/australian-teen-abdullah-elmir-isis-video.

Hage, G. (2003). *Against Paranoid Nationalism: Searching for Hope in a Shrinking Society*. London: The Merlin Press.

Hage, G. (2011). Multiculturalism and the Ungovernable Muslim. In R. Gaita (Ed.), *Essays on Muslims and Multiculturalism* (pp. 165–186). Melbourne: Text Publishing.

Hassan, R. (2015). *Australian Muslims: A Demographic, Social, and Economic Profile of Muslims in Australia*. Adelaide: University of South Australia.

Hopkins, P. (2007). Global Events, National Politics, Local Lives: Young Muslim Men in Scotland. *Environment and Planning A: Economy and Space*, 39 (5), 1119–1133.

Hopkins, P.E. (2009). Responding to the 'Crisis of Masculinity': The Perspectives of Young Muslim Men from Glasgow and Edinburgh, Scotland. *Gender, Place & Culture*, 16 (3), 299–312.

Howard, J. (2006). Address to the 50th Anniversary of Quadrant Magazine, Four Seasons Hotel, Sydney, 3 October. *Australian Government: PM Transcripts*. Retrieved from https://pmtranscripts.pmc.gov.au/release/transcript-22501.

Humphrey, M. & Islam, M. (2002). Injuries and Identities: Authorising Arab Diasporic Difference in Crisis. In G. Hage (Ed.), *Arab-Australians Today: Citizenship and Belonging* (pp. 49–87). Melbourne: Melbourne University Press.

Ipsos, Roose, J.M., & Turner, B.S. (2019). Global Masculinity Index Survey Developed and Conducted by Ipsos Public Affairs, Joshua Roose, and Bryan S. Turner. June.

ISIS (Islamic State of Iraq and Syria). (2014–2016). *Dabiq*, 5 July–31 July. Al-Hayat Media Centre.

ISIS (Islamic State of Iraq and Syria). (2016–2017). *Rumiyah*, 5 September–31 July. Al-Hayat Media Centre.

Jones, M.L. (1993). The Years of Decline: Australian Muslims 1900–40. In M.L. Jones (Ed.), *An Australian Pilgrimage: Muslims in Australia from the Seventeenth Century to the Present* (pp. 63–96). Melbourne: Victoria Press.

Kabir, N. (2005). Muslims in Western Australia, 1870–1970. *Early Days: Journal of the Royal Western Australian Historical Society*, 12 (5), 550.

Kabir, N. (2006). Muslims in a 'White Australia': Colour or Religion? *Immigrants and Minorities*, 24 (2), 193–223.

Mandaville, P. (2002). Muslim Youth in Europe. In S.T. Hunter (Ed.), *Islam: Europe's Second Religion: The New Social, Cultural, and Political Landscape*. (pp. 219–231). London: Praeger.

Manne, R. (2004). *The Howard Years*. Melbourne: Black Inc. Agenda.

Markus, A. (2001). *John Howard and the Remaking of Australia*. Crows Nest, NSW: Allen & Unwin.

Noble, G. (2007). Respect and Respectability amongst Second-Generation Arab and Muslim Australian Men. *Journal of Intercultural Studies*, 28 (3), 331–344.

Omar, W. & Allen, K. (1996). *The Muslims in Australia*. Canberra: Australian Government Publishing Service.

Poynting, S. (2006). What Caused the Cronulla Riot? *Race and Class*, 48 (1), 88.

Roose, J.M. (2013). Contesting Islam through the 2012 Sydney Protests: An Analysis of Post-Protest Political Discourse amongst Australian Muslims. *Islam and Christian–Muslim Relations*, 24 (4), 479–499.

Roose, J.M. (2016). *Political Islam and Masculinity: Muslim Men in the West*. New York: Palgrave.

Roose, J.M. (2019). Research Interviews Conducted by the Author, October–December.

Stevens, C. (1989). *Tin Mosques and Ghantowns: A History of Afghan Camel Drivers in Australia*. Melbourne: Oxford University Press.

Stevens, C. (2005). Mahomed, Gool Badsha (1875–1915). In C. Cunneen (Ed.), *Australian Dictionary of Biography*. Carlton: Melbourne University Press.

Stokes, G. (2004). The 'Australian Settlement' and Australian Political Thought. *Australian Journal of Political Science*, 39 (1), 5–22.

Tabar, P. (2007). 'Habiibs' in Australia: Language, Identity, and Masculinity. *Journal of Intercultural Studies*, 28 (2), 157–172.

United Nations Human Rights Council. (2016). UN Commission of Inquiry on Syria: ISIS is Committing Genocide against the Yazidi, 16 June. *United Nations Human Rights: Office of the High Commissioner*. Retrieved from https://www.ohchr.org/EN/NewsEvents/Pages/DisplayNews.aspx?NewsID=20113.

8
RELIGION, MASCULINITY, AND THE NEW POPULISM

This book sought from the outset to understand how and why Western liberal democracies have fallen into their current state of political turmoil, creating the vacuum necessary for a new breed of demagogic strongmen to emerge. The book explores two critically overlooked themes in the emergence of contemporary populism: religion and masculinity. It has done so through five interrelated theses, four of which that have already been outlined, and a fifth and final solutions-focused thesis which will emerge through this chapter's process of synthesis. By both looking back through history and at contemporary contrastive cases, the book casts new light on the use of populism as a political tactic in the pursuit of power.

The book's first thesis is that the decline of citizenship, the welfare state, and key social institutions has created an intellectual and social vacuum that can be exploited by those using populist tactics. Citizenship has deteriorated. In its current usage in the political lexicon, citizenship has become a bureaucratic mechanism for excluding people: migrants, refugees, and those who displease us, including criminals and terrorists. The modern state, governed by a professional class of politicians, absolves itself of responsibility for global challenges or contributing to their solutions by hiding behind an increasingly thin veneer of 'national interest'. National interest has increasingly come to mean a narrow, partisan interest tied to the electoral prospects of the political party in power. Yet, despite these developments, in recent decades the academic field of citizenship studies has grown exponentially. There has been a shift in the literature from classical conceptions of citizenship (and a critique of the limited rights inherent within) to identity-based conceptions of citizenship, which have emancipatory potential because they propose equal rights but have expanded so broadly as to strip the concept of its essence, which is balancing rights *and* responsibilities.

This book proposes a return to a reinvigorated classical citizenship, albeit one stripped of its cultural baggage. I adopt here the sociological definition proposed by

Turner (2016) and Marshall (1950), amongst others, that citizenship must ensure the full rights of participation (legal, political, social, and industrial) and balance these rights with obligations and responsibilities to contribute to wider society. This applies especially to corporations, which adopt corporate personhood and are afforded many of the rights, protections, and abilities to act enjoyed by humans, yet continue to dodge taxes and undermine employees' industrial rights. A key element proposed by Shklar (1990) in the United States should have a wider international resonance: the right to work. The concept should be extended to the right to dignity in work. Dignity has increasingly been stripped from blue-collar men, in particular, and it is steadily being eroded through the increasing casualisation and contract-based working conditions of white-collar workers.

I explore the intersection of citizenship and the welfare state, in particular the value propositions underpinning both. It is safe to assert that Beveridge, Keynes, and Marshall did not oppose capitalism per se. However, they acknowledged the significance of ensuring freedom from want and creating a social safety net to capture those workers who found themselves temporarily unemployed. Such protections for citizens required government spending, active government intervention when necessary, and the development of a collectivist suite of government-funded social services, a model that spread in the post-World War Two era. Whilst these key figures who shaped post-war economics and conceptions of citizenship stood to varying degrees in opposition to the establishment, they were also driven by an underlying Christian socialist ethos that 'stood in opposition to the selfish and materialist tendency' of economic systems (Andrews 2017: 959). Their beliefs were derived both from their educations and their social and professional networks, including, most notably, William Temple, the Archbishop of Canterbury and author of the book *Christianity and the Social Order* (1941). The University of Oxford, the University of Cambridge, and the London School of Economics were particularly important wellsprings of intellectual influence in this period. Despite the successful transplantation of post-war, value-driven social and economic models to many countries across the Commonwealth and, to a lesser extent, the United States, they struggled to survive in subsequent decades in the face of a sustained onslaught from neoclassical economists, particularly those associated with the University of Chicago, who operated at the individualist end of the political spectrum.

Neoliberalism sprang first and foremost from the Chicago School of economic thought, though currents existed at universities across the United States and Europe. Key scholars, including Friedrich Hayek and Milton Friedman, contributed to the development of the Mont Pelerin Society, an anti-government-intervention, pro-free-market think tank that disseminated neoliberal ideas globally. Perhaps most importantly for the aims of this book, neoliberalism was influential in all three contexts examined: the United Kingdom, United States, and Australia. It undermined both state intervention in the economy, a key principle of Keynesian economics, and traditional citizenship by focusing primarily on private property rights, individual liberty, free trade, and an unencumbered market in which there is no role for external influencers, such as trade unions. In this context market exchange emerged 'as an ethic in itself' and a substitute for 'previously held ethical belief', including the Christian socialist underpinnings of the welfare state. In the neoliberal economy, institutions of organised religion and trade unions alike operate in increasingly barren and, indeed, actively hostile social, economic, and political environments, which are contributing to their significant decline.

As explored in conjunction with the second thesis, religion has become increasingly defined by dogmatic claims to the possession of 'truth'. To varying extents trade unions and Labour parties have become dominated by a professional class that does not work alongside those they represent. Bureaucratic union leaders are separate from their members, and they enjoy a degree of security that is increasingly absent from the lives of the working-class. Similarly, whereas politicians were once both members and representatives of the workforce, they too are increasingly professional politicians out of touch with the daily lives of their constituents. The decline of key institutions that once offered workers a sense of solidarity, place, and dignity has created of a vacuum of intellectual, moral, and political leadership, which has been exploited by demagogues who deploy populist tactics to attain power and to achieve political goals.

Field interviews in what may be termed centres of populist support were instructive. Interviewees often reduced religion to identification with a culture, rather than observance. For many, where religion did permeate lives, cultural and language barriers inhibited interaction and the development of the solidaristic dimension outside of narrow communities.

Trade unions, while they were valued by men in both Birmingham, UK, and Hazleton, PA, were seen either as relics of a bygone era or as being only interested in the needs of a select few. Insecurity and precarity defined many interviewees' daily lives. A sense of loss and feelings of being left behind were pervasive. Those men who expressed anger focused it primarily on two key areas: welfare, which was viewed as gaining something for nothing rather than as assistance from the state for those in need, and migrants in the immediate area, who were accused of taking jobs, unfairly obtaining housing, and bringing crime. Bridging social capital between communities was almost non-existent, particularly amongst the older generation of white working-class men and recent migrants, be they Muslim or Latino. In the Australian context, those joining the Islamic State movement were not recent migrants, but second- and third-generation Australian-born young men disconnected from traditional institutions of citizenship, such as trade unions, mainstream community mosques, and political parties. The disaffected turned to small groups at the fringes of the community that promised the opportunity to articulate an alternate source of meaning.

The second thesis is that demagogic actors use religious motifs and narratives to strengthen their populist appeal. At the same time, organised religion also seeks to leverage populism to gain greater political influence. This latter point stands at odds with the perspective that religious actors are naturally opposed to the exploitation of social divisions.

Notwithstanding great strides made in interfaith work and ecumenicalism in recent decades, claims to the possession of universal truth are essential to the successful emergence and development of religions. A consideration of key figures in the history of Christianity and Islam, including St. Thomas Aquinas (Catholicism) and Ibn Taymiyyah (Islam), reveals that religious competitors are represented as 'false prophets' and 'transgressors', subjected to vitriolic statements that directly target their claims to the possession of 'truth', and threatened with expulsion (or worse). If this sounds similar to contemporary populist strategies, the link is solidified by considering the textualism and tactics of Martin Luther, the sixteenth-century German professor of moral theology who systematically singled out Catholics, Muslims, and Jews for extreme contempt and scorn. The ferocity of his campaign led to the emergence of the Protestant denomination and continues to shape world history to the present day. Key contemporary textualist religious actors deploy similar populist tactics, including attacks against the religious establishment, public attacks against other religions, attacks against women's rights, and promises of an imagined national community comprised of the majority faith.

Religion played a key role in the development of the United States by migrants fleeing religious persecution. Religious freedom and the separation of church and state were constitutionally protected, serving as a pivotal break with Europe and creating a fertile terrain for the development of new Christian denominations, many grounded in a Protestant theological base. Whilst constitutionally secular in the sense that the establishment of a state church was prohibited, the United States ultimately became home to the largest Christian population on earth, with much higher levels of religious observance than the old world that continue to this day. The country is particularly important in understanding the emergence of new religious traditions, including Pentecostalism, that compete with more established denominations for adherents and political access. Religious politics in the United States are particularly contested as competing groups make claims to possession of universal truth, which explains, in part, why the country has apparently higher levels of religious textualism.

Secularism, in practice, operates on a spectrum ranging from multicultural countries that allow legal pluralism in relation to civil matters and religious observance in public spaces to the militantly secular laïcité societies that strictly enforce the division of church and state in favour of national identity. There is no one model of secularism that fits all contexts. In some cases, it has quite simply gone too far in demanding complete conformity. Yet the concept of the separation of religion and state has played an important role in mitigating the potential for religious conflict. It has been written into human rights instruments ensuring freedom of religion or belief. However, secularism has come under increasing attack from religious activists and scholars alike. Religious activists decry the secular state for depriving them of the right to practice their faith as they wish, a critique more applicable to militant configurations than mainstream ones. More recently, concerted efforts by scholars pushing religiously-inspired agendas have drawn attention the apparent deficits of secularism and have attempted to assert a greater role for religion in public life.

The background regarding the emergence of Christian denominations, the political conditions in which they thrive, and contemporary debates about secularism is necessary for understanding the internal theological and political cleavages that have developed within the Christian denominations and Islam. It assists in understanding how they lead to close cooperation between textualist religious actors and populists. The book considers the contrasting examples of Pope Benedict XVI (2005–2013) and Pope Francis (2013–) to explore contestations within contemporary Catholicism. Pope Benedict self-consciously fashioned himself as a 'reference point for European unity' and a symbol of 'Christian civilisation'. His defining moment was his 2006 Regensburg Address, which contrasted the Christian tradition, grounded in rationality and non-violence (and by extension 'truth'), with an irrational and violent Muslim god (Benedict XVI 2006). The speech was delivered five years and a day after the 9/11 attacks and just months after the London bombings. Controversial as it was, it served the purpose of staking the Christian claim to Europe, the high moral ground (non-violence), and exclusive possession of universal truth. Pope Benedict's message is complimentary to those propounded by demagogic figures across the Western context to this day. It served as a clarion call to traditionalists and textualists throughout the Catholic Church.

Benedict's replacement by Pope Francis, the first Jesuit pope, saw a more progressive theological line come to the fore, including an almost immediate call for dialogue with Islam and tolerance dealing with Muslim migrants in Europe. Pope Francis's progressive approach, including a more liberal stand on Catholic social teaching, mobilised fierce opposition from conservatives and textualists within the Church, including Cardinal Burke, an American who had close, but eventually renounced, links with key populist strategist Steve Bannon. A broad coalition of conservative think tanks simultaneously rejected collectivist approaches to economics, actively promoted neoliberal economic approaches, and mobilised to push the hard-line Catholic fundamentalist agenda that became influential with politicians to the right of the political spectrum in the United States and, more broadly, across Western and European contexts. Fundamentalist Catholics formed relationships with populist political parties, including Lega Nord in Italy, the Orbán government in Hungary, and the Law and Justice Party in Poland, where the separation of church and state is becoming increasingly fragile. In other contexts, minority Christian groups have sided with those challenging established political power, and State religious institutions have sided with the state against those seeking to usurp their power and influence.

The presence of Islam in Europe is a key pivot for debates about the compatibility of Muslim populations in the Western context. Muslim migration has increased significantly in recent years. Muslim populations will constitute a significant minority within decades. Indeed, in some cities this is already the case. One aspect of the intense hatred of Muslims is the belief that they constitute a 'fifth column' intent on seizing political power and Islamising society. Islam, like

Christianity, has its theological divisions, including most obviously the Sunni–Shiite split. In Western contexts, political divisions between moderates and Islamists within Sunni Islam are key. Islamists, drawing on scholars, including Ibn Taymiyyah, assisted greatly in expanding the reach of Islamic State narratives in Western Muslim communities. Like their Christian counterparts, they use populist tactics, including the idea of a powerful and corrupt wider society and a claim to exclusive ownership of a divine universal truth.

Catholicists, like Islamists, seek a return to the past – an imagined era of greatness when religion and the nation state were inextricably linked. Religious leaders in this context move from being marginalised figures to central leaders of the nation-state with the power to shape the daily lives and actions of its citizens. Catholicists have aimed their sights on Europe, particularly in Poland, Italy, and Hungary. Islamists seek the establishment of a caliphate ruled by Islamic law. In this context, where the religious and the political are increasingly enmeshed, it is evident that a highly-calibrated, responsive secularism is more important than ever.

Interviews and fieldwork conducted for this book revealed that religion is less important to working-class men targeted by populist mobilisation than issues related to competition for resources, housing, state support, and local crime. In short, working-class men were disaffected and felt a sense of being wronged. For Muslims a feeling of being wronged may relate to the process of misinterpellation grounded in institutionalised racism. Religion became a way of branding the visible 'other', as in Birmingham, UK, although the city's history of race relations demonstrates that black migrants also faced significant discrimination. Hazleton, PA, is instructive in this regard. The original inhabitants of European-Christian backgrounds who signalled migration as an issue shared the Catholic faith with the individuals and groups that they criticised. They could not draw upon religion as an othering mechanism. For Latino communities it was a cohering mechanism. The largest Catholic church in town, St. Gabriel's, was a formerly Irish Catholic Church that had fallen into disrepair. It experienced a significant revival, of sorts, when Spanish-language services and materials attracted Hispanic Catholics to the congregation. The language of the new demagogues, when it pertains to religion and identity, appears to only resonate when there is close physical proximity between the religious or ethnic minority being singled out and the wider community. Despite their hostility to Latino migrants, not a single individual interviewed in Hazleton stated that Islam or Muslims constituted a threat to their way of life. Populist messages targeting religion are far more likely to resonate with religious and political groups that already possess deep ideological underpinnings antithetical to the 'other'.

Generational differences also played a role in populist messaging. Older men were more likely to stand opposed to migrants and minorities compared to younger men, who grew up with and attended the same schools and workplaces as more recent arrivals. Paradoxically, the younger generation of Muslims in Western contexts were more likely to become foreign fighters with the Islamic State movement. It may be that, on the one hand, an older generation of white working men may be unsettled by a perception of too much change happening around them, whilst, on the other hand, younger Western Muslims may view key institutions as inherently discriminatory and the wider society as hostile in ways that their migrant parents are not attuned to.

The third thesis explored within the book is that populist hyper-masculinity, irrespective of the national context in which it is displayed, is indicative of deep-seated social and emotional injury. This injury is compounded by feelings of loss, whether real or imagined, and victimisation.

A sense of loss is a key theme across the book. It may be loss of culture, power, and prestige, as in the case of Christian churches in Europe and the United Kingdom. Increasing numbers of people turning away from the church combined with high migration created a sense of marginalisation and, indeed, victimisation. While progressivist strands of religion assert the need to develop trust and mutual respect as a basis for the church's continued viability, particularly among working people, textualists aggressively pursue dogmatic approaches that seek to regain what has been lost. Fundamentalist textualists work closely with demagogic figures to attack secularism, fundamental human rights, and migrants. This has played out in the United States, where conservative Catholicism has flourished. In Europe evangelicals also closely align with demagogic figures in what they consider a battle to maintain their influence. In a similar vein to textualist Christianity, Islamists seek to regain what has been lost: a caliphate as the basis for global Islamic governance. The Islamists' worldview perceives a global war on Islam. Muslims are subjected to humiliation, shame, and violence on a daily basis. The caliphate is positioned as the only solution to this state of affairs. Whilst the Islamic State movement was based in Syria and Iraq, it sought to bring the war to Europe through terror attacks. In the case of both the Islamists and Catholicists, the perceived loss of power and status is equated with humiliation and shame. It is experienced as a visceral physical and emotional injury.

When I started this book, I did not expect to uncover the extensive animosity and hatred evident in the so-called 'manosphere'. I delved into the subject in greater depth than first planned. Working- and lower-middle-class masculinities are grounded in real-world struggle defined, to draw upon Guy Standing's frame (2011), by alienation from labour, anxiety due to precarious work, anger due to downward social trajectories, and anomie based in a deficit of moral guidance and social bonds. Data reveals that men form the primary base of support for the new demagogues. Many of these men enact 'subordinated' hyper-masculine identities, which are driven by humiliation, social injury, a sense of a lack of respect and recognition, and a perceived stripping of honour and dignity. Key data from the Ipsos survey revealed that about half of the men in any of the studied contexts believed that their incomes were stable and secure. About 70 per cent of men across the countries surveyed believed that hard work would help them build a better future. A similar number believed they could make a better life in their country, although the percentage was much higher amongst Australian Muslim respondents. Flipping these figures, it becomes evident that between one third and one half of men felt precarity and instability in their daily lives. Furthermore, the neoliberal concept of meritocracy did not resonate with them. Hage's (2011) concept of misinterpellation, broadly framed as the process of shattering that occurs when an individual realises that the social possibilities they once thought open to them (and they were told were open to them) are closed, may be equated with John Keane's (2016) observation that supporters of populism no longer 'feel held' in the arms of society. As Jack Barbalet (1993) observes, frustrated attempts to satisfy needs are likely to evoke strong emotions, including depression, fear, and anger.

Emotions played out in interviews in an unexpected manner. In speaking about the challenging circumstances they faced as individuals, interviewees in both Birmingham and Hazleton were quite matter of fact. They spoke with a sense of resignation about their own lives. Working-class solidarities were evident in the genuine camaraderie men demonstrated as I spoke with them in public contexts. They clearly felt comfortable and 'at home'. This was also evident among those I spoke with in Muslim communities. Pub, bars, cafés, or restaurants have very similar etiquette and cultural practices the world over. As a white male researcher and, perhaps, due to my outsider status and Australian accent, I was able to cut across class lines and engage on friendly terms. What was surprising was the extent to which genuinely friendly men's dispositions turned when they talked about the 'other' against whom they held deep-seated resentment and anger, be it Muslims, Latinos, or welfare recipients perceived to receive favourable treatment from the government. In Birmingham, one individual in a group conversation, who had listened and remained largely quiet, sat up when I mentioned the Christchurch terror attack. He pulled out his phone to show me a video of the attack that he had saved on the phone. On another occasion in Hazleton, a light-hearted discussion about the local area suddenly turned serious when the topic of welfare card fraud was brought up. Physical dispositions and the tone of voice adopted by those speaking changed. The proposition that migrants were not working hard was treated largely with incredulity by those from migrant backgrounds that I spoke to, who also inverted the anti-minority stereotype by accusing members of the white working class of lacking motivation and being unwilling to work hard. Yet, it was evident that beneath the veneer of joviality there was a deep-seated animosity grounded in social and emotional injury.

Because I was only able to conduct interviews with a handful of family members of Islamic State fighters, propaganda videos and blogs made by Australian fighters were instructive. Young men switched almost instantly from nebulous discussions of their lives in Australia to calls for the slaughter of Australians. Across the spectrum of men discussed in this book, it was evident that a powerful anger derived from a sense of loss and deep-seated social and emotional injury was bubbling just beneath the surface. The messaging of demagogic populists exploited this emotional undercurrent.

In the absence of intellectual and moral leadership and solidaristic bonds, we have seen the steady erosion of working-class honour and dignity. In a climate of disaffection, a very small, but active group have focussed on their victimhood status. Survey data suggests that the numbers would equate to approximately five per cent of men. Collectively, of course, it represents tens of millions of men across the countries examined within this book alone. This ties in directly to the next thesis.

The fourth thesis of the book is that the combination of religious invective, social injury, and wounded masculine pride signals the emergence of a new form of violent extremism that can have global implications. In an environment of alienation, anxiety, and expulsion, anti-women prejudice has migrated from its traditional base in organised religion to the online 'manosphere', where it has developed into a virulent new strain that advocates extremist violence against women.

In this context masculinity, defined broadly as 'what it is to be a man', has been weaponised. The new demagogues home in on those men who may occupy what are often referred to as 'subordinated' masculinities, giving them a sense that those in positions of power over them, such as hegemonic masculinities or women speaking and acting out of place, can be taken down. The end state of this weaponisation of masculinity results in what I term an 'ideological masculinity' underpinning male supremacism. Using various degrees of symbolic, institutionalised, and physical violence, it attempts to reassert men's control of the public and private domains.

Ideological masculinity operates along the spectrum of beliefs and actions that has come to be known as the 'manosphere'. At the soft end of the spectrum lies traditional religious prejudice against women. For example, evangelical men's movements reconnect with a Christian 'warrior' masculinity to reassert men as the heads of households, regain control over women's bodies, and relegate women to household and caregiving roles. Alt-right groups, such as the Proud Boys, operate in a similar manner. They seek to 'reclaim' masculinity from political correctness. They assert that women are genetically predisposed to stay at home and raise children. Such groups, influenced to varying degrees by religious textualism, claim a need for violence and occasionally enact violent acts. Concepts such as the 'Red Pill' have become prevalent across the alt-right, which wants to 'wake up' wider society to what they perceive as the real problem, including feminism and women's rights.

The MGTOW: Men Going Their Own Way movement is indicative of the spread of anti-women groups and sentiment grounded in a sense of victimhood. Religion is viewed as having let men down. Men see themselves as victims of a system designed to crush masculinity and punish men, which is facilitated by modern organised religion. Women are represented as predatory, selfish, and materialistic. They pursue their needs at the expense of loyal men. In this context women are parasitical and need to be rejected. Whilst members of MGTOW forums discuss violence against women, other key figures, such as Paul Elam and Roosh Valizadeh, openly advocate physical and sexual violence while hiding behind a thin veneer of meme culture and satire. Their activities have not escaped the attention of key anti-hate organisations, such as the Southern Poverty Law

Centre, who have labelled organisations founded by Elam and Valizadeh as hate groups.

It is clear that hatred of women is central to the 'manosphere'. In this context, women must be denied positions of faith and political leadership, subordinate themselves to men, resign themselves to meeting their husbands' needs in the domestic sphere, and produce the next generation. It represents a fantasy return to the tropes that have been central to feminist criticisms of patriarchy for many decades. Not only does a desire to return to binary patriarchal gender roles persist, it appears to be gaining momentum as groups of men organise online. Increasingly, demagogic leaders employ anti-women language when engaging their political base.

There is, however, an extreme end of the ideological masculinity spectrum. The 1989 Montreal massacre at an engineering school targeted women because they were, according to the perpetrator, 'all fucking feminists'. Feminists, in particular, are the targets of threats of sexual assault and physical violence online. A new direction in violent extremism can be traced to the recent emergence of 'incels' (involuntary celibates) prepared to kill women on the grounds of their gender and for perceived past rejections. This form of violent ideological masculinity is rooted, not in religion or nationalism, but in gender. 'Victimised masculinity' becomes the primary identity affiliation. Women are perceived as enemies and oppressors. In the context of what the World Bank describes as a 'global pandemic' of violence against women, it is essential to correctly identify and label this violence in order to develop policy solutions to it.

Feminist scholars have an entire lexicon for describing misogyny and prejudice against women. Some call this behaviour 'masculinism': 'the ideology that justifies and naturalises male domination' (Brittan 1989: 4), and the 'ideology of patriarchy' that requires 'curbing the influence of feminism' and 'revalorising masculinity' (Blais & Dupuis-Déri 2012: 22). Yet this alone does not describe or capture aspects of the contemporary environment, such as illegal activity or the ferocity of the new anti-women activism. Drawing on work around masculinism, we must recognise male supremacism as an inherently political ideology.

Foregrounding the ideological dimension of male supremacism brings this emerging form of violent extremism firmly within the remit of law enforcement agencies within the United States, United Kingdom, and Australia. Public policy must treat male supremacists' calls for violence against women as seriously as other forms of ideologically motivated violent extremism. The end state of male supremacism is the subordination of women to men grounded in deep resentment and indeed hatred, which places it on the same spectrum as far-right and Islamist violent extremism.

Male supremacist behaviour is also abundantly clear in the actions of the Islamic State, which sexually enslaved women and designated their roles as domestic and reproductive – raising male 'cubs of the caliphate'. The Islamic State's actions are part of a long history of fundamentalist religious actors drawing upon literal readings of religious texts to subjugate women and commit grave acts of sexual and physical violence, which have shaped wider society to this day.

Recent terror attacks against women on the basis of their gender are the tip of the proverbial iceberg. Endemic violence against women in online spaces occasionally filters into the real world. The power derived by men committing violent acts of ideological masculinity belies their self-perception as victims. When demagogic populists promote the notion of male victimhood and the marginalisation of men, they feed this deep undercurrent of anti-women hatred. Yet if anything (Islamic State aside), the men I spoke with, both married and unmarried, were largely supportive of the women in their lives. They were comfortable in the presence of women. It became evident that there was a disconnect between the experiences and perspectives of these men and the 'manosphere' and male supremacism. The fact that I primarily spoke to older blue-collar men may have impacted this impression. The Ipsos data points towards a higher likelihood that younger men under the age of 35 hold prejudicial attitudes toward women. Nonetheless, it appears clear that the largely online world of anti-women ideological masculinity does not resonate with either the daily lives of blue-collar working men or broader Muslim communities. This suggests that anti-women messaging by demagogic figures may appeal to some men, but not those traditionally associated with patriarchal working-class attitudes.

The fifth and final thesis of the book is that, paradoxically, potential conceptual and policy solutions to the challenges posed by the new populism are to be found in both its religious and hyper-masculine dimensions.

This book at times discusses what are typically considered negative aspects of religion: textualism grounded in claims to possession of a universal truth; the emergence of highly politicised forms of religion centred on gaining political power, such as Islamism and key factions within Catholicism; vitriolic outbursts and extreme violence against competitor faiths; anti-women prejudice; efforts to obtain or retain exemptions from state regulations or laws; and ongoing attempts to call secularism into question. As the book has demonstrated, textualist religious leaders have worked closely with populist figures throughout history, particularly when it assists them in gaining political power.

However, far from condemning religion or embracing militant secularism, I assert here that religious values grounded in concern for the common good have a significant role to play in a secular society. Christian egalitarian values and a concern for the vulnerable underpinned the development of the welfare state, Keynesian economics, and classical citizenship. Granted, the values and works were context specific and, thus, susceptible to the prejudices of the time in which they were written. Nonetheless, they formed the basis for post-war prosperity that shaped the world of the present moment. In a world defined by neoliberal economic and social policies, where market exchange has become a value in and of itself, moral and ethical foundations are lacking. Indeed, economic and social policies lack any vision of a future where citizens feel a sense of belonging and feel they are 'held in the arms of society'.

Secularism simultaneously preserves space for citizens to contribute to public life while it erodes society through claims for religious exemptions based on gender and sexuality, attacks from scholars, and political favouritism that promotes some religions over others. In a world where religious diversity is increasing, particularly across Western contexts, and church attendance is diminishing, there is an urgent need to reassert secularism as being key to good democratic governance and a healthy public sphere. Secularism creates a space for developing a consensus, rather than competition. It extends beyond the ecumenical and interfaith movements. It is a broader societally based conversation. By cutting through the privilege of the dominant denomination or faith, what Bhargava refers to as 'institutionalised religious domination' (2001: 92), a reinvigorated secularism can expose demagogic and textualist claims, including anti-women and anti-human-rights views, to sunlight rather than allowing them to hide behind opposition to a nefarious 'other', obfuscation, couched language that enables deniability, and anonymous social media accounts.

Masculinity

This book has also spent considerable time exploring a spectrum of what might be considered negative dimensions of masculinity: textualist religions that attempt to reimpose patriarchal conceptions of the family and gender roles, the manosphere, male supremacists, incels, and men who advocate for or enact terroristic violence against women on the basis of gender. Demagogic populists have successfully tapped into elements of anti-women prejudice in running their campaigns, whether attempting to win an election or recruit activists and fighters. They use anti-women sentiment in a bid to appeal to those who feel they occupy subordinate masculinities or subscribe to a narrative of victimhood, providing them with a sense of hegemonic masculine empowerment otherwise lacking in their daily lives. Yet it is argued here that masculinity is not and should not be viewed as the problem *per se*. Restoring the dignity of work, job security, and citizenship grounded in values-based responsibilities in order to balance rights-based claim making is key to the development of healthy masculinities that stand opposed to anti-women prejudice and demagogic hyper-masculine signalling.

Decades of neoliberal economic policies enacted by powerful figures on the right, such as Margaret Thatcher and Ronald Regan, and appropriated by traditional leftist Labour parties have fundamentally altered the form and structure of modern work. Men, in particular, have been displaced from traditional roles that emphasised heroic physical labour and employment where workers lived in the same locale as their workplace. In this traditional context, trade unions and churches offered intellectual guidance and solidarities with fellow workers. They provided spiritual, moral, and ethical direction and a sense of community, particularly for blue-collar men. The demise of these traditional institutions in combination with the professionalisation of Labour-oriented political parties has created a significant intellectual, moral, and political vacuum. It is a context where working men lack a voice. The economic and social impacts of neoliberalism have been amplified in the context of social media, a powerful force multiplier for demagogues seeking a constituency to attain power.

At some point, dignity in work, respect, recognition, and stoicism were replaced by a sense of victimhood. Victimhood is not righteous outrage or the moral courage to speak up in the face of a more powerful other. Rather, it is a need, as Campbell and Manning (2014) argue, to seek validation of victim status from others. The manosphere, male supremacism, and incels all demonstrate victimhood status. Yet the question remains: Who makes up these groups? This research focused primarily on blue-collar working men as the base of populist support. It emerges that the blue-collar male voters at the geographic heart of an election that changed national political trajectories were not keyboard warriors tapping out violent anti-women or anti-minority treatises in their evenings. However, these blue-collar men felt and voiced a profound sense of loss and alienation from the political process. Exclusion from and marginalisation by professional political parties added to their sense of voicelessness, producing a deep-seated anger that belied working-class stoicism. However, their anger was not targeted at the abstract economic principles driving work precarity and chain migration, though they possessed a strong working knowledge of neoliberalism's form and function. Rather, they directed it at the most visible and perhaps easiest targets: minorities and welfare recipients. Outsiders and others who could be looked down upon.

In this sense, it appears that the manosphere and anti-women activism have much broader class and geographic support. This is important, as there is a tendency to view alienated and angry working-class men as the root cause of many of these issues. In fact, they extend much more broadly across the class spectrum, including into the white collar professions where the negative impacts of precarity, anti-discrimination legislation, and greater competition for employment are increasingly felt.

Restoring to working men a sense of honour, dignity, respect, and recognition must be a priority of public policy making. This includes removing the barriers of institutional racism, which act as a metaphorical glass ceiling for workers (men and women) from non-white backgrounds and prevent them from developing upward social trajectories beyond a certain point. The Black Lives Matter protests that swept the globe in June 2020 are indicative of just how much work remains in this regard, especially in an environment where black and brown citizens' lives are at risk in encounters with state actors and powers. At the same time, every effort must be made to tackle gender-based discrimination as well as identify and address male supremacism as a potent form of ideological masculinity and violent extremism. Dealing with inequality – racial and gender – acknowledges the vital links between work and responsibility (grounded in service), the individual development of a healthy intrinsic sense of honour and self-respect, and extrinsic recognition.

This requires the development of highly calibrated, evidence-based policies that, where necessary, strongly encourage the private sector, which has increasingly lacked accountability to wider society, to develop meaningful training and secure work offering upward social trajectories. Initiatives may require subsidies, a dirty word in the lexicon of neoliberal economic policies. A measure of state coercion and intervention may also be required to ensure the survival of the right to industrial citizenship, particularly after four decades of anti-union legislation and union busting. Unions provide solidaristic bonds and their concerns for the health of workers and fair pay offer a healthy alternative to the focus on pure profit that has become pervasive.

It is important to weigh up the economic cost of such policies with the potential social cost of not countering the prevalence of neoliberalism, particularly in the post-COVID-19 environment. To this extent it is worth considering how governments of past generations dealt with post-war conditions and the return of solders from the battlefield by investing heavily in infrastructure projects. Where such initiatives did not occur, large groups of disenfranchised men formed the base of radical far-right political parties, which led to further conflict.

It is also vital to balance the economic with the social. It must be a key imperative to restore honour and dignity to working-class (and increasingly white collar) men by developing and instilling in them a sense of duty to the community. Gender equality must be embedded in every facet of this restoration, with a particular emphasis on the young men among whom anti-women attitudes are particularly prevalent. In an era where rights-based claim making and identity politics have come to predominate, this requires a paradigm shift. In the past, citizenship-based service to the nation was defined through service in the military, often through conscription, or other mass participatory activities. This has been replaced by weak citizenship, where the individual's only service obligation to the nation is in the form of reciprocal obligation arrangements for welfare recipients or community service as a form of light punishment for criminal offenders. Other avenues for representing one's nation have become limited. For example, the professionalisation of sport means there are significant barriers that prevent most people from serving and aspiring to represent their country. For an individual to provide a service to their nation on a full time basis, it requires high levels of education and cultural capital.

I stop well short of renewed calls for conscription of young men and women into the military, which creates as much work for the professional armed forces as it does for recruits. But I urge governments to think creatively about institutionalising service as a key aspect of citizenship. Opportunities exist. In Australia community-based volunteer fire brigades and food and logistic service providers battle catastrophic bushfires without pay. The United States Peace Corps places volunteers in communities around the world. The National Health Service in the United Kingdom recruits volunteer responders. All excellent examples of responsibility-based citizenship that embed gender equality, build a sense of honour and dignity, and provide exceptional community support. There is still a role for duty and responsibility to one's community and nation in a globalised world. Governments would be well advised to invest considerable resources now, prior to the emergence of new extremist groups or the further development of nascent ones.

Lest the urgency of the task be considered minor, it is important to remember what happened in the decade following the 2008 global financial crisis: the emergence of global populism, the arrival of the Islamic State as a global terror threat, the British referendum to leave the European Union, the election of Donald Trump and many other demagogic populist leaders across Europe and the global South, and the appearance primarily online (for now) of the 'alt right', manosphere, and incels. The impact of the COVID-19 pandemic on a global scale promises to dwarf the effects of the 2008 financial crisis. There will undoubtedly be increased unemployment and further detrimental impacts on already precarious and insecure workers. In a context where increasing inequality and insecurity has resulted in even the middle-classes turning to food banks, we can expect to see an intensification of populist tactics. Negative social developments, such as anti-women and far-right agitators, are likely to increase. Blame will be directed toward faceless and corrupt 'elites', women, and superfluous populations, including migrants. Increased nationalism will promote division and divisiveness.

In this context, social media must be treated as an extension of the public street where the general principles of citizenship apply and individuals required to act accordingly. Social media and the wider internet have become a parallel universe where individuals can use anonymity, pseudonyms, and fake accounts to troll, make hate filled statements, and incite social division. These polarising statements can shift public discourse towards the normalisation of extremist language. This is not to mention non-regulated currencies, such as Bitcoin, that can fund such movements. None of these behaviours are acceptable in our streets, however, have become the norm on our computers and phones. Attempts to regulate online activity are usually framed as authoritarian and state overreach into the private sphere. This is a false premise, however, that has contributed as much as any factor to the rise of the new demagogues and populism. Leaving aside important issue of safeguarding privacy in search engines, communications, and private commerce, a step as simple as ensuring that individuals using social media forums must use their own names would arguably bring a measure of civility and respectful dialogue to an otherwise largely unregulated space. Citizenship education accompanying such a step would teach of the potential societal consequences of making socially divisive comments. Individual freedoms and choices would remain, yet those seeking to divide society would no longer be able to hide behind fake accounts and names.

States must reengage the possibility of a return to classical, value-infused citizenship bound in rights and responsibilities, but without the cultural baggage. It is, as Heater stated three decades ago, citizenship that can tame the divisive passions of other identities (1990). A Christian socialist ethos infused the origins of the welfare state, Keynesian economics, and Marshall's bundle of rights and responsibilities with a commitment to egalitarianism and concern with the vulnerable. A reinvigorated secular society showing neither fear of nor favour to established religion opens a space for a values-based discussion as to the ultimate aim of social policy.

With the COVID-19 pandemic decimating global economies, it is the right time to consider alternate economic pathways. On 3 April 2020, the editorial board of the *Financial Times* called for 'radical reforms – reversing the prevailing policy directions of the last four decades' (Financial Times 2020). The conservative financial newspaper's board also called for the foresight of the Beveridge Report with its commitment to universal welfare (Financial Times 2020). Such a call is unprecedented amongst the financial establishment. Perhaps this has become so difficult because neoliberalism as an economic approach, which rejects the place of morality, has developed its own dogma to which politicians and policymakers alike cling. Like textualists, they adhere to prescriptive canons centred on free markets and efficiency, no matter the social impact, in the misguided belief that unadulterated and unfettered free markets lead to prosperity for all.

In developing an alternate economic path forward, we might look to the exemplars of Birmingham, UK, and Philadelphia, PA, two great cities close to my heart that were the birthplaces of the industrial revolutions that were pivotal to the emergence of the global industrial age. The Lunar Society in Birmingham and Junto Society in Philadelphia (which evolved into the American Philosophical Association) brought together some of the great scientists, mathematicians, natural philosophers, manufacturers, theologians, poets, and entrepreneurs of the era. These associations were centred not on maximising efficiencies and profits, but on mutual bonds of friendship and the furtherance of scientific, moral, and political inquiry. Their collective intellectual, scientific, and commercial outputs played a large part in the one of the most significant revolutions in human history. One can only imagine their impact had these societies included women. In a context defined by the commodification of knowledge, attacks on universities, and a narrow focus on profit, any government seeking to define a pathway out of a predicament that will saddle nations with debts and burden generations to come would do well to consider the manner in which values, creativity, and intellectual inquiry are at their most powerful when a consideration of the greater good is central to their ambit. Combined with a renewed and vigorous commitment to inclusive citizenship and secularism, governments worldwide can chart a new direction based on the common good.

To return to the aims of the book in conclusion, this work sought to understand how and why Western liberal democracies have become dominated by a new class of demagogic strongmen. It is clear that a wide and complex array of factors have shaped these developments. I attempted to home in on two overlooked factors: religion and masculinity. These two factors clearly extend into understanding the wider economic, cultural, and political factors shaping the emergence of the new demagogues and a populist epoch. This book by no means has all the answers to our current (and likely future) predicament, however it foregrounds the centrality of a reinvigorated and inclusive values-based citizenship as a key step in the right direction.

References

Andrews, D. (2017). Keynes and Christian Socialism: Religion and the Economic Problem. *European Journal of the History of Economic Thought*, 24 (4), 958–977.
Barbalet, J.M. (1993). Citizenship, Class Inequality, and Resentment. In B.S. Turner (Ed.), *Citizenship and Social Theory* (pp. 36–57). London: Sage.

Benedict XVI. (2006). Faith, Reason, and the University: Memories and Reflections. Lecture Transcript, delivered at Aula Magna of the University of Regensburg. 12 September.

Bhargava, R. (2011). Rehabilitating Secularism. In C. Calhoun, M. Juergensmeyer, & J. VanAntwerpen (Eds.), *Rethinking Secularism* (pp. 92–113). Oxford: Oxford University Press.

Blais, M. & Dupuis-Déri, F. (2012). Masculinism and the Antifeminist Countermovement. *Social Movement Studies*, 11 (1), 21–39.

Brittan, A. (1989). *Masculinity and Power*. Oxford: Basil Blackwell.

Campbell, B. & Manning, J. (2014). Microaggression and Moral Cultures. *Comparative Sociology*, 13 (6), 692–726.

Financial Times. (2020). Virus Lays Bare the Frailty of the Social Contract: Radical Reforms are Required to Forge a Society that Will Work for All'. *Financial Times*, 4 April.

Hage, G. (2011). Multiculturalism and the Ungovernable Muslim. In R. Gaita (Ed.), *Essays on Muslims and Multiculturalism* (pp. 165–186). Melbourne: Text Publishing.

Heater, D. (1990). *Citizenship: The Civic Ideal in World History, Politics, and Education*. London: Longman Group.

Keane, J. (2016). Populism and Democracy: Dr Jekyll and Mr Hyde? *OXPOL Blog*, 3 November. Retrieved from https://blog.politics.ox.ac.uk/populism-and-democracy-dr-jekyll-and-mr-hyde.

Marshall, T.H. (1950). The Problem Stated with the Assistance of Alfred Marshall. In T.H. Marshall (Ed.), *Citizenship and Social Class* (pp. 1–9). Cambridge: Cambridge University Press.

Shklar, J.N. (1990). *American Citizenship: The Quest for Inclusion*. Cambridge, MA: Harvard University Press.

Standing, G. (2011). *The Precariat: The New Dangerous Class*. London: Bloomsbury.

Temple, W. (1941). *Christianity and the Social Order*. London: SCM Press.

Turner, B.S. (2016). 'We Are All Denizens Now': On the Erosion of Citizenship. *Citizenship Studies*, 20 (6–7), 679–692.

INDEX

Acton Institute 67
Aggrievement 82, 84, 141
al-Baghdadi, Abu Bakr 2, 16, 87, 167, 178
Alienation 9, 10, 11, 13, 80, 83, 90, 94, 95, 102, 105, 111, 136, 163, 174, 178, 189, 198, 200, 204
Alt-right 4, 88, 89, 90, 92, 94, 97, 105, 118, 200
Amazon 154, 157, 158, 162
Anger 7, 9, 10, 11, 12, 14, 25, 73, 83, 85, 86, 95, 99, 100, 104, 105, 111, 120, 136, 140, 150, 163, 177, 178, 181, 182, 183, 184, 185, 188, 189, 194, 198, 199, 204
Anglicanism 26, 42, 43, 124, 125 (See also Church of England)
Anti-Semitism 17, 56
Anxiety 7, 10, 11, 13, 70, 80, 83, 84, 85, 90, 94, 102, 104, 105, 111, 120, 136, 150, 163, 169, 178, 181, 183, 184, 188, 198, 200
Archbishop of Canterbury (See also William Temple, Justin Welby) 13, 26, 28, 63, 112, 122, 193
Archbishop of Krakow 68
Asad, Talal 60, 61
Asia 2, 43, 45, 85, 113, 116, 130, 132, 133, 134, 135, 169, 172
Attorney-General's Department (Australia) 101
Australia xi, xii, 7, 8, 15, 22, 24, 36, 37, 39, 40, 41, 43, 45, 51, 58, 68, 70, 84, 89, 94, 96, 101, 102, 103, 104, 167–177, 179, 184, 185, 186, 187, 188, 193, 194, 198, 199, 201, 205; White Australia Policy 168–171
Autochthonic politics 85

Bannon, Steve 44, 66, 67, 70
Barbalet, Jack 12, 25, 83, 199
Barletta, Lou 16, 145, 160, 162
Beierle, Scott 96
Berezin, Mabel 4, 7
Berger, Peter 60
Bergoglio, Jorge Mario (See Pope Francis)
Beveridge Report 38, 206
Beveridge, Sir William 26–28, 45, 193
Bhargava, Rajeev 61, 203
Bible 54, 91
Bilardi, Jake 187
Birmingham 7, 15, 111–117, 124–129, 132, 134–137
Bitcoin 206
Black Lives Matter 204
Blair, Tony 36, 41
Blue-collar xiv, 16, 39, 40, 41, 83, 87, 104, 105, 132, 140, 141, 147, 155, 156, 162, 163, 193, 202, 203, 204 (See working-class)
Blue Labour 4
Bolsonaro, Jair 85
Bourdieu, Pierre 35
Brexit (See European Union Referendum)
Bridging Social capital 135, 194
British Union of Fascists 112, 113

Brubaker, Rogers 4, 10
Bureaucracy 82, 124, 192, 194
Burke, Edmund 58
Burke, Raymond (Cardinal) 66–68
Bush, George W. 33

Caliphate / *Khilafah* 1, 2, 13, 16, 64, 167, 170, 178, 180, 187, 197, 198, 201
Cambridge Apostles 28–29
Cambridge University 28, 29, 33, 45, 57
Capitalism 3, 33, 35, 39, 98, 131, 193
Careerism 40–41
Casanova, Jose 60
Catholic Church xi, 9, 44, 54–55, 63, 65, 68, 105, 125, 161–162, 196–197; Catholic Clergy 67, 70; Catholic News Media 67, 68; Catholic Church in Australia 43, 70; Catholic Church in Hungary 69, 74; Catholic Church in Italy 68, 74; Catholic Church in Poland 68–69, 70, 74; Catholic Church in United States 44, 66–68, 74, 145, 160–162
Catholic Church Sexual Abuse 9, 44, 145
Catholic conservatives 34, 44, 54, 65–66, 70, 89, 196, 198; Catholicists 9, 74, 88, 197–198
Catholicism 54, 56, 62–63, 66–70, 74, 151, 195–196, 198, 202; Catholic 31, 39, 42, 43, 53–54, 57, 60, 63, 64, 65–68, 70, 74, 89, 124–125, 143, 145, 152, 160–161, 195–197; Roman Catholic Doctrine 57, 66
Cavanaugh, William 60
Charlottesville 88
China 22, 62, 147, 148, 151
Christian 1, 13, 28, 43, 53, 73, 121, 122, 127, 134, 142, 152, 161, 162, 180, 193, 194, 195, 196, 197, 206; Christian Churches 9, 10, 44, 45, 55, 73, 74, 136, 198; Christian civilisation 9, 196; Christian denominations 53, 58, 112, 124, 195, 196; Christian Europe 70, 121, 134, 197; Christian heritage 13, 121; Christian identity 10, 52, 65, 70, 134, 136, 152; Christian immigrants 45; Christian institutions 45, 58; Christian-Islamic dialogue 64, 65, 196; Christian leaders 70; Christian Minorities 62, Christian missionaries 53, 85; Christian moral values and principles 28, 35, 45, 60, 69, 121, 123, 160, 202; Christian Prayer, 59; Christian right 151, 152; Christian theology 122; Christian tradition 64, 196; Christian unity 44;
Christian voters 124, 151; Christian warrior masculinity 200
Christian Militia (See Catholic News Media)
Christian Nationalist Crusade 56
Christian Research Association (Australia) 43
Christian Socialist 28, 45, 122, 193, 194, 206
Church Militant (See Catholic News Media)
Church of England 44, 55, 57, 58, 112, 122, 123, 124, 125
Churchill, Winston (bust) 119
Citizenship xii, 4, 6, 7, 8, 9, 14, 22, 23, 24, 34, 35, 37, 38, 39, 44, 74, 82, 137, 146, 156, 189, 192, 193, 205, 206; Citizenship education 206; Classical or traditional citizenship 2, 23, 24, 30, 31, 36, 51, 192, 193, 202, 206; decline / deterioration / erosion of 7, 8, 15, 21, 22–24, 39, 46, 51, 192, 194; Equal citizenship 29, 82; Industrial 16, 26, 39, 205; Marshallian citizenship 24–26, 29, 30, 31, 35, 38, 105; Political citizenship 26; values-based / inclusive citizenship 16, 74, 203, 206, 207; Weak citizenship 37–39, 205; Women's 30
Civility 142, 206
Clinton, Bill 36, 140, 158
Clinton, Hilary 11, 140, 141, 150, 151, 152,
Common good 30, 31, 51, 52, 163, 202, 207
Connell, Raewyn 12, 81
Conscription 205
Conversazione Society (See Cambridge Apostles)
COVID-19 Pandemic xii, 1, 2, 5, 16, 22, 23, 27, 38, 45, 126, 127, 153, 163–164, 205, 206
Cox, Jo 110
Cronulla Riots 173

Dabiq Magazine (See Islamic State)
de Tocqueville, Alexis de 58
Demagogue 1, 2, 6, 7, 9, 10, 12, 13, 15, 16, 21, 22, 46, 52, 53, 63, 73, 74, 80, 83, 87, 97, 105, 117, 118, 119, 120, 147, 162, 188, 194, 197, 198, 200, 203, 206, 207
Democracy xii, 1, 2, 3, 4, 6, 14, 17, 21, 23, 24, 27, 31, 36, 37, 58, 60, 62, 86, 102, 147, 181, 182, 192, 203, 207,
Democratic Party (US) 11, 36, 140, 141, 152, 162 (See also Bill Clinton, Hilary Clinton and Barack Obama)
Department of Homeland Security (United States) 101
Dignitatus Humanae Institute (See also Steve Bannon) 66

Dignity 8, 9, 11, 12, 14, 15, 16, 29, 42, 66, 82, 83, 94, 129, 130, 135, 136, 137, 157, 193, 194, 198, 199, 203, 204, 205
Disgust 182, 183, 188
Dishonour 16, 184
Divorce 70, 84
Duterte, Rodrigo 85

Economy xi, 2, 3, 8, 9, 10, 11, 12, 13, 15, 16, 21, 22, 24, 25, 26, 27, 28, 29, 30, 31, 32, 33, 34, 35, 36, 37, 38, 39, 40–42, 45, 61, 67, 72, 82, 83, 84, 86, 90, 94, 97, 98, 105, 110, 111, 114, 115, 117, 126, 129, 132, 133, 135, 141, 142, 143, 144, 145, 147, 148, 149, 153–156, 158, 162–164, 171, 174, 176, 185, 187, 189, 193, 194, 196, 202–207
Elam, Paul 92, 99, 200, 201
Elites 1, 3, 4, 5, 6, 38, 9, 10, 52, 61, 62, 72, 82, 84, 93, 111, 141, 147, 149, 151, 172, 178, 206
Emasculation 13, 90
Emotion, Emotional 1, 5, 6, 7, 8, 10, 12, 14, 15, 73, 80, 83, 120, 126, 150, 173, 176, 177, 181, 184, 185, 188, 198, 199
English Defence League (EDL) 117
Erdogan, Recep Tayyip 64, 183
Ethno-nationalism 81
Europe / European 2, 10, 33, 36, 51, 52, 54, 55, 57, 58, 59, 64, 65, 66, 67, 68, 69, 70, 71, 73, 82, 115, 118, 121, 123, 125, 126, 132, 134, 135, 142, 144, 145, 160, 162, 167, 169, 170, 176, 187, 189, 193, 195, 196, 197, 198, 206
European Left 36; European Christianity 10, 59, 63, 65, 69, 70, 73, 121, 134, 196, 197, 198; European Jews 56; European Muslims 55, 67, 70, 71, 176, 196; European Parliament 15, 68, 117; European Secularism 52, 59; European Union / EU 1, 2, 7, 15, 22, 55, 64, 74, 86, 110, 111, 116, 117, 118, 121, 122, 123, 124, 125, 126, 129, 132, 134, 142, 189, 206; European Union Referendum (Brexit) 1, 2, 7, 15, 22, 74, 86, 110, 111, 118, 119, 121, 123, 124, 129, 132, 134, 135, 142, 206; European University Institute xi; European Wars of Religion 51, 54
Evangelical xi, 1, 9, 13, 28, 45, 62, 87, 105, 151, 152, 198, 200
Evidence-based policies 204

Fabian Socialist 26
Falwell Jr. Jerry 151

Far-right 1, 59, 66, 68, 69, 70, 71, 81, 82, 85, 88, 101, 110, 116, 117, 118, 120, 142, 172, 201, 205, 206
Farage, Nigel 2, 5, 13, 15, 85, 86, 110, 117–122, 132, 136
Fascism 3, 113, 135
Fear(s) 10, 12, 71, 73, 82, 83, 87, 89, 133, 136, 147, 169, 183, 184, 199, 206
Femicide 97, 99
Feminism 59, 87, 89, 90, 98–99, 102, 200, 201
Fertility 84
Fertility rates 61, 71
Fidesz party (See Hungary)
Fifth Column 71, 72, 148, 196
Financial Times 206–207
Foreign fighter 1, 13, 16, 22, 87, 175, 176, 186, 188, 197
Friedman, Milton 31–35, 193

Generation 1, 9, 32, 71, 129, 132, 158, 160, 163, 174, 177, 179, 194, 197, 201
Germany 56, 64

Habermas, Jürgen 60, 71
Hage, Ghassan 12, 83, 168, 177
Harvey, David 8, 27, 35, 45
Hate 17, 32, 56, 69, 87, 89, 90, 91, 92, 94, 99, 100, 95, 136, 140, 154, 157, 160, 183, 196, 198, 200–201, 206; Hatred of Women 90, 92, 95, 97, 99, 202
Hawke, Robert (Bob) 36, 171
Hayek, Friedrich 28, 31–34, 35, 193
Hazleton (See Pennsylvania)
Heyer, Heather 88
Hispanic 146, 148, 152, 153, 157, 159, 160, 161, 162, 163, 197; Latino 145, 146, 156, 160, 162, 163, 194, 197
Hobbes, Thomas 52
Holocaust 69
Honour 8, 9, 11, 12, 13, 14, 15, 21, 81, 83, 94, 176, 179, 180, 181, 184, 185, 188, 198, 199, 204, 205
Hope 2, 56, 64, 131, 132, 157, 158, 187
House of Commons (United Kingdom) 40, 41, 101
Howard, John 37, 40, 171, 172, 173
Humiliation 7, 12, 82, 83, 179, 181, 184, 189, 198
Hungary 2, 69, 70, 85, 196, 197; Fidesz Party 70

Ibn Abd al-Wahhab, Muhammad 178
Ibn Taymiyyah 54, 72, 178, 195, 197

212 Index

Identity Politics xi, 2, 4, 8, 9, 10, 14, 25, 39, 40, 51, 52, 65, 68, 69, 70, 73, 74, 84, 90, 105, 121, 142, 151, 163, 205
Ideological masculinity 12, 15, 80, 87–88, 97, 99–102, 105, 200–202, 204
Illegal Immigration Relief Act (See Immigration)
Immigration 16, 43, 67, 68, 110, 113, 114, 116, 118, 119, 123, 130, 131, 132–135, 145, 146, 147, 151, 158–160, 162, 164, 169, 172, 188
Incel 12, 88, 94, 95–96, 97, 101, 105, 181, 201, 203, 204, 206
India(n) 2, 61, 85, 113, 116, 129, 170
Individualism 30, 82, 163
Industrial revolution 98, 111, 112, 135, 142, 143
Infrastructure 27, 145, 205
Injury 2, 7, 8, 10, 12, 13, 14, 15, 80, 83, 176–177, 198, 199, 200
Innocence of Muslims Protest 174–75
Intercultural understanding 137
Internment 61, 173
Iraq 16, 61, 117, 121, 172, 198
Irrationality 60, 64, 66
Islam xi, 2, 9, 10, 13, 16, 42, 52–56, 59–61, 64–67, 70–74, 105, 116, 121, 124, 133–136, 152, 167–171, 173–178, 180, 183, 186–189, 195–198, 201; Islamist(s) 2, 64, 70, 72, 74, 88, 116–117, 173, 175, 178, 183, 197–198, 201
Islamic State (ISIS) xi, 1, 2, 7, 9, 12–13, 16, 22, 61, 65, 83, 87, 116–117, 167–168, 172, 174–76, 178–189, 194, 197–199, 201–202, 205; *Dabiq* Magazine 16, 175, 178–183, 185, 188; *Rumiyah* Magazine 16, 175, 178, 179, 181–184;
Italy 2, 68, 74, 133, 196–197; Lega Nord 68, 196

Jędraszewski, Marek (Archbishop) 68–69
Jefferson, Thomas 58, 112, 143
Johnson, Boris 2, 111, 120–121, 136
Joppke, Christian 51, 61
Judaism (Jewish) 42, 43, 53, 56, 85, 105, 152

Kaczyński, Jarosław 68–69
Keating, Paul 36, 40, 171
Keynes, John Meynard 26–27, 28, 29, 31, 33, 45, 193
Keynesian Economics 9, 24, 27, 31, 32, 33, 35, 38, 39, 45, 171, 193, 202, 206
Kingstanding, Birmingham 7, 15, 111, 117, 124, 126–127, 130, 131, 133, 136

Knights of Columbus 67, 89
Knights of the Republic Order 67

Laïcité 59, 195
Latino (See Hispanic)
Lattimer Massacre 144
Law and Justice Party (See Poland)
LGBTIQ 9, 62, 68, 69, 70, 99, 100
Lega Nord (See Italy)
Legatus 67
Lépine, Marc 97–98
Locke, John 57–58, 142
London School of Economics 3, 26, 31, 45, 193
Lunar Society 111, 112, 143, 207
Luther, Martin 54–56, 73, 151, 185

Mackert, Jurgen xii, xiii, 24, 35
Madison, James 58, 143
Mahmood, Saba 61
Malcolm X 113
Male Supremacism (Supremacist) 12, 15, 80–109, 200, 201, 202, 204
Mansophere 13, 88, 89, 90–95, 97, 99, 101, 102, 104, 181, 198, 200, 201, 202, 203, 204, 206
Marshall, Alfred 24
Marshall, T.H. 8, 24–31, 45, 193
Marx, Karl 5
Marxism/ Marxist 25, 39, 40, 59, 98
Masculinism 98–99, 201
Masculinity xii–xiii, 2, 6–16, 80–81, 83–85, 87–88, 90, 93, 95, 97, 99, 103, 105, 118–121, 126–127, 129, 131, 133, 142, 150–153, 155, 156, 158–159, 162–163, 167, 175–176, 179–181, 185, 189, 192, 198, 200–201, 203, 207; Masculinities 11–12, 15, 81, 83, 156, 168, 176, 198, 200, 203; Muslim masculinities 168, 176–178
McCrae, Donald 3
McDowell, Linda 11, 83
McInnes, Gavin 88, 89, 93
Mead, Lawrence 29, 82
Media 21, 67, 82, 88, 92, 120, 149, 156, 167, 173, 174, 176, 185
Mediocrity 84
Melbourne 7, 173, 179, 186, 187
Men Going Their Own Way (MGTOW) 12, 90–92, 104, 105, 200
Meritocracy 4, 8, 82, 127, 129–130, 153, 155–157, 186–187, 199
Middle-class 10, 80, 83, 84–85, 90, 125, 126, 129, 135, 149, 150, 158, 198, 206
Midlands Enlightenment 111

Index   213

Milbank, John 4
Minassian, Alex 96
Minorities 3, 15, 41, 44, 61, 62, 85, 86, 114, 116, 121, 132, 133, 136, 142, 158, 159, 172, 173, 178, 187, 188, 189, 196, 197, 199, 204
Misinterpellation 12, 83, 102, 177, 184, 185, 186, 189, 197, 199
Misogynism 81, 96, 102, 104, 149, 180, 201
Modi, Narendra 85
Moffit, Ben 4
Mont Pèlerin Society 31, 193
Morality 7, 9, 35, 41, 42, 45, 52, 183, 207
Mosely, Oswald 112, 113
Mudde, Cas 10, 81
Multiculturalism 15, 23, 42, 43, 59, 85, 110, 115, 116, 117, 160, 163, 168, 170–172, 173, 174, 177, 187, 195
Muscular Christianity 13, 105, 122
Muslim 1, 7, 9, 10, 16, 42, 43, 52, 54, 55, 59, 61, 62, 64, 65, 67, 69, 70, 71, 72, 73, 74, 85, 87, 90, 99, 116, 121, 124, 130, 134, 135, 136, 161, 167–179, 181–185, 187–189, 194, 195, 196, 197, 198, 199, 202

Napa institute 67
Narratives 6, 7, 9, 10, 11, 12, 13, 14, 15, 21, 62, 73, 80, 83, 92, 101, 116, 125, 130, 141, 159,-160, 168, 178, 185, 194, 197, 203
National Health Service (NHS) 27, 38, 205
National Socialism 3, 56, 69
Nationalism 2, 81, 117, 168, 187, 188, 201, 206
Neoliberalism 8, 11, 31, 34–39, 40, 41, 45, 83, 129, 132, 162, 172, 193, 203, 204, 205, 207
North Atlantic Treaty Organisation (NATO) 2
Nostalgia 1, 2, 21, 122, 142, 147

Obama, Barack 119, 140, 141, 147, 158
Orbán, Victor 69, 70, 85
Orwell, George 11
Oxford University 26, 32, 45, 57, 122, 142, 193

Panama Papers 38
Parsons, Talcott 29
Patriarchy / Patriachal 61, 81, 88, 93, 98, 99, 181, 201, 202, 203
Penn, William 57, 142
Pennsylvania 7, 16, 57, 112, 140–146, 148–149, 151, 153, 163; Hazleton 7, 16, 143–146, 150, 152–164, 194, 197, 199; Hazleton CAN-DO 144–145, 154; Luzerne County 16, 141, 143, 147, 150, 152; Philadelphia 57, 140–143, 159, 207; Scranton 140–141, 145, 148–151, 161
Pentecostalism / Pentecostals / Pentecostal 42, 43, 45, 62, 74, 125, 135, 136, 161, 162, 195
Poland 2, 68, 69, 74, 196, 197; Law and Justice Party 68–69, 74, 196
Political Islam xi, 71
Pope Benedict 63–66, 68, 70, 196
Pope Francis 44, 63, 66, 67, 68, 74, 196
Popper, Karl 31
Populist / Populism xii, xiii, 1–17, 21–25, 44, 46, 51–52, 55, 62, 65, 66–74, 80–86, 90, 97, 105, 110, 117, 119–122, 124, 130, 132, 136, 141, 147, 149, 151–152, 162–163, 168, 172, 175, 178, 188, 192, 194–199, 202–207
Powell, Enoch (Rivers of Blood Speech) 113–114, 117, 133, 135, 160
Prakash, Neil 182, 187
Priestley, Joseph 112
Private Sector 14, 39, 204
Politician(s) 1, 6, 8, 17, 22, 32, 38, 40, 41, 45, 52, 67, 69, 70, 71, 72, 110, 119, 120, 121, 132, 135, 136, 152, 163, 172, 174, 194, 196, 20
Professional / Career Politicians 1, 8, 22, 41, 192, 194
Protestant xi, 54, 57, 58, 60, 73, 122, 151, 195
Protestant Reformation 54, 73
Proud Boys 88–89, 200

Quran 178

Rape 93, 94, 105, 167, 180
Rationality 60, 62, 64, 70, 91, 196
Ratzinger, Joseph (See Pope Benedict)
Reagan, Ronald 33, 40, 203
Reddit 95
Red pill 90, 92, 200
Refugee 68, 69, 70, 121, 132, 169, 170, 192
Regensburg Address (Pope Benedict)
Religion xi–xiv, 2, 3, 6, 7, 9, 10, 11, 14–17, 28, 35, 42–44, 46, 51–54, 56–65, 67, 70, 71–74, 82, 87–91, 94, 97, 99, 102, 104, 121–122, 124, 126, 134, 136, 142, 151–152, 158, 160–162, 169, 172, 175–177, 186–187, 189, 192, 194–198, 200–203, 206–207; Religious 2, 4, 5, 7–10, 12–16, 24, 28–29, 40, 42, 44–46, 52–55, 57–63, 72, 73, 81, 89, 94, 97,

101, 104, 105, 112, 116, 125, 134–135, 142, 145, 152, 162, 170, 187, 194–195, 197, 201, 202–203; Religion and women 12, 87–90, 91, 104–105, 200, 201; Religious authority / leaders 9, 12, 15, 52, 63, 65, 70, 105, 121, 155, 161, 197, 202; Religious freedom / liberty 58, 61, 67, 112, 142, 152, 195; Religious institutions 9, 42, 44–45, 63, 196; Religious intolerance 8, 13, 15, 57, 135, 200; Religious literacy 62; Religious minorities 44, 142, 197; Religious principles / values 40, 45, 51, 202; Religious textualism 195, 200, 201, 202; Religious tolerance 57, 59, 196; Religious traditions 60, 136, 195; Religious violence / conflict 60, 65, 74, 195
Republican Party 85, 140, 141, 147, 151, 152, 152, 162–63 (See Ronald Reagan)
Resentment 7, 10, 14, 25, 73, 80, 84–85, 86, 90, 94, 97, 100, 105, 118, 135, 142, 157, 199, 201
Respect 12, 25, 44, 61, 65, 83, 93, 123, 130, 155, 157, 176, 189, 198, 204
Responsibility 6, 14, 16, 23, 34, 35, 36, 37, 38, 45, 52, 136, 186, 188, 192, 204, 205
Revenge 11, 83, 95, 182
Rights and responsibilities 6, 23, 35, 192, 206
Rivers of Blood speech (See Enoch Powell)
Rodger, Elliot (Incel, manifesto) 95–96
Rome xi, 67, 167
Rumiyah (See Islamic State)
Rushdie, Salman 171
Rust Belt States 141, 142, 147, 149

Sadness 120, 150, 181, 184, 185
Salafi (st) 9, 70, 72, 116, 167, 173, 174, 178, 186
Salvini, Matteo 68,
Saudi Arabia 72, 171
Schröder, Gerhard 36
Secular / Secularism 4, 10, 15, 16, 29, 43, 44, 52, 55, 58–62, 64, 66, 70, 71, 72, 74, 85, 151, 152, 188, 195, 196, 197, 198, 202, 203, 206, 207
Securitisation 4, 22, 63, 71, 175, 176
Shiite 72, 197
Shklar, Judith 29, 30, 82, 156, 193
Social Media 1, 2, 13, 55, 97, 105, 168, 174, 203, 206; Pseudonyms 206; anonymity 85, 95, 99, 203, 206
Socialism 25, 26, 32, 34; Christian socialist 28, 45, 193, 194

Somers, Margaret 38
Southern Poverty Law Centre 88, 99, 100, 200–201
St. Thomas Aquinas 53, 54, 195
Standing, Guy 11, 81, 83
Stoicism 12, 84, 204
Strikes (Birmingham) 115
Sunni 54, 72, 178, 197
Symbolic Violence 87, 104
Syria 16, 117, 121, 198

Tarrant, Brenton 168
Tawney, R.H. 26
Taylor, Charles 60
Temple, William Archbishop 26–28, 112, 193
Textualism xi, 53–54, 72, 74, 90, 189, 195, 196, 198, 200, 202, 207
Thatcher, Margaret xi, 32–34, 37, 40, 42, 114–115, 132, 172, 203

The Birmingham Blitz 112
The Road to Serfdom (See Hayek)
Thompson, Matt the Very Reverend 125, 128, 132
Toronto 96, 102
Trade Union (s) 2, 8, 14, 15, 16, 21, 24, 25, 26, 30, 32, 34, 39–41, 42, 45, 46, 83, 114, 115, 128–129, 135, 136, 141, 145, 154, 155, 162, 193, 194, 203, 205
Trojan Horse Affair (Birmingham) 116
Trump, Donald 1, 2, 5, 7, 13, 16, 22, 55, 66, 69, 74, 85–86, 87, 89, 119, 120, 140–142, 145–152, 162, 163, 189, 206
Trust 5, 9, 61, 102, 125, 111, 198
Truth Claims 53, 58, 59, 72
Turkey 2, 64, 85, 169
Turner, Bryan S. xii, 23–24, 30, 37, 102, 193

Uighur 61
Ummah 9, 72, 184, 185
United Kingdom xii, xiii, 1, 7, 15, 22, 24, 38, 39, 41, 43, 45, 51, 74, 84–85, 89, 94, 101–102, 104, 110–111, 114–118, 120–122, 126, 136–137, 143, 152, 167, 171, 175, 189, 193, 198, 201, 205
United Kingdom Independence Party (UKIP) 7, 13, 15, 86, 110, 117–119, 121
United States of America xii, xiii, 1, 10, 15–16, 22, 29, 36, 39–43, 51, 57–58, 66–67, 73–74, 82, 84–85, 88–89, 99, 101–104, 140, 142, 144–148, 152–160, 162, 164, 171, 175, 189, 193, 195–196, 198, 201, 205

Universal Declaration of Human Rights 59
University of Chicago 31, 32, 33, 93
University of Potsdam xii, 4

Valizadeh, Roosh 93–94, 99, 200–201 (See also Mansophere)
Vatican xi, 62, 66, 68, 126; Second Vatican Council 44, 62, 66, 68, 126
Victimhood 8, 12, 16, 83, 84, 92, 94, 181, 199, 200, 202, 203, 204
Victimisation 9, 13, 84, 85, 88, 198
Violent Extremism 2, 8, 12, 13, 81, 82, 97, 99, 100–101, 104, 116, 200, 201, 204
Volunteer 38, 205
Vulnerable 12, 14, 184, 185, 202, 206

Wallace, George 147
Warrior 13, 16, 179, 180, 200
Welby, Justin 63, 123,
Welfare 24–31, 36–37, 41, 112, 115, 136, 156, 157, 194, 199, 204, 205, 207
Welfare fraud (perceived) 130, 133, 156–157, 199
Welfare State 7, 8, 9, 14, 15, 21, 23–24, 26–29, 31, 36–38, 45, 51, 112, 192, 193, 194, 202, 206
West Midlands (See also Birmingham) 15, 113, 117
White Nationalism (See also Nationalism) 117
White Privilege 84, 137
Williams, Roger 57
Woodhead, Linda 44, 124
Working-class xiv, 8–12, 14–15, 39–41, 82–85, 87, 90, 98, 111, 114, 117–119, 123, 125–126, 128–130, 132, 134–137, 140, 147, 155, 194, 197, 199, 202, 204–205; Working-class solidarities 8, 21, 39, 114, 130, 135–136, 156, 162, 194, 199 (see also blue-collar)
World Health Organisation 2, 96
World War I 31, 63, 112, 135, 144, 169
World War II 24, 32, 112, 132, 170, 193

Xenophobia 132, 169

Yazidi 61, 167, 178, 180
Yiannopoulos, Milo 65

Printed in the United States
By Bookmasters